"The 90-Day Soulmate Plan is mother at your side reminding you or your p̶ experiential process will guide you through five steps to not just find a partner, but even more importantly raise your vibration, clear out your past, love yourself, and call in a true match. Over the years of our friendship, Sarika's teachings and heart have helped me heal and close the past and invited me to open to more love in my life. I'm so grateful she has put her well-tested method into a book for all the access. Follow her simple process and see your life and relationships transform."

HeatherAsh Amara, author of Warrior Goddess Training and The Five
Secrets to Happy and Healthy Relationships with don Miguel Ruiz Jr.

"If you are truly ready to have heart opening, soul-stirring, forever love in your life, run (don't walk!) to Sarika Jain to show you the way. She possesses the deep wisdom and practical knowledge to firmly place you on a successful path to love."

Arielle Ford, author of The Soulmate Secret

"Sarika is perfectly suited to be a master teacher of romance. And because she's playing her cards right, her authentic resonance will surely open a beautiful harmony of romance for those lucky enough to read her warm and intimate book. But make no mistake, she means business. In her results-driven approach, she offers a practical step-by-step process for you to bring love into your life like drawing a moth to a flame. Follow her approach and you will surely find the kind of juicy, fulfilling love that will satisfy your soul."

Alexander Dunlop, author of Play Your Cards Right:
A Sacred Guide to Life on Earth

"Sarika's words always leave me uplifted, curious and somehow knowing myself and the world better. Her writing is multi-layered, rich and holds a potent space for self-exploration and discovery. I'm so grateful that she's chosen to share her wisdom in the form of this book and support women in stepping into their divine feminine power. Anybody who reads The 90-Day Soulmate Plan and allows Sarika to guide them through this magical process is sure to be more deeply connected to love in every possible way. What a gift!"

Nicola Humber, author and Founder of The Unbound Press

"Sarika is the epitome of a feminine goddess. She lives and breathes all that she teaches. This book is truly a vessel for her to share all her innate (and hard earned!) wisdom. If you are ready for deep intimate connection... read this, it will guide you to your ONE!"

Chrisa Zindros Boyce, Executive Coach

"This book is an absolute gift that needs to be savoured and actively experienced in a deeply nourishing way, as it opens your heart to more love in all areas of your life. Sarika so generously shares experiences from her own life and an incredible range of practices that will not only support you to find your soulmate in an aligned way that honours your needs, but deepen your connection with yourself and remind you of the love that you truly are. This in itself is life-changing and everyone needs to read it."

Tara Jackson, author of Embodied and Embodied Business

"In this book, Sarika has radiated light and wisdom through an engaging work of higher love. Her warmth, connection and explanations of the physics of resonance and energetic alignment allow for an emotional as well as intellectual experience. The practical and fun methods she shares help activate one's higher calling towards becoming grounded in their uniquely authentic state of grace and flow.

Inspiring steps towards heart-centered living, Sarika will help you cultivate a state of inner and outer alignment, live in your soul purpose, and recognize your own deep connection to the divine. She lovingly educates and holds space to help one release personal barriers and raise their consciousness around love. Pathways are illustrated for finding more connection, purpose, meaning and fulfillment through the alchemy of self-compassion and fostering healthy relationships. Such interconnectedness is just what we need to bring peace, harmony, tranquility, and heaven on earth!"

Dara Goldberg, Ph.D., Spiritual Psychologist,
author of Awaken Your Inner Goddess

"The 90 Day Soulmate Plan is a beautifully written book that weaves together both personal stories with practical tips to guide people on their journey to love - a love that begins within our own hearts before we can truly embrace the nourishing, passionate, connected relationship we dream of.

Sarika shares her experiences of the dating rollercoaster as a young, successful woman in Manhattan and the chance meeting with a chain-smoking Romanian gypsy psychic who showed her there was a different path to follow after yet another painful breakup. In learning to look within, Sarika uncovered the power of unconditional love which ultimately led her to meeting her true soulmate within just a few months.

This gorgeous book is the perfect guide for women (and men) who are tired of dating, fed up with meeting the wrong people and simply want to meet someone who shares the same values and dreams."

Lorraine Pannetier, author and intuitive
copywriter for lightworkers

"Sarika is a potent woman, a goddess, a soulful sister whose writing comes from her divine truth. She weaves her words with authenticity and love, holding a sacred space for the reader to become curious and explore her 90-Day Soulmate Plan with courage and confidence. If I had not yet found my soulmate, I would be thrilled to have this book in my possession."

Brier Heart, author of Take Off Your Armour and Have a Cup of Tea

"When I first contacted Sarika, I was at a point in my life where I knew something was just plain wrong with my energy. I was doing everything 'right' in my life as far as work, life, etc., but my romantic relationships would not flourish, no matter what. I also had financial hardships and other life areas seemed stagnant. I had tried almost everything on my own, but I realized through prayer and God's guidance that I needed help removing energetic blocks, specifically blocks in my heart.

This healing process is opening up all destiny paths in my life. My gifts are getting stronger, and doors are being opened in all areas of my life.

I met a man two months into working with Sarika and fell deeply in love. It is very helpful to have Sarika to help guide me through this relationship, as I have not been able to manifest a real relationship for sixteen years prior to meeting this man.

I would recommend other women to embark on this path if they feel like they have so much potential, dreams and vision for their lives, but no matter what you try, it's like something keeps stopping you or standing in your way. Sarika will help guide you out of this dark place and into the light to embark on manifesting into your true energetic self and manifesting your true Goddess nature, abounding with infinite love, hope and possibilities."

Laura S., healthcare professional

SARIKA JAIN

THE 90-DAY
Soulmate
PLAN

Get out of your own way and attract
the Higher Love you deserve

ISBN 978-1-913590-29-1 Paperback
ISBN 978-1-913590-30-7 Ebook

The Unbound Press
www.theunboundpress.com

Hey unbound one!

Welcome to this magical book brought to you by The Unbound Press.

At The Unbound Press we believe that when women write freely from the fullest expression of who they are, it can't help but activate a feeling of deep connection and transformation in others. When we come together, we become more and we're changing the world, one book at a time!

This book has been carefully crafted by both the author and publisher with the intention of inspiring you to move ever more deeply into who you truly are.

We hope that this book helps you to connect with your Unbound Self and that you feel called to pass it on to others who want to live a more fully expressed life.

With much love,
Nicola Humber

Founder of The Unbound Press
www.theunboundpress.com

May we unleash the powers of the divine feminine and masculine moving into sacred union. May we create a world of higher love, healthy relationships and true fulfillment.

CONTENTS

Step 3: Discover Your "Wow! Factor":

Align with Your Unique, Feminine, Sexual Self - 191

Step 4: Prepare for Lasting Love - 225

Step 5: Love and Date with Confidence - 267

Introduction

[Author's note: In this book, for the sake of simplicity and based on my personal experience of coaching women and men, I am referring to a traditional relationship between men and women in the heterosexual sense; however, this is in no way diminishing the validity of the teachings and lessons for people of all genders and sexual orientations, as long as the essence of relationship between the feminine and masculine principles are understood. While masculine and feminine energies reside in both men and women, it's important to recognize the interplay between the masculine and feminine to generate 'polarity' and sexual chemistry.]

Dear one,

How would it feel to know that you're on the right path to meeting your soulmate and life partner – a man who's emotionally available and committed to you?

Or, if you're in a relationship, you're creating a partnership that's juicy, loving and *lasting*? Wouldn't it be amazing to know that you're breaking through emotionally draining patterns, and on the road to creating a meaningful, fulfilling relationship that feels easy and harmo-

You feel safe, loved, powerful and sexy... and irresistible. You are a radiant goddess and a magnet for healthy love.

You know that a juicy, intimate relationship that transcends old, painful patterns – and is connecting on every level... mental, emotional, spiritual, physical – is your birthright. A relationship based on evolution, heart connection and sacred principles around love.

Moreover, all of your significant relationships, at home, work and with friends, are thriving and joyful. Positive people and abundance are flowing to you... *synchronistically.*

The question is, how can you achieve this kind of love?

It starts by creating the conditions for healthy, lasting love to enter your life.

The 90-Day Soulmate Plan **is your roadmap to help you do just that.**

You've worked hard in your career and are successful and have a great life already.

Yet, you know that there's a part of you itching for more...

...of being with a wonderful man, and maybe even having a child or two (or more!). To go on adventurous travels, build a beautiful home with the smell of home-cooked meals wafting through the air, host family and friends as a couple, and have date nights in romantic restaurants. Have pillow talk into the wee hours of the morning, chatting away about your wildest dreams and desires. You're so excited about your love for each other... that you want to share it with the world, and you're fueled by a sense of purpose and passion.

Yet, you are dating and feel stuck – almost at your wit's ends about what you're doing wrong. Why men disappear or don't text back.

Or, your relationship is starting to wear on both of you, and you feel drained from doing all the work and are frustrated with his lack of communication and unpredictability. *You secretly wonder if it's going to last.*

At some point, romance feels like a job and you're starting to dread it.

You feel lost, confused and doubtful, wondering if you're ever going to be really, truly happy inside.

> *"Men seem to be interested in me and then lose interest for some reason I don't understand."*
>
> *"I'm more tolerant and understanding towards my man as I learned my lesson from my previous relationship. Yet these efforts don't seem to be appreciated enough and I don't know what I should have to do to keep a healthy relationship."*
>
> *"I'm afraid of failing and picking the wrong person… and getting hurt again."*
>
> *"I'm really busy and don't have much time to spare for dates that usually go nowhere."*

You're done with playing games and pointless dates. Of being in relationships in which you're always giving and having to work hard to make things work, or where he won't communicate and withdraws when he's triggered.

You know that you deserve <u>way more</u> – a loving, easy relationship with a man who rocks your world, a love that feels blissful and transcendent. You know that your soul won't settle for less.

You're a Love Goddess, a magnetic, irresistible force of nature who can capture your man's heart and raise you two higher. A woman who's wise, loving, powerful and sexy, and knows what she's doing when it comes to her relationships.

Your dating and love life needs to reflect who you are deep inside.

———

When I started dating to find my life partner in my twenties, I would ask, "How do I meet a nice, successful, handsome man who wants the same things as me, has the same relationship goals and is someone I feel safe, loved and cherished with?" I wanted someone who matched my ethnic background, whom I could relate with, had my back and would miraculously get me. I assumed that when I would meet the person, I would feel butterflies in my stomach and simply know, and chemistry would be off the charts! Secretly, I also wanted to be saved from being single, and ideally have a man jump through hoops to be with me.

Yet, when I experienced disillusionment in my love life, and processed my heartbreak and grief over what I had lost, I could see the world a little differently – a new possibility began to emerge.

I realized that my views were potentially immature and based on a false reality that I had constructed to feel safe and secure. When the rug was pulled from under my feet, I began to search deeper. I discovered that what I wanted in life was more nuanced and profound. If I *were* to get into a relationship, I wanted it to have more connection and purpose. I wanted to approach my life differently and seek to understand what it means to be *fulfilled*. As I began dating again, I began to ask myself:

- *How can I be my most authentic, loving, powerful self?*
- *How do I date in a way that's conscious and joyful?*
- *How do I know if I have found the right partner?*
- *How can we communicate better with each other?*
- *How can we keep the spark alive forever?*

If I was honest, these are questions I've always had, yet never articulated – in fact, I didn't even know if these were possible for me. I knew in my heart that I wanted a Higher Love with my life partner, one that was truly extraordinary in which we felt we were transcending an old relationship paradigm that no longer worked for us, and creating connection on *every* level – mentally, emotionally, spiritually, physically.

What I'm grateful to share is that I am now with a man, my soulmate, who asks these very questions about love. Having this compass has guided us in taking our flirty courtship to a place of being in an intimate, juicy marriage and the ability to consciously parent our two little ones. We're able to ride the waves of rupture and rapture with a sense of grace, curiosity and even joy. I feel a sense of peace and contentment that I've never felt and have a sense of inner security that feels unshakable.

Which leads me to you, dear one.

If you're excited about this kind of love, then you're in the right place, at the right time.

In this book I'll be sharing the exact principles and techniques I used to find my partner, and steps you can begin taking to creating the life that your soul desires and *knows* you deserve. A life of love, fulfillment and authenticity.

Whether you're single or your relationship is feeling shaky and you're determined to transform this part of your life, following The 90-Day Soulmate Plan will set your heart and mind free to create a love life that takes you higher!

But first, let me tell you a little bit more about my experiences in love.

My Story

It was 2:00 am on January 30th, 2012. I woke up, sobbing into my eggshell-colored cotton duvet. There were smoky mascara stains on the edges of my sheets. I was shaking and in a state of shock.

The prior evening, I had met my fiancé for dinner at an upscale Mexican restaurant in Midtown Manhattan. I was thirty-two, in my prime, getting married to Mr. McDreamy. He was an Indian doctor that I had met online just a year prior – the man I *knew* was "the one" for me. I was so proud and relieved to finally achieve my dream of getting married and settling down with a kind, handsome man who was also such a catch.

I wore an elegant cream sweater, diamond drops in my ears, had straightened my hair and wore just enough make up to accentuate my luscious lips and my inquisitive, bewitching eyes.

It had been almost a month since we'd seen each other. As he walked in, he looked like a stranger. There was a stiffness and cool distance about him, and his expression looked both scary and comical.

When I saw him from my bar stool, I braced myself for the conversation we were going to have. I hugged him warmly, and he gingerly returned the embrace. My heart sank. *I had been there before.*

I was going to be a warrior, put aside my ego, and work through whatever tough patch we were going through.

As we sat down and ordered, we caught up briefly. He had moved to upstate New York for work, and we were just starting with wedding planning which seemed to not be getting anywhere.

As we ate silently, I started to ask him what was going on. I offered my apologies for my own outbursts and the fights we were having. I joked about our wedding planning and how we seemed to be stalled. He acknowledged all of this, and before I could continue, he stopped me.

"Sarika, I can't do this with you. I am breaking off our engagement."

My heart sank.

Throughout my twenties I had done everything to find my soulmate. I had read every book under the sun on dating and catching a great man, done courses, sought dating coaching support. I visited astrologers and performed rituals to clear my "troubled relationship house."

Interestingly, I had become so proficient in dating that even though I worked full-time as a management consultant on Wall Street, by evening I was moonlighting as a dating coach for women, many of whom found their partners.

In my personal life, though, I was plagued with painful patterns that didn't seem to go away. By some stroke of grace, I never had problems necessarily meeting great men or even dating them – in fact, most men I dated were everything on my list – handsome, educated, kind, even *evolved* in some way. We had romantic, fulfilling relationships with plenty of potential.

Yet I always ended up getting dumped and my heart broken.

I was determined to find my soulmate, no matter how frustrated I felt. Each date I went on, I patted myself on the back, often picking myself up after being ghosted or going on what I considered the longest date *ever* with Mr. Condescending or Boring (or both). Even after going on over a hundred first dates, and going through periods of feeling jaded and hurt, I somehow managed to always stay positive and optimistic and kept my faith burning alive.

In my relationships, I did what I could to be caring, feminine, sexy, mysterious and fun. I was agreeable and easygoing with men, although I had enough of an edge to keep things spicy. I was a master at flirting. I rarely acted insecure or jealous, and I was always willing to meet men more than halfway. My parents had taught me to be adjusting to a relationship, as is with my Indian heritage and being a woman, and I did that to a 'T' (albeit in a modern context of seeking equality and partnership in marriage). I played by "the rules" for getting married to a smart, successful, handsome man, and becoming the dream woman that men sought after.

7

When Mr. McDreamy and I started dating, he pulled out all the bells and whistles, wining and dining me, discovering the world with me. We shared our secret desires and fears into the wee hours of the night over cuddles and wine, traveled to near and far romantic destinations and dreamt about our future. We were having the time of our life together and were looking forward to spending our life together.

After a year of dating, he proposed to me at the riverfront overlooking Brooklyn Bridge, and I practically died with excitement – I felt like I was in an Indian Bollywood movie! We had an epic engagement party, inviting dozens of friends and family to celebrate with us, many of whom flew in from around the country. Indeed, it was a big moment – the moment I had been waiting for since I was a young woman.

I was ecstatic… and mostly, I felt like I had conquered the world and had solved the greatest mystery of all – falling in love and finding my mate.

So, I couldn't understand why this man was breaking up with me.

Yet, if I'm honest, I could sense that things were going to the pooper – fast. The month prior to our breakup, and perhaps even many months before, my body started telling me something wasn't right. I had my first panic attack on a flight during one of our travels, in which I fainted and hit my face badly which created a permanent scar. After our engagement, I felt a constant anxious knot in my stomach, along with nausea. There were growing disagreements between us. Every time I felt him pulling away, I would work harder to make the relationship work. I found myself stifling my words around him, not knowing how to communicate my discomfort with things that bothered me. We regularly drank our problems away or found other distractions, rationalizing that since we're good, well-meaning people, everything will work out. *After all, our parents' generation did fine, right?*

As I walked home alone on the cold, wintry night, I wanted to end my life. I fantasized about jumping into the East River.

As I lay in my bed, I wished this could all go away. I felt incredibly embarrassed, ashamed and deeply alone. I also wondered if he had made a mistake, because I was clearly his ideal partner (wasn't I?).

I wanted answers; *something* to change about my fate. I related to the female protagonist in Federico Fellini's film *Nights of Cabiria* who searched endlessly for love in Rome, only to be robbed and pushed over a cliff by her fiancé.

It was then, at 2:00 am, when I awoke, and a voice came from my heart that said, "I need spiritual healing".

I didn't know anything about this mysterious voice, or even what the words *spiritual healing* meant.

The very next day, as I roamed aimlessly, zombie-like, on my busy Manhattan avenue, I encountered a sign that said, "Psychic readings for $10." *Something drew me in.* Even though I had seen signs like this in the past, I avoided them like any reasonable person would.

Walking in, I met the woman who would go on to be my mentor and friend for the next four years. She was a chain-smoking Romanian Gypsy psychic named Pat.

She told me, *"You are deeply blocked and you're limited by your negative thinking about yourself and your life. Your heart and sexual chakras are blocked. If you don't recover from this broken relationship and clear your blocks, you will keep attracting the same patterns over and over, like a magnet. It will be like Groundhog's Day."*

I sat in shock, not understanding. I literally had done everything possible to make my love life work, and yet I was staring into an abyss because of the despair I felt.

Trying to grapple with what she was saying, I asked for more details.

"You are going through a spiritual crisis. If you want him back, then you really need to heal your heart and understand the ways you were sabotaging the relationship, and why. If it's the right relationship, he will come back."

9

Just a few years prior, I had gone to a ten-day silent meditation retreat in the Himalayas in India, known as Vipassana. Although one of the most arduous experiences I've endured, by the end of it, I had come out with newfound clarity, a sense of happiness and lightness. I had vowed to continue practicing meditation and pursuing spiritual growth, but by the time I came back to New York City and began working in my competitive workplace, while spending my free time dating to meet Mr. Right, I forgot.

At this very moment, however, I was skeptical of what she was saying. A chain-smoking Romanian Gypsy psychic, no less!

And yet... I was at my wits' end. I had lost everything – my dreams, my self-image and faith in life – and I felt stuck and exhausted.

She asked for $20,000 in cash and would guide me in healing over the next few months. I would meditate, pray to God, heal spiritually, and learn my lessons. I would learn about love, and the ways in which I was blocking myself.

Should I do this? The doubt arose in me. The side of me that always felt like I could do it better, smarter, cheaper... was there.

Looking at my alternatives, however, and feeling a sense of deep *resonance* – **I took a leap of faith into the unknown.**

Meeting my Soulmate

I began a journey of catharsis and recovery. I prayed, did healing practices, rituals and meditations, and began a process of examining my beliefs, patterns and thinking. I was a caterpillar in a vulnerable, messy blob of a chrysalis, becoming a butterfly without even knowing it.

The pain from the breakup was immense but knowing that I had a backstop and someone to hold the heartache with me helped tremendously as I wept with grief on New York City subways or screamed with rage into my pillow, making sense of my loss.

I came across spiritual teachings of different forms and found a community of people focused on meditation, service and kindness. While on this journey of understanding what love was really about, for the first time I was meeting my true soulmate friends who were also on a search for understanding what it took to lead a meaningful, fulfilling life.

I also traversed the path of reconciliation with my ex, which was incredibly scary and vulnerable. After I cut energetic cords with him (which I now somewhat jokingly call the "Ex Files"), understood what had happened, and even met him again to see whether we could make things work, I consciously decided to let him go. In due course, I even began to feel grateful for him for pushing me onto this path of finding myself!

I started to learn to have a respectful, joyful relationship with myself and see myself as my own soulmate. I found out that I'm actually a very lovable, spirited, gifted woman – and that I deserved happiness and true fulfillment.

I wasn't a late bloomer – I was at the perfect place, at the right time. I didn't suck at love – I merely didn't have the right tools for healthy relating.

I started to feel a sense of peace… and saw new possibilities in my life. It was like the murky clouds had cleared before my very eyes. I felt a deep sense of gratitude for the countless ways I was being loved and supported, the beauty of the world around me and for the experiences in my life.

I was stepping into a divine feminine path – one of deep self-love, awareness and pleasure, being deeply connected with my body, sexuality and emotions, and feeling a sense of limitlessness and empowerment. I discovered new sides of me, including my hidden talents in healing and psychic abilities, and opened up to my soul's purpose which helped me feel more aligned and grounded in myself.

I noticed that things were flowing in my life through grace, ease and synchronicity. I didn't have to struggle anymore!

A friend once told me when I complained to him about a man, "Sarika, love flows in the path of least resistance," implying that the relationship I was experiencing seemed too difficult to continue.

I didn't understand what I now knew – that it was in releasing my resistance to love and my own sabotage patterns, and opening my heart to giving and receiving genuine, unconditional love, that I saw miracles flowing to me! I met new friends in my local park who would give me gifts like new dresses, people on the street complimenting me on my radiance, or restaurateurs offering me complimentary meals. I felt such a deep level of kinship with everyone around me, and my heart was brimming with joy and a sense of self-confidence. Even my work was getting easier – I moved from working with toxic people to having a new boss who let me work from home twice a week and take long vacations, which was unheard of at my company.

I was becoming a magnet for love, and I was entering into a state of inner and outer alignment.

Ninety days after I began this path, I met a special man.

Even though we saw each other every week in our meditation circle, we hadn't really spoken to each other. As luck would have it, a friend connected me to him, saying, "I think you and Krishan have a lot in common and really need to talk!"

At a retreat, I noticed him gazing at me intently, yet gently. I felt a flutter in my heart and noticed that he was indeed handsome. I found the courage to walk up to him. We slowly began chatting away, and twenty minutes became an entire evening, which then became a series of e-mails and random long walks at night over several months. We laughed, listened to each other's stories and struggles, hung out in parks and held space for our visions. I shared things with him that I hadn't with anyone else.

I sometimes joke that Krishan was nothing on my "list" – he was five years younger than me, his name was similar to my ex's (I know, right?), he was on sabbatical and was living at home at the time with his parents. Yet he was exceptionally open, self-aware and vulnerable. This man was not the kind of "smart, successful," debonair (and emotionally unavailable) man I had ached for before in the past. Yet, we clearly had a connection… and I just let my curiosity lead the way.

Instead of jumping into a relationship with Krishan, I began to date consciously and joyfully. I discovered a new way of dating online and meeting men and found that the men I was attracting were of much higher quality. I was actually enjoying dating for the first time – it no longer felt like a game I was playing.

Right after our first "official" date, in which we spent the day together wandering through New York City, Krishan left for pilgrimage in Spain, the Camino de Santiago. We wrote long, beautiful e-mails to each other, and I would secretly wait to see his message pop up on my phone. Even though we longed to write and see each other, we allowed the flame to burn softly, and stay openhearted to whatever life was pre-senting us. I had no idea if he would meet someone while he was trav-eling – and for the first time in my life, I was ok with it, because I wanted him to be happy, no matter what.

And yet, when he came back to America, the first place he arrived from the airport was my apartment. When I opened the door, I found myself rejoicing!

We now have a cozy, beautiful home together and two enchanting daughters. We had our dream wedding in India in the city where the Buddha attained enlightenment, Bodh Gaya, with our entire family and many of our friends present. We are aligned in our values and even have similar trains of thought. Sometimes I feel like he can read me better than I can. I love his uniqueness and quirks, and he loves mine –

and we thrive off our differences (although these very things trigger us too). His sense of humor has me splitting at my seams.

I can safely say that being with Krishan has been the most magical experience of my life. There are times when I feel like I'm soaring, and he is the proverbial wind beneath my wings, my heart whisperer, my divine protector and lover. He tells me, "I have been looking for you my whole life. You are the answer to my prayers, my eternal fire, my reason for living. If it weren't for you, I would still be single and possibly a monk by now!"

Your Love Destiny

Now, having personally gone through this recovery and awakening in my love life, and having mentored countless more women and men in finding their mates, **I've found that the most effective path to meeting and *keeping* your man is one that is both holistic and transformational.**

I have newfound respect and awe for the power of love and its ability to heal us and turn us into more divine, radiant, potent versions of ourselves – wherein we become better lovers, mothers, wives, daughters, sisters, friends and colleagues. Love is inherently transformational, lightens our spirit, makes us kinder, generous, wiser, more radiant and openhearted. We connect with ourselves and the universe in a deeply profound, intimate way, and make our relationships unshakably strong. Love is the compass that guides us during the darkest nights of our soul and helps us meet and transcend our fears and insecurities with grace and strength. When it comes to our partner, love has the ability to elevate our relationship higher and higher, evolving our world for the better through it.

However, not only is love is misunderstood, but as modern women (and men), we are grossly unskilled at relationship building

and we struggle with our own insecurities and sabotage patterns, especially in intimate relationships. We start off with pure intentions but get hurt and sidetracked through our own behaviors and subconscious blocks. Moreover, **we attract circumstances and relationships that inevitably lead to suffering and struggling, over and over.**

What do some of the patterns look like?

... Getting your heart broken, over and over – or by a man you thought was "the one"

... Being ghosted by a man you thought was interested in you

... Dating men who are emotionally unavailable

... Getting entangled with a narcissist or being in an abusive relationship

... Losing yourself and your identity in relationships; struggling with low self-esteem or deep insecurity

... Feeling afraid to speak your truth; walking on eggshells around your partner

... Feeling like your relationship is simply taxiing around, not going anywhere

... Having poor health related to stress from your relationships

... Not feeling safe, secure and cherished in your relationship

... Turning to addictions, like alcohol, smoking, men, social media, etc. to escape your pain

These patterns have a way of chipping away at your soul and makes it even harder to get out there and trust that you will meet someone. Your light begins to dim, and you become jaded, losing faith in life. You begin to wonder if you are even worthy of love and fulfillment.

Another unfortunate factor in our painful love life is our education system and the lack of role models. Education around making relationships work is bare to none in our society and we have to rely on a relationship blueprint we receive from our own parents. To thrive in a relationship requires commitment and study in subjects that are not widespread or understood, while at the same time gaining mastery over our own psychology. Personally, I searched far and wide on how to make love work – and yet I received my most profound education from a Romanian gypsy psychic and a Zen Buddhist monk!

Practicing love is both an art and a science, and translating it from lofty ideals to day-to-day interpersonal relating takes tremendous skill. The path of love is also one of truth-seeking – uncovering what's really true for you, understanding what holds you back from achieving your soul's desires, and bringing utmost honesty and integrity into your relationships.

As high-achieving yet openhearted women, we *want* more from our lives, and we want to end the cycle of suffering that we're seeing manifest in our own love lives or we saw in our parents'. We recognize that we're being shortchanged by the existing narrative around love and dating – even our purpose and careers, and that somehow we're not living out our true potential. We know that there is a kind of relationship that's possible that connects us on every level – mentally, emotionally, spiritually, physically… and our souls won't settle for less.

There is a love revolution and paradigm shift waiting to happen – and if you're reading this book, you're part of it.

Over the last decade I've studied everything I can to help people find love that's *real* and fulfilling with the least amount of pain and heartbreak, while coaching countless women and men in stepping into their greatest potential in relationships.

Through dating and turning our relationship into a successful marriage and mentoring other women and men in dating and love, I've learned the exact steps to release your inner barriers, step into your feminine power and attract a partnership that resonates with you at a soul level. How to date in a conscious, joyful way with the least amount of heartache. How to create a passionate relationship with a magical, sexy man that fuels your mind, body and spirit; one in which you both transcend what's holding you back from total connection, ecstasy and fulfillment.

Now I want to share this with you during your own Love Goddess journey in attracting and creating a life and relationship on your terms.

"Your task is not to seek for love, but merely to seek and find all the barriers within yourself that you have built against it." ~ Rumi

If you're willing to do the inner work of releasing your barriers and raising your consciousness around love, then miracles and healthy love *will* flow to you; it's only inevitable.

Now, at this point, if what I'm sharing with you doesn't resonate or doesn't feel right to you, then I would encourage you to stop reading this book and find another resource supporting your love life. I mean it!

My desire is for you to trust your own intuition and have the courage to follow a path that feels aligned for you.

On the other hand, if you're curious (and even a little skeptical), and a) you've done everything already for your love life and you're still feeling stuck, b) you're just coming out of a relationship, or c) are ready to consciously forge a *higher* kind of soulmate relationship with your partner – then I invite you to read on and follow the path that this book takes you on.

You have to tap into what *resonates* for you – and the way resonance feels for many is like a quickening in heart rate, maybe even a combination of fear and excitement. In fact, the more you go on this journey, the more resonance you will begin to feel, which is an essential part of calling in your dream relationship.

The goal of this book is to support you in taking steps in getting into energetic alignment with your soulmate and learning the secrets of how to date like the Love Goddess you truly are.

When and how you meet your mate is of course up to divine timing and how committed you are to showing up to your love life. The good news is, when you're aligned you will find everything in your life, including dating, your close relationships, and even your career, feeling smoother and even joyful.

Why ninety days, though? It takes three months for all your cells in your body to regenerate and for you to rewire your thinking around love and develop healthy relationship habits. In this time period you can completely rewrite your story while upgrading your physiology and psyche for a higher kind of love. You'll be stepping into a more divine, wise, loving version of yourself that can see through B.S. and establish relationships in your life on your terms.

"The moment you change your perception is the moment you rewrite the chemistry of your body." ~ Dr. Bruce H. Lipton

You will begin to create a solid, unshakable inner foundation based on the principles of self-love, and you'll see its impact rippling into every part of your life – including creating intimate, juicy relationships that your heart always longed for.

My intention through this book is to *activate* your mind, body, and spirit, the parts of you that are inherent yet hidden, waiting to be to be unleashed as you step into becoming the sexy, confident and radiant Love Goddess that you truly are.

Through following the framework and exercises in the book, you will become relationship-ready and open to meeting Mr. Right, someone whom you connect with on every level. Your man will be in awe and have deep respect and gratitude for you – and no doubt he'll want to be around you for life. You're his Queen!

So, lady… are you ready to take the journey your heart and soul have been waiting for?

Let's get started!

————

"And the day came when the risk to remain a tight bud was more painful than the risk it took to blossom." ~ Anais Nin

How to Do This Book

Embarking on your soulmate journey is both exciting and nerve-wrecking.

First of all, if you've made it here and you are committing to your 90-day love transformation, congratulations! You've made the right choice in investing your time and energy into a process that has worked for anyone who has done it.

In order to make the most out of your ninety days, I would recommend you read all the materials and do each of the exercises involved, one at a time. I will also be providing meditations, rituals and practices. **Don't worry about doing additional research or work related to the concepts being shared – simply stick to the materials and exercises provided.** Later on, you can do a deeper dive in each area – I have been studying all these topics for nearly a decade and keep finding areas for my love life to heal and blossom.

How to do the book by week

Preparation: Read Introduction and Part I: Creating Love That Lasts

Begin the 90-Day Journey: 5 Steps to Calling in Your Soulmate. *(Note: This is guidance; please follow your own intuition in how to pace yourself and adjust accordingly.)*

Step 1: Be a Love Magnet

Week 1: Mental Well-being; Spiritual Well-being

Week 2: Emotional Well-being

Week 3: Physical Well-being

Step 2: Heal Your Heart & Close Your "Ex Files"

Week 4: Heal your Heart – From Yourself

Week 5: Heal your Heart – Mother Wound

Week 6: Heal your Heart – Father Wound & Release Your Ancestral Blocks

Week 7: Heal your Heart – Close Your "Ex Files"

Step 3: Discover your "Wow!" Factor

Week 8: Awakening Your Sexuality

Week 9: Activating the Divine Feminine Within

Week 10: Aligning with Your Purpose & Igniting Your Passion

Step 4: Prepare for Love

Week 11: Feng Shui Principles for Calling in Love & Establish Your Queendom

Step 5: Date & Love with Confidence
Week 13: Enlightened Dating Principles & Getting Started
with Dating

(Note: You can download and print out the weekly plan here:
https://sarikajain.com/Soulmate-Plan-Resources/)

As you're getting started, think about the next ninety days as a
sacred container for yourself and practicing self-love. The more you
invest in yourself in this area of your life, the more you'll reap the
rewards. Here are some ways to prepare your sacred container:

1. Commitment

As you're starting, make the decision to continue this program for
ninety days. Let the universe know, by declaring, "I hereby declare that
in these next three months, my love life is taking priority and I am going
to show up each and every moment I can for it, come what may!"
There's something really powerful about putting a stake in the ground
and creating the conditions for this sacred process. Commitment begets
rootedness and focus, allowing all sorts of magical forces beyond your
wildest imagination to come in and play.

There are going to be many times when you want to give up. For
instance, you might start feeling like what I'm sharing is hogwash or
that somehow this process doesn't apply to you. The moment you begin
to feel something is "too much", you might seek a back door like quit-
ting, some sort of addiction like getting on social media or even complaining to a friend. This is a sabotage pattern that regularly shows up

in our lives and stops us from reaching our full potential. I would say – face it with love and courage.

Know that the path of love will help you reach the highest destinations that no other road can take you to.

2. Dating

I strongly recommend that you take a hiatus from dating for at least two months. Deactivate those apps to not invite temptation. In fact, I would recommend that you only begin dating again when you feel that genuine spark of desire inside (and not coming from a place of urgency). This is because the process of untangling from the past, creating a strong inner foundation and rewiring for healthy love takes effort and focus. It's important to stay clear of emotional triggers that will derail this precious process. If you get back too quickly to dating, you risk going "one step forward, two steps back" in your dating patterns. I want you to experience your love life blossoming like a rose!

Likewise, if you're in a relationship, let your partner know that you're going to be spending time concentrating on your inner well-being for the next ninety days, and graciously ask him to support you in getting the space you need. This doesn't mean you're not going to be there for your man. In fact, you'll show up as a better version of yourself when your own cup is full!

3. Time and space

Think of the next ninety days as love detoxing and recovery. Set aside several hours a week to focus on your love life, if not more. There's no better use of time than extraordinary self-love and self-care. If you're doing other programs, I would recommend you stop, as each program is potent and transformative on its own. Disconnect from the news, media and all outside influences as much as possible to create mental and emotional space for detoxing, and focus on eating healthy foods and getting exercise. Spend time in nature, meditate, pray, and simply be, when you have free time. Let your friends and family know that you'll be a bit busy focusing on self-care, and let go of social engagements for a while, if your schedule is overwhelming.

Sometimes we have to prioritize the most important things in our lives. I've learned that my love life has to be my top priority in order for me and my family to be happy and healthy, always. If there isn't a bit of sacrifice, then great things can't be achieved, right?

We've been taught that our careers are most important, along with taking care of others, while our love life should somehow emerge naturally. This is far from the truth! In fact, the lack of time and space for love is what's holding men and women back from engaging meaningfully with each other and breaking down relationships. Studies have shown that the greatest cause of illness comes from stress in relationships. *Our relationship health is ultimately what defines our happiness,* so investing as much time and energy as possible and even receiving relationship education is essential.

4. Doing this program with others

I have found that having a group of like-minded people around me as I embark on a sacred journey is vital. People who believe in love, healing and transformation and can see you in your greatest potential; with whom you can share about your experience honestly while also holding you accountable. Of course, having a mentor, therapist or coach is powerfully supportive, as well.

Whether you're working with someone or doing this program your own, I would recommend creating a pod with other women and meeting once a week to share experiences or do some of the exercises together. *Sometimes, a transformational journey can feel lonely and isolating.* Plus, you'll enjoy your love journey a heck of a lot more when you're laughing through your gaffes and celebrations with others! In these gatherings, try to agree on an agenda and a time limit, and choose a facilitator. You can even start with a twenty-minute meditation. It's important to create a judgement-free zone, where you're there to witness each other with compassion without trying to fix or give each other advice. Affirm and celebrate each other's successes! As women, we need each other's friendship, appreciation and affirmation to thrive.

5. Materials

During this book, I'll be sharing some practices, meditations and rituals, some of which may require taking a bath with rose petals, "saging" your place (sage is a type of plant that, when burned, creates smoke that will energetically clean your environment), worksheets, using a candle, or making a vision board using magazine cutouts.

However, there's one item that you will keep throughout: a rose quartz crystal, which you can buy from any spiritual bookstore or online. Ideally, you want one that you can place on your heart for a meditation every morning, which I'll be sharing below.

Rose quartz is a crystal with tremendous healing abilities, especially in the area of heart healing and allowing for love to flow into your life. Sometimes when I'm wearing rose quartz jewelry, people say I'm glowing.

When you get your rose quartz, you can clean it by either placing it under moonlight, in a pot of soil, or in water with rock salt overnight. The next day, you can rinse it and pat it dry, and hold it in your hands, praying and sending loving energy to the crystal.

Fun fact: Our hands have powerful energy, especially when we direct our healing intention through them, and can be used on ourselves or our loved ones.

After cleaning the stone and praying to it, you can make a decree: "I ask to release all old programs in this stone and set a new intention for the stone to support me in healing my heart and becoming a conduit for love."

The stone will be your best friend throughout your love journey.

6. Morning ritual (very important!)

Perhaps the most important way to heal your heart and mind is to have a daily morning ritual. The first thing you should do as soon as you wake up is to do something positive, *before* your mind gets busy and distracted with negative thinking and mundane tasks of the day. Your morning ritual will set the tone for the rest of the day, and doing this every day, without fail, will be what creates lasting results – outside of everything else that you do in this book. You will find that just doing this morning ritual will change your life. Note: If you're feeling some resistance with this, know that this is common. Our ego is resistant to being told what to do, especially when it's healthy or involves sticking to a routine which requires discipline. Simply bring awareness and have compassion for yourself. Remember, it's only for the next ninety days!

When you wake up, list ten things that you are grateful for out loud. Feel the gratitude inside out. You can think, "I'm grateful for this bed and having a safe place to sleep; I'm grateful for having food, water and safety; I'm grateful for my job and income…" You could even be grateful that you're not in a toxic relationship – really a huge blessing!

Gratitude is the most powerful energy for receiving grace and attracting what you desire in your life. Gratefulness sets you up for being open to receiving – and remembering that your life is a gift. If you can live in that space, you'll feel a heart opening.

Then, placing the rose quartz on your heart, as you're lying down, pray to your higher self/universe/God for ten minutes for surrender, grace, healing, love, forgiveness. You can think to yourself, "I am open to love, grace and healing entering my life" over and over.

Say the below affirmations in front of a mirror. Affirmations have a powerful way of rewiring our thinking and creating the environment for deeper, more subtle changes to take place. If you can do this before going to bed, that would be great too.

- I accept my life.
- I accept my parents.
- I accept this body.
- I am worthy of God's love.
- I am worthy of a happy, healthy, abundant life.
- I am worthy of healthy, fulfilling relationships.
- I love myself, my mother, my father, God.
- God, my mother, my father, love me.
- I can change.
- It's OK for me to heal.
- I can grow.
- It's OK for me to grow.
- It's OK for me to thrive and express my aliveness in the world.
- I am safe in the world.
- I can distinguish friend from foe.

Place an energetic shield on your body. Envision a permeable, translucent golden egg (or another visual that feels resonant) around you, take one or two mindful breaths, and declare with a smile, "May only things of my vibration or higher enter my field." Sometimes I mimic creating the egg around my body with my hands as I'm saying these words, so as to infuse my intention.

(Note: For ease, I've included the morning ritual and affirmations which you can download here: https://sarikajain.com/Soulmate-Plan-Resources/)

PART I
CREATING LOVE THAT LASTS

Cultivating Your Love Garden

Emily's anxiety attacks, or "episodes", were becoming more regular. She had been dating Robert for over a year, and she could feel him pulling away. The more he seemed distant, the more she clung to him and the more her panic took over her body, paralyzing her, sometimes to a point where she felt she couldn't breathe.

During our coaching, Emily began her Love Recovery journey. She began to calm her mind and body, observe her sabotage patterns, and look deeply at her personal habits. She saw she needed to unlearn what she had about love and relationships and bring in new love practices for herself. She realized her anxiety was due to past hurts and her fear of abandonment. Her sabotage patterns and relationship habits were hard-wired and unconscious. When she felt insecure, she resorted to old coping mechanisms like clinging, threatening and bargaining, which pushed Robert away, causing her to feel even more mistrustful.

Emily began to heal and nourish her own heart, mind and spirit and expand her consciousness around love, first with herself. Through this process, Emily became the grounded, sexy, compassionate version of herself, reclaiming her inner Love Goddess, which naturally attracted Robert and brought forth his desire for connection. Now, a few years later, they are happily married with two beautiful sons, and have a juicy relationship based on mutual understanding and adventure. She is the compass and he's the driver of their ship!

As you're beginning in your Love Recovery journey, it's important to first form a firm understanding about what love is and isn't, and how to **begin cultivating the conditions for love and grace to show up in your life.**

As I've discovered through the years, so much of our understanding about love is plain wrong. We've been fed lies from our media, society, movies, and education system, which has left us woefully unprepared in making relationships work – in fact, so much of our schooling ends up promoting ideas on competition, perfectionism and worldly success which drives wedges in our relationships. On top of that, unbeknownst to us, we've been programmed into believing that there's something fundamentally wrong and unlovable about us, and that love is about fulfilling a long list of needs that somehow never gets met. The less those needs are met, the more we feel undeserving, which creates low self-esteem and loss in trust and faith that we'll ever get what we want. What a self-fulfilling prophecy!

In recent years, **I've had a chance to rethink my purpose for being, which I've come to realize is about being my most loving self and sharing this love with others.** I used to be confused about what all of this meant and how to achieve that and felt like love was a game. "Don't hate the player, hate the game" was my motto when dating.

Now, when I think of love, I think of it as a **sacred garden that I'm constantly cultivating.** When my love garden is thriving, I almost don't have to think about what's going to grow, or who's going to come garden it with me... it happens magically, and life often surprises me.

Most of us barely have a seedy strip of land that we could consider our "love garden." In it, the soil is mostly barren, and while some of the seeds planted are of understanding and compassion, many of the seeds include insecurity, greed, grief or anger. We may forget to provide light or water and other nutrients. Our garden is overrun by weeds which sabotage the growth of the flowers and fruit trees we plant. However, by surrounding it with beautiful faery lights and putting up a sign that says, "Free garden to play in!", we hope that someone great will come and join us – and that through some sheer stroke of luck and providence, the garden will turn into a magical paradise. Instead, we attract vagabonds and bored teenagers who trash our garden further with broken beer bottles and piss, taking an inch or two of the garden with them.

After my last break-up, I felt like there was no love left for me in the world. I saw myself as a loveless blob, a street urchin – someone God left behind – and just felt immensely pitiful about myself. I felt insanely jealous of my friends having the best times of their lives with their men, traveling the world, having kids, getting promoted at their jobs. I wondered if I was capable of truly loving and if anyone could possibly love me.

Today, I see my main job as a gardener. I spend a lot of time nourishing my soil through self-love and unconditional love practices. I mindfully unearth my deeply entrenched seeds of contempt, greed, fear, and I've been planting and watering my seeds of compassion, joy and other positive traits. I am constantly weeding – observing and getting rid of sabotage patterns that want to destroy my love garden. I water, providing sunshine and the right nutrients to my garden, like meditation, being in a state of pleasure and healing my heart and limiting beliefs. I keep learning how to plant and support different heart-opening aspects to grow in my garden, like my romantic relationship, raising happy, healthy children, cultivating genuine friendships and sharing my gifts in the world in an uplifting way. I invite like-minded friends to join me in dancing and singing in this gorgeous sacred ground. From time to time, I am surprised by the random new fruits and fragrant flowers that keep showing up in my little paradise, along with playful butterflies, fairies and pollinating bumblebees. My garden is thriving, abundant and magnetic, if I might say so myself!

> Journal: How would you describe your love garden?
> How would you like your love garden to look and feel?

What are some ways that we destroy our garden, and how do we cultivate the most beautiful love garden for ourselves?

As a Love Goddess, the first thing you have to master is your understanding of how love and relationships work, and your unique role in all of this. You'll get to see that there's nothing wrong with *you* – rather, the cards are stacked against *all* of us, and learning to navigate the maelstrom of relationships is the work of the humble yet determined love warrior.

(Note: In this chapter, I'm asking you to dive deep. We're going to the roots, so you can examine your blocks that prevent you from stepping into your love potential – this is where the foundations are laid, so stick with me, Love Goddess! The journal prompts provided are merely suggestions, so use them in a way that feels good. Going through the process in the rest of the book will help you release your blocks – so if you're fretting, not to worry.)

Law of Karma

(Note: In this section, we're talking about karma as a concept of cause and effect, especially for conscious actions you'll be taking in your life going forward. This is by no means downplaying trauma you may have experienced in your life, or saying that something is your fault, such as sexual assault, childhood neglect or any form of abuse. I have the deepest respect for women and men who have endured such circumstances, many a time emerging with beautiful healing gifts and abilities.)

"Do to others as you would have them do to you." ~ Luke 6:31

Everything that you say or do to others has a lasting effect on people, which comes back to you through the law of karma. When you do something that hurts yourself or another, intentionally or unintentionally, it comes back into your life as a lesson to learn.

I'm sure you've heard people say, "Karma's a bitch!" When life throws you a curveball, or some of your relationships are floundering, you can be sure that karma's got something to do with it.

Life gives us relationships to heal our karma and learn our lessons, and to become better, more compassionate, kind, wise beings in the process. We learn so much about ourselves through each relationship, whether at home, school or work. Sometimes I wonder if there's such a thing as a random encounter.

I choose to look at every relationship situation from a karmic lens, whether it's learning about why I got dumped, holding space for my daughter's tantrums, dealing with a toxic boss or being deeply triggered by something my husband said or didn't say. Each dark night of the soul I go through (usually triggered by other people), I see it as an opportunity to heal or release something, and somehow, through divine guidance and support, find a way to transcend the painful situation with grace.

In this sense, none of us are victims – we're all on a personal growth journey, which supports us becoming closer to our authentic, loving, powerful selves.

Spiritual Blocks and Other Barriers to Love

Sometimes you see a pattern happening over and over in your life and you can't quite put a finger on why a certain situation seems like Groundhog's Day. When it only seems to be getting worse, then it may indicate that you're dealing with a **spiritual block** – a lesson you're meant to learn or resolve on a spiritual level. For instance, maybe you find yourself being broke constantly, getting your heart broken or constantly getting entangled with toxic people, like narcissists. The root could be something deeper, like a spiritual block which leads you to believe that you are unworthy of love, or have a karmic entanglement to clear. The block may even show up as in your body as an illness or disease, as self-help authors Louise Hay talks about in *You Can Heal Your Life*, and Anita Moorjani discusses in *Dying to Be Me*, each describing that their form of cancer came from deeply rooted places of self-loathing. This doesn't mean that there's something wrong with you – far from it. *These are ways our body or life circumstances are telling us to "Wake up!" and deal with situation at hand – often in a different, more holistic way.*

Before we're born, we choose our parents and our life circumstances to help us learn, based on the karma we're here to heal and areas we want to grow in, spiritually. I know that it's hard to fathom why someone would choose an abusive parent or experience rampant addiction in one's family, yet these are the very experiences we're here to recover from and find our sense of love, power and truth within. Inter-

36

estingly, some of the most compassionate, sensitive people I know had a toxic parent – they learned how to navigate challenging situations and swore to themselves that they wouldn't repeat their parents' pattern.

Our life experiences go on to shape our thinking and belief system, and we get certain memories imprinted in our psyches. We're prone to getting hurt (ask my daughter – she loves showing me her 'boo boos') and holding the pain in our bodies. Unfortunately, physiologically our body often remembers pain more than pleasure in order to help protect us and make safe decisions. The pain ends up piling up, and **we produce other blocks – mental, emotional, sexual, energetic, physical.**

These blocks are deeply subconscious – many stemming from our early childhood experiences, from conception to five years old. We learn how to deal with challenging situations, like a parent cold-shouldering one another or hearing words like "money doesn't grow on trees" or "love is about sacrifice" and in due course this becomes our *conditioning*. Simply put, all our life we're conditioned with how to respond to life's ups and downs – how to feel, what to say, how to react to different triggers. In fact, many parts of our personality are formed from unconsciously compensating for something that we feel is lacking or wrong with our parents or ourselves.

We also develop some deep fears early in life, like the fear of abandonment, of not being 'good enough' or being somehow 'bad' or unlovable. Usually, we have one core fear running our lives and we do everything possible to preserve ourselves from facing this fear (while turning it into a self-fulfilling prophecy), which sometimes seems crazy! For instance, if you're deeply afraid of being abandoned or losing yourself in a relationship, you may date unavailable men or be in long-distance relationships that never go anywhere.

When we have unresolved blocks and fears, we begin to have limited flow of life force in our bodies and we're operating from a place of survival. We're in a state of resistance to life. We begin to **unconsciously**

sabotage our life – like showing up late for meetings, putting our foot in our mouth, falling and tripping, getting sick or pushing people away. We end up creating a host of problems that we didn't mean to, and life begins to feel out of control. We feel like victims because things just don't seem to be going our way, and we feel that we're on a downward spiral.

> Journal: What may be some mental, emotional, physical or spiritual blocks showing up in your life? What are the physical symptoms, and what patterns do you see? What possible sabotage patterns are you seeing play out?

Wait Up! My Archnemesis is Leading My Love Life?

Do you ever wonder who that woman was that shrieked and acted insanely jealous when her man got a phone call from his ex or disappeared for an evening without telling her? Was that woman ever you?

It's amazing how we lose our cool and say and do things that seem "uncool" when we're feeling insecure or riled up. We end up saying and doing things that feel good in the moment but make us feel embarrassed in the end. Of course, there's nothing wrong with being 'real', but when we're not self-aware, we end up playing out an unconscious part of us that's secretly out to destroy us and our relationships.

Echkart Tolle, author of *The Power of Now*, talks about our "pain-body" leading the show in our relationships – which I see as a combination of our ego, accumulated pain and lifetime of conditioning. It's the reactive reptilian part of our brain. This pain-body paints a "cool, calm and collected" *chica*, but is ready to lash out or flee the moment it experiences something triggering. Its main goal is to shelter an insecure, fragile ego and a frightened inner child.

This pain-body *wants* you to be single because it wants to protect you from the outside world, and in turn, it sabotages your relationships. In these moments, though, we inadvertently generate more karma because we're coming from a place of causing even more suffering to ourselves and others.

For instance, let's say that your man withdraws. It may bring up an old fear that he's going to abandon you because he's pulling away. Your protective, defensive side lashes out, either sending you into an anxiety attack or getting annoyed with him, hurting him even more through your contempt or criticism. Whatever the pattern is, it will devour your relationship alive like a voracious honey badger going nuts on its prey – and in those moments, you don't have any control! Enough moments like this lead to a loss in trust and stability in a relationship, which causes your partner to pull further away.

Here's the other thing. The pain-body *loves* drama in its relationships and is constantly trying to itch that what can't be scratched. For instance, maybe you had an unavailable dad, or you've been hurt by men in your life. You've had to struggle your whole life to prove your worth, whether it's with your parents, your career and especially romantic love. Your pain-body may be wired to crave for the charismatic but distant and non-committal man that it thinks can fulfil that crazy, never-to-be-fulfilled desire of being loved and validated by that "unavailable man" in your life. If you had a narcissistic parent, your pain-body may want you to find a narcissistic partner. Or it may settle for a "good enough" relationship just to fulfill its needs for safety, only to find you constantly bored, hot and bothered.

When you're wounded, your chemistry is off, and you're wired to be attracted to dangerous men or less-than-perfect matches. On the

flip side, you can be so afraid of getting hurt that you squander your chances when the real deal shows up – what a doozy!

> Journal: In what ways does your pain-body show up in your relationships? What is its' personality, and what does it hope to achieve?

> Meditate: Can you offer love and compassion for your pain-body, perhaps even thanking it for protecting you till now, recognizing it as the hurt part of you that's been conditioned to behave in an unconscious way?

I share all of this to give you a perspective on the different ways that you are either attracting duds or ruining a potentially great relationship.

Here's the good news. In this book we'll be going through the A to Z of releasing all these blocks and noticing these patterns. By going through this process, you'll be aligning with your loving self. You'll be a warrior when it comes to whipping away your love blocks. You'll not only stop creating more negative karma, you'll be setting yourself up to attract Mr. Right.

Underneath your pain-body and blocks is a magnanimous, loving, omnipotent, radiant human being.

To gently release your blocks and allow for love and grace to enter your life and to live as powerfully as possible is what makes life super fun and interesting. It's almost like solving a somewhat maddening, yet fascinating scavenger hunt mystery to get to the treasure – and guess what – you're it!

Your soul is on a special journey of growth and love in a vehicle that's your human body, on our planet Earth, which is the ultimate school for your soul. That's why they say that we're divine beings having a human experience. As such, recognizing the spiritual nature of your life, especially when it comes to love, will drastically improve your human experience, and you'll open up to living with even more fulfillment than you could have possibly imagined.

The soulmate relationship you attract will be one based on true connection and healing – not on unresolved karmic issues or sabotage patterns.

Unleashing Your Feminine Power and Stepping into Higher Love

There's a superpower lying dormant in you, and that's your womanhood.

It's only in the recent years when I've asked myself the question, "What's so great about being a woman anyways?" that I got to go deep into understanding my power.

I found that I had deeply rooted biases about women given our patriarchal system and how men seem to have the upper hand, no matter what. It drove me nuts that I had to work so hard at both work *and* love, and somehow nothing I contributed was enough – men would get the promotions and bigger paychecks, find doting wives and most of all didn't have the burden of giving birth and childcare. My self-worth was linked to the deficiencies I felt women had – and on top of that, I perceived women having less power. In religious institutions around the world, women are hardly given the title as spiritual leaders, and certain religions state that women can never attain enlightenment because of their role of giving birth and being caretakers of others.

I secretly felt that being a woman was a curse.

Now I'm realizing nothing can be farther than the truth!

In ancient cultures around the world, feminine (and masculine) energies were esteemed. Pagan cultures which worshipped the Mother have long existed. In India, the sacred feminine has been revered; for instance, in Tamilian culture, girls and women are seen as embodiments of goddess Lakshmi – goddess of love, abundance and well-being. In ancient India, it was normal to see female gurus and spiritual aspirants. Unfortunately, society around the world has morphed due to modernization and colonization, diminishing the understanding of the inherent, divine nature of the feminine.

As women, we are the relationship leaders and the creators of family, society and culture. When we learn the secrets to relationship-building and we're deeply connected to our divine nature, our powers are unleashed. Spiritually speaking, the feminine seeks relationship, while the masculine seeks consciousness. As humans, we have both masculine and feminine energies. Yet when we women heal ourselves and allow feminine energy to flow through our bodies, which have a sacred role of creating and sustaining life, we operate at a higher, more unified state of consciousness.

We have the power of turning men to putty and playing at their heartstrings. There's nothing else that a man wants but being inside a woman. This sounds sexual – but it's deeper – men need women to survive, to feel loved, safe and nourished in a safe harbor – so much so that it hurts when they don't have that connection. Men are inherently vulnerable to a woman's love and approval.

William Golding, author of *Lord of the Flies*, said: "I think women are foolish to pretend they are equal to men, they are far superior and always have been. Whatever you give a woman, she will make greater. If you give her sperm, she'll give you a baby. If you give her a house, she'll give you a home. If you give her groceries, she'll give you a meal.

42

If you give her a smile, she'll give you her heart. She multiplies and enlarges what is given to her. So if you give her any crap, be ready to receive a ton of shit."

A couple of thousand years ago, men who were smart but greedy men got wind of women's power and created a whole system (think *The Handmaid's Tale*) to make women feel small and helpless to control and use them. Women were conditioned to believing that they had to conform to societal norms, like marriage and being dependent on men in order to survive the system.

If that patriarchal history isn't enough, we women are constantly targeted by media and corporations that dumb us down, force us to compete with each other and feel "not-enough."

While this has been true till now, women are waking up from this illusion. Whether it's lackluster relationships, thyroid or feminine health issues or deep-set anxiety and depression, the toll on women's lives is real. Women want to reclaim their true selves and recover from an abusive system that ends up hurting both men and women.

I'm not sharing this to make you hate men or the system (which includes women who operate with unconscious biases and oftentimes cause more harm than good) – rather, I want you to understand that **in order to enter a new paradigm of relationship, then you have to transcend this old, painful one – and begin to understand that you are greater than what you've been conditioned to accept.** This isn't about becoming equal to men in education and career and feeling a sense of redemption through it. Or simply about claiming one's financial independence.

It's about learning to really love yourself and claiming the parts of the feminine that have been repressed by society, like your compassion, creativity, intuition, sexuality and the powerful, unique, deep connection with the divine which no man can ever emulate, which I call the *divine feminine*.

43

To me, a part of being on a heroine journey is to unravel the special gifts I have available through my divine feminine side, while marrying them with my more developed, yet evolving masculine side.

I used to read dating books that would tell me to "be mysterious" and "keep him on his toes" through accentuating my sexuality, and I'd play games to increase a man's desire for me. Conversely, at work, I had to subdue my feminine and sexy side so that I could be taken seriously. There were a lot of conflicting boxes to tick!

Now that I'm embodying my feminine power, I don't need to manipulate a man to want to be with me – I instead tap into my God-given feminine qualities, and simply be myself, drawing men to me like bees to honey. In my career, I do my work with grace and ease, and am comfortable with my nurturing, intuitive, receptive, compassionate sexy side that's also strong and determined. This feels natural and *resonant.*

When a woman is in her divine feminine, men around her feel turned on and begin to step into their sacred masculine. When you're in your feminine power, you have the power of supporting your man becoming a rightful, wise, loving king, with his allegiance to serving, protecting and providing for you. A true Love Goddess (like Queen Cleopatra) can even inspire an entire army of men that are devoted to fulfilling her vision and mission. This isn't hyperbole or about gender stereotyping – this is in alignment with natural masculine and feminine energies that are waiting to emerge and flow through us and unite in this way.

The feminine energy is magnetic and has the power of manifestation. When you're embodying your feminine power, you begin to energetically draw in and create a new reality based on your authentic desires.

While awakening your divine feminine side is a lifelong journey, in this book you'll be taking the right steps in healing your relationship with your femininity and discovering sacred gifts that are waiting to be unleashed which will support you in your love life.

Vibrating at the Frequency of Love

"If you want to find the secrets of the universe, think in terms of energy, frequency and vibration." ~ Nicola Tesla

We were each born with a soul essence which vibrates at a certain frequency. I like to think of our soul's frequency like that of a tuning fork, which when struck begins to ring at a certain vibration. **When a tuning fork is struck, if there is another tuning fork of the same natural frequency, it too begins to vibrate, which is how resonance works.**

We each have a unique, beautiful frequency at which we naturally vibrate from the moment we are conceived.

However, over time, as crud develops on our tuning fork due to painful experiences and false beliefs, we begin to vibrate at a lower frequency, which creates misalignment. This may show up in your life as constant anxiety, personal conflict and depression. What you think, say and do seem to be off-kilter, and you might feel like a different person at home, work and your personal relationships. You get tired of wearing so many hats, living up to others' expectations, while watching your own life force dwindle away. In this state, you keep attracting relationships with men that just don't work out and you can't put a finger on it.

You must be wondering, *"So, Sarika, how the heck do we get into alignment anyways?"*

The most powerful way to "clearing your tuning fork" and stepping into your natural frequency is by following a journey of self-love.

Once you begin to take steps in learning to truly love yourself and commit to clearing your emotional baggage and inner blocks, you begin to align with your original frequency. The signal from your tuning fork will become clearer, and over time you begin to feel a sense of integrity in everything that you say and do, no matter where you are or whom you're with. You feel a sense of energetic alignment which invariably brings peace and tranquility within, even when life throws its curveballs.

When your thoughts, words and actions are in alignment with your soul vibration, your signal becomes clear. You begin to sync with people and opportunities you deeply resonate with, which is basically what synchronicity is. Inevitably... you *will* attract your soulmate.

This isn't woo-woo mumbo-jumbo – this is physics! Now that I've been studying energy, I realize that love can be seen as an energy or vibration that we can align with. It is an emotional state that's generated through our intention and actions.

Dear Love Goddess, your potent Love Recovery journey is only beginning, and no doubt, just by contemplating all that I have shared, you are raising your consciousness around love.

You now have a foundational understanding in what it takes to make a relationship thrive and why you attract certain patterns. In the rest of the book, you'll learn the secrets of stepping into your relationship potential and attracting love that takes you higher and higher!

Love Alchemy: 5 Tools for Massively Upgrading Your Love Life

After the breakup with my ex, I was done with toxicity and inauthenticity in my life. I would rather have nothing than to deal with any more drama. I was tired of dysfunctional work-place dynamics, working ridiculously long hours on projects that I didn't resonate with. My relationships with my family and friends were feeling superficial. I felt done with dating and was ready to give up. I couldn't put a finger on it, but somehow I felt that the common factor was "me." I was tired of pleasing, over-giving, avoiding certain people, feeling rejected, harboring irritation and anger at men and feeling jealous of others' happiness. My life felt half-lived, and everything felt hard and challenging.

After beginning my Love Recovery journey, I asked myself, "How do I know I'm making progress anyways? What if I'm repeating the same patterns and don't even realize it? What if I'm always destined to be single, no matter what I do? Maybe I'm the one who's meant to be alone."

Yet, I plowed through. I had plenty of resistance, self-doubt and bitterness. I was resolute that no matter what, I was going to conquer Love, or have her break open my heart and undo me, whichever one came first!

Through the Love Recovery process, I realized that I didn't need to fight anymore, nor seek control. I saw that I was more powerful than I thought I was, and that I was divinely supported. If I approached everything with love with the best of my abilities, using certain tools, then things would transform on their own, often into even better situations. Even situations which seemed like a curse were actually blessings in the end. Using the Love Alchemy tools, I was starting to get softer around my edges and less defensive or driven by desire to prove something or be someone else. I was able to face my fears and resistance head on, and I began to approach my sabotage patterns with more conscious awareness.

There was an "alchemy" happening within me, and I could feel the heavy energy within transforming. That inner transformation felt uncomfortable at times, and I could literally feel my anger and fear festering in me, wanting me to stop – yet, through patience and attentiveness, I watched it metamorphize into understanding and wisdom. My habits were getting healthier, and I was making better decisions that were coming from a place of personal truth and strength. I started to get in touch with my intuition and could navigate the world through my heart, feeling for resonance. I felt lighter, more curious and playful – and ultimately was having more fun.

Things were manifesting for me that were better, especially the things that I knew were true to my heart – like community, my well-being, discovering my unique gifts, getting more time off from work, reveling in nature and having time to relax and simply "be."

Best of all, while I was dating, the old patterns no longer bothered me, and I started attracting higher-quality men who were kind and respectful. I felt radiant walking around and I could see men turning to look at me. I felt a shift in what I could see in men and would sometimes be asked out on a date while I was walking! I could feel the magic of love at work within me, expanding my life and my horizons.

There's a spiritual power within you, that flows through you, and that is the power of love.

As you awaken your inner Love Goddess you will begin to see a shift in your outer world that mirrors your inner transformation.

However, as you're embarking on this journey of unrooting your blocks and planting new healthy seeds in your Love Garden, **you'll begin to notice resistance arise**. You may face laziness, self-doubt and general annoyance. You'll probably want to quit or distract yourself with your usual escape route like getting on social media, watching romance movies, opening up your dating app, or drinking, or claiming that this book sucks and won't work for you and complaining to a girlfriend.

You may also begin to encounter old wounds and patterns, or notice overwhelming emotion arise and not know what to do about it. Facing some drama with a family member or colleague will be par for the course. And while dating, you will face uncomfortable encounters, like meeting a great guy that you had a deep connection with who doesn't call you back for a whole gut-wrenching week. If you have kids, they will wield their superpower in finding your dark, stormy side and instigating it.

As I've discovered, being married doesn't get me off the hook either. Oftentimes I face fear, insecurity, anger or self-righteousness in my relationship with my husband. As we've learned through couples' counseling, the same traits that attracted us during the honeymoon phase are what triggers us later on! Being with one's soulmate is a never-ending road of facing one's own triggers, healing old wounds and finding deeper connection and understanding with each other through the process. *This is the process of moving from rupture to rapture in a relationship, leading to the couple's evolution. Love doesn't thrive in the status quo.*

In the journey of love, life throws us a wrench or two every so often to see how determined we are in opening our hearts, releasing old wounds and beliefs, and learning our lessons. *This is a good thing, and as a Love Goddess, I invite you to embrace this with courage and openness.*

You'll always have a choice as to how to respond to each situation, and if you choose the more loving option, then you will experience profound alchemy, along with more peace and harmony in your life. You will begin to bring down the walls around your heart and feel a heart expansion and even a sense of upliftment, drawing in more synchronistic experiences.

You will see how your words can melt a man's heart, or how your honest, sexy vulnerability creates a magical, potent environment for a relationship to thrive.

When you sow positive seeds in your Love Garden, you begin to manifest the very things in your life that your soul truly desires – a life of love and fulfillment.

Interestingly our soul also *needs* suffering for us to learn and grow. As the gardener of our Love Garden, we have the ability to compost our suffering into healthy soil, ripe for fruitful manifestation. As Thích Nhât

Hạnh once said, "There is the mud, and there is the lotus that grows out of the mud. We need the mud in order to make the lotus." Each of our blocks and suffering are potential areas for healing, alchemy and growth.

I'm not going to sugarcoat it: in life and love, there are going to be deeply uncomfortable times. You already know this from your own love life.

But here's the good news: the better you are at dealing with icky feelings within you, and the more you're able to make conscious choices when a difficult situation arises, the more you'll be able to transmute it to something greater. You grow your capacity in love, compassion and understanding, which allows you to handle even more complexity and nuance in your relationships – and thus, experience even more rapture and pleasure in your love life.

As you're beginning your Love Goddess journey and growing your Love Garden, I want to equip you with certain Love Alchemy tools that will serve you, no matter what situation arises. These are tools to be used and perfected throughout your life, so there's no rush! Instead, think of these as intentions.

Love Alchemy Tool # 1: Radical Self-Love & Self-Compassion

As you're aligning with love, the first place to start is by loving yourself, by being your own mother, father, sister and lover. Take a moment to close your eyes and imagine being held and comforted by someone in a compassionate way, maybe when you were a child. Now, can you imagine doing that for yourself?

The other night, I was feeling vulnerable and self-conscious about writing my book and was also feeling a bit shaken by the pandemic situation. As I lay in bed, instead of asking my husband to hold me (which of course is a wonderful thing), I decided to first love and honor myself, and each part of my body. I was proud of myself for putting myself out there and held the sad and confused parts of myself, saying, "I see you, dear one. I'm here for you. I won't abandon you. You are safe with me." I witnessed my emotions like an empathetic observer. I genuinely felt love and compassion for myself, held myself and caressed my body, while offering gratitude. My heart and soul felt so replete and buzzing! No doubt the oxytocin surge I felt replenished my being, to the point that even my husband could feel it.

Here's where the alchemy lay: *in that moment of practicing self-compassion, I was patching up old wounds of disconnection in my psyche of when I felt scared and abandoned as a young child. I was rewiring old pathways of unworthiness and creating an environment of love and safety within myself. The chemicals being released – the oxytocin, serotonin – were helping seal these new pathways. Isn't this beautiful?*

Transformation in one's life can only happen when we feel safe, loved and accepted – and the person who needs to offer it to us is ourselves. We have to be our greatest champions and cheerleaders, and honor and respect what our body and soul need.

This being said, here are a few additional pointers to support you in extending love and compassion for yourself:

Ask for what you need.
Receive all that is given to you with grace.

Strong, ambitious women have been taught that independence is a sexy quality. Yet I've found that the energy behind "I don't need anyone" and "I can do it myself" stems from a place of suffering – it is likely a defense mechanism for a childhood memory in which maybe it was dangerous for you to allow others to help you or seem like a burden in some way. While healthy independence is important as a transition phase from our childhood dependency patterning in order for us to succeed in love, we have to be able to move to *interdependence* – a healthy "give and receive" relationship with others.

A woman who accepts her vulnerability and can ask for help, and is in her receptive energy when she accepts help, heals these old wounds of independence and restores her divine feminine side. Asking for help could look like getting a therapist, a personal trainer, a personal assistant or even something simple like being in a grocery store and asking a stranger to help you reach for something on a shelf. Most people love helping and being in service (especially men, who find it irresistible to be around receptive women) and you are bringing back balance into your own life, and the world, by regularly asking for help and support. This is counter-intuitive to what we have been taught, as strong, independent women. *Yet, asking for what you need and learning to receive are two important daily practices of healing in love.*

Be accepting of your life, no matter what your situation.

One of the very things that we're here to heal is our constant worry of "there's something wrong with me" or "I need to change or fix my situation" – yet life (and love) can only move through us when we are calm, centered and, ironically, in acceptance. As we learned through the Law of Karma, there are certain events playing out in our life, and our life is the accumulation of everything we have been through, relation-ships we've had, our beliefs, etc. As such, it's empowering and vital for you to say, "I accept this present moment. I know I can handle this," while paradoxically acknowledging and honoring your desires.

Your body and mind may resist acceptance, seeking backdoors and distractions like reading self-help books, watching TV, guzzling alcohol – but those are ways that we try to escape our reality and continue our state of denial. I find that when I'm having a hard time accepting, I go out and be in nature, which inherently calms my nerves and connects me back to myself.

Personally, I've found that acceptance and trust were huge areas for me to heal and learn – it seemed that my muscle memory was geared towards distrusting the current situation and seeking a way out. It was painful for my body to simply be present. However, after several months of practicing acceptance, I was able to relax my over-driven nervous system and begin to truly enjoy the present moment. I also had to build my "trust muscle," where I would constantly use affirmations like "I trust in life" or simply, "I trust, I trust," as I walked around or made decisions that were uncomfortable yet I knew were in my highest interest.

Give yourself permission to do whatever the heck you want and need, including making mistakes (which, guess what – there are none!)

So many times, we as women seek permission from others to do what we know is good for us. Whether it's asking for time off, spending money on something really important, switching jobs or taking a break from dating, rather than listening to our own intuition, we feel we need to hear it from someone else. It could be something really basic, like not being around family when you need a break or saying no to something that could be over-extending yourself. In the self-love journey, you're going to learn to do whatever you think you need to do, give yourself permission. As long as your intentions are good, it's ok to make mistakes. Life is all about experiments and discovering your inner truth, however windy the road is.

Forgive yourself often.

We're conditioned to constantly doubt ourselves and beat ourselves up for saying or doing something wrong. Whenever you feel that way, remember that you're human and doing the best you can. So forgive yourself and "fugget about it!" as they say in New York. When you do so, you begin to create an environment in which vulnerability is ok, which fosters creativity and experimentation. You become less defensive and more open to making difficult choices. One of my favorite phrases I use with myself is, "Even if I think I've made this mistake, I love, accept and forgive myself." I then work to clean up any mess I've made, if needed.

Love Alchemy Tool #2: Sitting Through Triggers and Discomfort

Ah, love and dating, and all the feelings it evokes! The main thing here is for you to acknowledge that you will feel a range of emotions, and while I'll be covering emotional well-being in the next chapter, I want to share tools for dealing with fear, resistance and triggers.

Fear

Probably anything worth pursuing evokes fear and self-doubt. We're miserably afraid of failing, feeling rejected and getting hurt, *especially* when it comes to love. Yet, as I've learned over the years, the best way to deal with fear and self-doubt is to not give any mind. Fear is *False Evidence Appearing Real*, is based on the past or a future eventuality, and is rarely indicative of what is going on in your life. In most instances, fears don't actually pan out. In fact, the more you spend your energy focusing on fears or fostering them, the unhappier you become, bringing even more suffering. So, as much as possible, don't pay attention to fear or self-doubt, and simply bring yourself to the present moment. Try to respond to the situation with love or just simple awareness. You can also pray for divine support, healing and wisdom, or practicing loving kindness meditation, where you send love to yourself and others, which is what I often do in times of uncertainty. In doing so, you transform your fear by not feeding it, and send out positive, intentional vibes of what you *do* want to create.

Here's a fun fact: sometimes fears actually point us in the direction we truly desire to go. I remember being deathly afraid of becoming a mom, because I fretted about losing my independence and not being able to do "do it all" in terms of my work. Yet over time I realized that what I *really* wanted was to have kids and – check this out – be a stay-at-home mom, depending on my man financially. For a smart, successful woman, this seemed like a death-knell – yet this was what my heart wanted. You can't make this up!

Lastly, Susan Jeffers, a psychologist, shares in her book, *Feel The Fear And Do It Anyway*, sometime our fear of helplessness is way worse than not taking action at all – so taking action, in spite of your fear, is the most empowering thing you can do.

Resistance

Remember in physics, when they talked about Newton's third law, "For every force, there's an equal and opposite counter-force"? Well, I can't think of a bigger force than love.

When you have resistance arise, like irritation, laziness, despair or any other form of discomfort, try to be with the discomfort, meditating and breathing through it. Acknowledge your physical symptoms and sensations and name your resistance. You can say, Robert De Niro-style in *Analyze This!*, "You... You... You're good, you! I see what you're doing here!" while laughing away your resistance like the naughty child it really is. If you're having a lot of aversion and noticing your addictions rising, bring it up with an accountability buddy or someone who's on the side of you achieving great things in your life. Get the support and cheerleading you need, and simply push through and keep showing up for your love life.

Triggers

Let's face it, people are going to trigger you – there's no way out of it. But here's the alchemy that's possible – when you look at a trigger as something to heal within yourself, then you can view these relationships from a transformational lens. If your colleague rubs you the wrong way, your mom says something that embarrasses you, or one of your Instagram friends brags about her recent travels with her new man, instead of blaming your annoyance and discomfort on them, look within yourself to see what is reflected within you. Where are you insecure, or where do you see a similar trait within yourself? Sometimes we might look at someone and berate their flaws – yet those are the very qualities that may be existing in us that need to be witnessed and healed.

So, how do you deal with triggers? First, create the time and space for being with them, maybe during meditation. Allow yourself to look and breathe and be with the sensation, but not too long. Acknowledge the trigger, and allow the feelings and sensations to arise, without getting into the story. You'll find that the trigger will slowly start to dissipate, and over time you'll find yourself more accepting of the situation or person. *This is a powerful way of knowing you're making progress in your love life.*

"The only way out is through." ~ Robert Frost

57

Love Alchemy Tool #3:
Be Discerning in What You Think, Say and Do

"You only have control over three things in your life – the
thoughts you think, the images you visualize, and the actions
you take." ~ Jack Canfield

Another vital Love Alchemy tool is having true discernment and
wisdom about everything that you say and do. Remember in the last
chapter, we talked about The Law of Karma? Well, here's your chance
at ending negative karma in your life, once and for all!

Here are some pointers on how to be, think and act in love:

- First and foremost, it's important to **take responsibility for
your actions.** Apologize when you've hurt someone, even unintentionally. Having regret, and sincerely apologizing takes a great deal
of personal strength. If you make a promise or commitment, keep
it, come hell or high water. Integrity is crucial in living a life of love.
If you feel overwhelmed, say no to people – it's ok! I find myself
saying no to most things because I know I need plenty of buffer for
rest to be able to show up for my loved ones with presence and joy.
Less is more, they say!

- **When you're in doubt, do and say nothing.** If you're confused,
let me explain. We live in a world where being over-reactive is
normal. Yet, I've found that simply being silent and present, especially when I'm triggered or excitable, is profoundly transformational. I used to be a smart-ass and make jokes, many a time insult-
ing people in the process, or letting people know if I didn't agree
right off the bat. All these encounters, which I thought nothing of,
ended up hurting my loved ones over time. I've rubbed people the
wrong way and eroded trust. I've really had to learn to curb my ten-

dencies of speaking and acting without thinking, trying to fix others' problems, or giving advice. Instead, I now mostly listen while focusing on my breath, trying to understand the other person, and speak with mindfulness; I rarely act unless I really have to, and when I do, I always seek out a non-violent path.

• **Curb your habits around gossiping and complaining** about others or yourself. From now on, I would encourage you to be respectful of yourself and others, and as such, be mindful and kind in your speech. Your words, thoughts and actions have an energy that can boomerang back to you while hurting others. Drama, be gone!

• **Keep your personal endeavors close to your vest and share with very few people.** We live in a TMI (too much information) world, where we water down what's sacred to us. Recognize that there are certain things that are in a fragile state, like your love life, old wounds that you're healing or talents that you are exploring, and you know others' doubts, jealousy and opinions would taint it. In these instances, feel free to keep it to yourself or share it with a confidante.

• **Don't take anything personally.** This is one of the most important lessons I learned from *The Four Agreements* by Don Miguel Ruiz. Whenever a man stands you up or your sister says something callous to you, don't think it's about you. Most of us are walking around with unprocessed emotions and wounds, doing unconscious things, speaking directly without thought, and react when we're triggered, as I've shared above. Therefore, people are speaking and acting from a place of suffering that's usually their own. Don't take it on yourself. Instead, learn to look at people and smile at each of their quirks or inconsistencies – we're all human, doing the best we can.

• **Let go of the need to be "right"** and simply allow the other person to have their own perceptions and experience. A lot of times we try to impose our own knowledge and way of doing things on others, which creates an experience of controlling and suffering. *In the moments where you feel that tug, notice the sensations coming up within you.* Recognize that you're rewiring old tendencies of seeking power and domination in love; instead, you're creating a world where everyone can be themselves.

• **Love sometimes requires a great deal of patience, sacrifice and generosity.** Now this doesn't mean that you need to be a martyr and over-give. Rather, when you're in various situations, you will be called to do what you deem as right in order to serve and protect others (or yourself), even if it requires a great deal of your time, energy and resources. For instance, maybe you have to give a large amount of money to a loved one, or you have to spend a great deal of time caretaking for a child, your sick spouse, or an elderly family member. With your partner, you may have to practice a great deal of patience and understanding while they're going through their own meltdown. This really is love in action and having the wisdom and patience to be with all of the physical and emotional struggle is where the alchemy happens.

Love Alchemy Tool #4: Be Unreasonable

Here's the thing about love that no sane, rational person can get around – love, and our heart's desires, are unreasonable. That's right – if you really follow your heart, you'll be led to seemingly dangerous, exciting new places, and even the possibility of falling in love! A woman who's in touch with her passion and purpose is unreasonable in how she loves, is an unfettered bird that flies freely, singing her soul song. She's unafraid and paves her own path. This is a magnificent sight to behold.

When you're connected with your heart and coming from a loving place, you may start to do unreasonable things – call the cute guy that you normally wouldn't, play hooky from work (one of my favorites), end the relationship that's been draining you yet giving you a sense of security. You might end up passing up a promotion, falling for your electrician who is a beautiful human being and is perfect for your soul, or start writing a book of poetry for the hell of it.

You lose your egoic handrails, and instead align to your principles and what *resonates* with your personal truth and gives you pleasure. You begin to trust the wisdom that what's good for your soul might not be the case for others, and that you don't need to do things to meet others' expectations. You'll begin to bring down those walls that were created when your heart got hurt in the past.

As you continue to do unreasonable things and allow Love Alchemy to work through your body, mind, and spirit, **you'll find yourself connected with your intuition, which is even stronger and more refined than your instinct or impulse** – two immature, reactive responses that have likely led you down the wrong path before, and made you distrust yourself or life.

Your intuition will arise as a whole-body knowing, one that combines the intelligence of your gut, your womb, your heart and mind.

You will begin to find that as you take unreasonably loving steps in your life, the universe comes to your aid and supports you. Sure, there may be some disappointments and learning moments as you refine your intuition, yet it's in this space of non-judgement and exploration where miracles lie.

If you're looking for an example of what unreasonable living is, check out Nick Vujicic who wrote *A Life Without Limits: How to Live a Ridiculously Good Life*. Here's the catch – this man has no limbs! This handsome, hilarious, faith-filled man wrote about his heart-opening yet gutsy adventures, and how to live beyond one's normal expectations.

Lastly, as children do, revel in play and pleasure. Lighten up! When you're living in the moment, being present to all your feelings and everything around you, you begin to feel alive, and carefree. This doesn't mean you can be irresponsible and date everyone under the sun – it's not a hippy kind of liberation – rather, it's about recognizing life is about fulfillment, joy and exploration, which can only happen in the present moment.

Love Alchemy Tool #5:
Meditate Often and Practice Mindfulness

The last, but perhaps most important Love Alchemy tool is meditation and mindfulness. I cannot stress enough the power of building quietness in our bodies, so that we can detox old habits and become observers of our reality. I know I wouldn't have been able to rewire my old, habitual thoughts and reactions without meditating and practicing mindfulness.

If you look at a calm lake, you can see a couple of feet down – maybe all the way down to the bottom. But on a windy day, the waves cause the rocks and sediment to be strewn about. The only thing that can bring the lake to clarity is stillness, when the sediments start to slowly settle to the bottom. There is a serenity in being a part of such a scene.

We all have the capacity to find that level of serenity within us. We can be in the eye of a tornado, where the world around us is moving with rapid turbulence, while the inside is calm. We're able to view the circumstance with a sense of peace and knowing that "this too shall pass." I know it may seem rather drastic and far away from your current reality. Yet, I can tell you that it's possible, and when you do feel it, you will feel a sense of inner freedom.

What do I mean by stillness? Isn't thinking supposed to be a good thing? People always talk about keeping a mind busy in order to stay healthy. We have been taught to keep our brains busy with academic degrees, books, and now, the internet.

Yet, studies have shown the impact of an overactive mind. The front part of the brain (the prefrontal cortex) becomes hyperactive in analysis. This leads to examining different fears of things that don't exist and living in a state of constantly strategizing to avoid pain and control chaos. As high-achieving women, being in our heads has become part of the norm, and yet it affects us in our love lives. In dating or in a relationship, an overactive mind becomes the playground for the devil, where you're constantly evaluating your partners' mood and behaviors, wondering whether you'll be safe, loved and connected. This is a scary place to be in a relationship.

Being in your head doesn't allow for you to become connected with your body and the wisdom that exists in the thirty trillion cells in your body. You become disembodied, unable to really feel or to be present to life and everything around you. Decisions and choices from this place are ultimately made from the ego, or your thoughts from that day. They aren't coming from a place of groundedness or connection with your true self.

There is another part of you that is powerful and intelligent – your heart. According to the HeartMath Institute, your heart has its own mind, and has an electromagnetic field that's 5,000 times stronger than that of the brain. Your heart is the doorway to the mystery of life, to universal wisdom, and of course, true, unconditional love.

Ancient teachings from both Western and Eastern traditions expound on the ultimate creative and natural intelligence that a woman's womb and reproductive system has. From the ability to conceive, birth and nurture a baby from a place of nothingness to maintaining the complex hormones in a woman's body, it is nothing short of a miracle. From a mystical point of view, the womb has the energy to help a woman be able to manifest things in her life, including a partnership, her career, and so much more.

Likewise, the other parts of our body hold deep wisdom and strengths. I will share in more detail about the miraculous nature of our body, but at the moment, I simply want to bring awareness to the immense possibilities that are within your body.

Love cannot exist only in the mind. It's a full-bodied experience, and the heart leads the way in creating the flow of love through us, and around us. When we're tapped into our whole body, we create a field of consciousness around us, and we can connect to every part of us – mental, emotional, physical and spiritual. When we act in our relationships from this place, it is healing – even if you're having an argument.

Stillness forms the basis of such levels of connection and awareness within us. It helps curb our natural habit energies of running towards pleasure or fleeing from pain and brings us to a consciousness of what is. You see things clearly from a place of inner freedom. You tap into the wellspring of vitality that's within your body, from your soul and spirit, that's connected to a higher divinity. You can literally experience heaven on earth when you're in the state of pure stillness.

While doing this book, if you do up to twenty minutes a day of sitting in silence, become more present and mindful during the day and simply focus on your breath while you're doing your activities, you'll notice a quick and stark difference in the quality of your life. You'll be able to move quickly in healing yourself and manifesting everything your soul desires! I know that this seems like a tall claim, yet you will begin to see the natural grace and love that wants to flow into your life as you gently allow it to.

I've included a guided meditation you can do daily, which you can download here at https://sarikajain.com/Soulmate-Plan-Resources/

There's a power that's waiting to be unleashed *through* you, and that is the power of love. You are a Love Goddess, an alchemist, someone who can turn times of uncertainty or discomfort into pleasure and healing. In nourishing your Love Garden, you're creating your haven, and inviting a sexy, loving, caring man to join you.

I'll end this chapter with a powerful poem by Saint Francis of Assisi:

Lord, make me an instrument of your peace:
where there is hatred, let me sow love;
where there is injury, pardon;
where there is doubt, faith;
where there is despair, hope;
where there is darkness, light;
where there is sadness, joy.
O divine Master, grant that I may not so much seek
to be consoled as to console,
to be understood as to understand,
to be loved as to love.
For it is in giving that we receive,
it is in pardoning that we are pardoned,
and it is in dying that we are born to eternal life.
Amen.

PART II
5 STEPS TO CALLING IN YOUR SOULMATE

STEP 1: BE A LOVE MAGNET

Discover Your Loving
Self through Self-Love

Ariane was no stereotypical ambitious woman climbing the corporate ladder at all costs. As a leader in her company, she managed her teams with empathy and wisdom, and had a passion for personal development. She also made plenty of time for her family and was the bedrock for her loved ones, always willing to go the extra mile to help out or be a compassionate listener.

However, her love life was full of drama. She had never experienced a healthy relationship. While at graduate school, she attracted a charming, romantic man. He was smart and successful and anyone who met him initially thought he was handsome and caring. Ariane intuitively had her doubts, yet she felt deeply attached to him. Their sexual chemistry was off the charts and being around him gave her a feeling familiarity and comfort.

After the initial honeymoon phase, he started becoming more controlling. He distrusted Ariane's family and friends and encouraged her to alienate herself from them. He made it clear that their relationship was her only priority. He would sometimes spiral down into emotional lows, pulling her into his self-pity and depression mixed with anger. She would fret about his emotional state, listening to him for endless hours. Despite all of that, she felt conflicted because she loved him and thought he was "the one". She was losing herself and started seeking more space. Even as she began pulling away, he pushed stronger to stay in her life.

Her workplace was also quite challenging. It was competitive and unrelenting, and her boss was toxic. She found herself slogging long hours, trying to appease him, to no avail.
Ariane felt like a part of her was dying inside, and she knew she needed a reset button.

Through our coaching work together, she began to quietly disentangle herself from the difficult relationships, energetically. She focused on creating a healing container for herself and began to love herself in a way that she never knew was possible. As an empathic person, she was overly sensitive to others' needs and was always there solving others' problems, almost to a default. This time, she learned how to be there for herself, emotionally and physically. She was building her inner foundation.

Through the process of loving herself, she saw her intuition and discernment grow. She began to radiate with a sense of inner confidence and a strong self-knowing. She started to enjoy her own company, seeing herself as her own soulmate. In terms of her ex, and other similar men, she learned how to assert herself, and gracefully untie the draining relationships through energetic clearing and firmly setting physical boundaries. She determined what balance worked for her in terms of work and her relationships.

At some point, Ariane knew she was worthy of a better job, and through feminine grace and synchronicity, manifested her dream job in a Fortune 100 company that was much more supportive of her talents. Her new boss turned out to be empathetic as well – and her greatest champion.

Ariane began dating with ease and a sense of play for the first time in her life. She finally understood deep within that she was worthy of a relationship with a man who honored and respected her – but she had to first create a healthy relationship within herself. She began dating men who were kind and respectful of her – a change! She felt sexy, magnetic and was having fun getting to know men. Ariane vowed never to simply fall into a relationship just because it simply "felt right" from the get-go (her old pattern) – she would allow self-love to lead the way in helping her find her mate and creating a solid foundation of understanding, respect and trust from the beginning.

The Power of Self-Love

"The most exciting, challenging and significant relationship
of all is the one you have with yourself. And if you find
someone to love the you you love, well, that's just fabulous."
~ Carrie, Sex and the City

One of the primary lessons we're here to learn on this planet is how to love ourselves. It sounds like a somewhat straightforward task – go get your nails done, ask for a raise, follow your dreams!

Yet, in my experience, self-love is a sort of spiritual discipline. It comes from a deep place of yearning to "know thyself," to heal our old wounds, and to live our greatest potential. It's an understanding that we're each magnificent, worthy of love, and have a right to lead an extraordinary life that tickles our heart.

I know it seems contradictory to how many people live – follow a path to success, make our parents proud and secure a relationship that turns into marriage. Have two kids and live in a gorgeous house with white picket fences, growing your savings account while climbing the corporate ladder at work. While this formula may work for some, it doesn't work for many, especially for heart-open women who want more, and are drawn to living a life that feels aligned to their soul, which feels unclear in the beginning.

Here's the good news: *When you begin to foster a healthy relationship with yourself, everything else – your love life, career, home, children – follows naturally. Self-love is the way to building that primary relationship.*

The benefits of self-love are limitless. You begin to accept and love yourself, overcome your own self-doubt and feel a deep sense of worthiness. You set healthy boundaries, figure out what makes you happy and what doesn't, and learn how to speak your heart. You ask for what you want, in a compassionate way. You cherish and are kind to yourself, and act from a place of deep self-awareness. You're curious about your mind, body and spirit, and see your body as a temple. Your negative self-thinking vanishes, and you feel free from all your guilt, shame and regret. Your heart is open to healthy love and new possibilities.

You feel emotionally resilient because you've already created your inner foundation. You begin to lean into the mystery of who you are – you are way more than your physical body – you are an infinite, multidimensional goddess with so many untapped talents, brimming with unconditional love.

All of these may seem far away for you. You may be skeptical at first, because common dating advice tells you that if you act and dress a certain way, learn the "game of love" and behave mysteriously, you will be a magnet for love.

Yet, when you really, truly love yourself, you don't need to act anymore. You're deeply connected with your feelings and needs, your femininity, and trust what your soul desires. There's no wishy-washiness – you intrinsically *know* you are a woman of value, and you aren't afraid of expressing yourself and asking for what you desire. You can be your most truthful, loving self – a refreshing way of being in today's manicured and sculpted world.

When you do reach this place, you have the ability to attract *anything* you want, through synchronicity. Remember how I talked about the tuning fork, and returning to your original frequency? The right circumstances begin to automatically align with you, without the normal struggle that we're all used to.

You begin to shine your own light, and soon enough, people are attracted to your radiance. Adoring men, career opportunities, and financial abundance begins to flow to you – things that naturally belong to you, because you have aligned your essence with our loving, benevolent universe that *wants* you to be happy and to experience heaven on earth.

> "You, yourself, as much as anybody in the universe,
> deserve your love and affection." ~ Buddha

When you reach this place of self-love, you begin to see yourself as your own soulmate, as someone to love and cherish.

On a spiritual level, the world is your mirror. The more love and approval you have within yourself, the more you will model it to

those around you to give it to you, and energetically, you begin attracting that kind of love. On the flipside, if you have an abusive, dismissive relationship with yourself – that's what you will attract. In fact, even if you attract a wonderful man, the relationship will eventually get molded into this painful pattern.

Most importantly, you learn the Art of Love, which you first master with yourself. Most of us start out with broken relationships with ourselves and inflict our way of loving on others. We cause hurt and wounds to our loved ones, unintentionally, and get trapped in painful patterns. We say things we don't mean, let our insecurities drive our behavior and pretend to be someone we're not. We don't know when to say no, and by the time we assert our boundaries, it's too late.

> "Your ability to love another person depends
> on your ability to love yourself." ~Thích Nhat Hanh

You will find that your ability to love in a way that promotes freedom, compassion and understanding begins with yourself – and when you love others, these qualities will spill over.

Just through self-love, you will see a complete repatterning in all your relationships.

In the beginning, it may feel uncomfortable for you to assert your need for space and offer yourself self-love. It may be going against the grain, depending on the culture you've grown up with. Yet, you must make a commitment to rewire these old tendencies of self-denial and approval-seeking, and take a stand for generating your own happiness, which originates through self-love.

This chapter will give you the foundation to practice self-love on every level – mental, emotional, physical and spiritual. By doing all the exercises in this chapter with commitment and discipline, you will become a master in loving yourself.

You will step into being a Love Magnet and begin to see love flowing to you just through this chapter.

To really see where you land in terms of your sense of self-love and fulfillment in different areas of your life, let's start with a self-assessment.

EXERCISE: SELF-ASSESSMENT: MY HAPPINESS & WELL-BEING

On a scale of 1-10, where **10** is representing **I Agree Very Much/ Alignment** and **1** is representing **I Don't Agree/Difficulty:**

- I feel happy, healthy, content, and have peace-of-mind. I feel a sense of love and appreciation for myself. _____
- I have surrounded myself with positive friends, mentors, family, and community. _____
- I follow beautiful and nurturing self-care habits. _____
- I know my purpose and contribution to the world. _____
- I am connected to my feelings. _____
- I can express my feelings to people in my environment.

  _____

- I am comfortable with both my femininity and masculinity.

  _____

- When it comes to my sexuality, I can express it openly and freely to my partner. _____
- It's easy for me to communicate my desires. _____
- I'm handling financial matters and decisions with ease and grace.

  _____

- I love my physical body. _____

Take a look at your scores in each of the areas. There is no good or bad, so this is not a time of self-judgment. It gives you an idea of what you need to take extra care of during this program. The higher the levels, the more confident you will feel, and you can be sure that you are emanating love. We will go through all of these throughout the book.

Mental Well-Being: Generating a Loving Mindset

One of the first places I start when I coach women is the mind – it is the biggest block that women face when it comes to love. *Everything is energy, including our thoughts – and whatever we think, we attract.* Somehow as women, we got the memo to perpetually beat ourselves up and have a somewhat diminished view of ourselves, in small and big ways.

In this section, we'll be focusing on what it takes for you to have a solid, confident, unshakable mindset – one that isn't deterred by the outside world. One that *knows* you're worthy of love and is your biggest champion. "I think, therefore I am" is a true statement, and how you think affects everything in your body – your emotions, physiology, and ultimately, the energy and vibe you give off.

Experts estimate that we think between sixty thousand to eighty thousand thoughts a day. Isn't that unbelievable! I garner that nearly ninety percent of our thoughts are self-critical or just plain negative. I know that seems like a lot, but I invite you to spend a day simply observing your thoughts. How many times a day do you say, "Uggh, I wish I weren't so [fat, ugly, unlucky, pick your adjective]" or "How could I have been dumb enough to say that! I'm such a hopeless disaster." These thoughts are like our own inner evil stepmother.

When I ask people to share their negative thoughts during coaching sessions, they can go on and on for nearly an entire hour listing unflattering thoughts in every area of their lives – their career, relationship with their parents and siblings, love life, dating, body, looks, money – the list is endless.

Thoughts are like energy packets that are released from our brain and they persist forever. Our ether is made up of billions upon billions of thoughts, starting all the way from the beginning. Think of the franticness of our society, and all the sound waves from sources like people's conversations, their thoughts, and the media. **When your mind is not strong or is prone to negative thinking, it can tune into thought and sound waves of similar frequencies, just like a radio or television transmitter. You begin to "tune into" those waves, and they amplify or even feed your own negative thinking.**

Thoughts are really powerful in how your body behaves and whether you are happy and healthy. Physiologically, when you think negative, self-critical thoughts, they generate feelings such as fear and anxiety, which go on to create bio-chemical reactions that can paralyze you, disconnect you from your body and cause hormones like adrenalin and cortisol to be secreted, creating a frazzled energy in your body.

On the flipside, when your thoughts are calm and self-nurturing, you begin to brim with joy and serenity, and your body concocts healthy, mood-lifting hormones like serotonin and dopamine, which go on to help promote vitality in your body. Literally, your thoughts have the ability to make your life heaven or hell. Negative thoughts solidify imprisoning belief systems that limit you in your potential and turn you into a jaded, disempowered being. Moreover, through conscious or unconscious stories and thoughts, you generate emotions that get harbored as stuck energies in your body, which over time turns into disease.

As you can imagine, in terms of relationships, negative thoughts have the ability to make a relationship crumble. Not only do you attract a relationship based on what you think of yourself, you can also cause damage to a relationship by being unconscious or fearful in your actions. For example, if you feel insecure with your partner and something is bothering you, you may waver between blowing up or walking on eggshells, which creates uneasiness in the relationship. If you're critical and judgmental of yourself, invariably you'll find yourself dragging others into your misery, by judging and criticizing them. Men feel uncomfortable around women who are judgmental, which slowly erodes their sense of safety and freedom in the relationship.

When I see that I am judgmental of others (which used to happen so often), I look within to see which parts of me I still judge, feel shame about or criticize. I can tell where I am, in terms of my self-love, based on how triggered I feel by others.

What if, instead, you had a loving relationship with yourself, where you were your own champion and best friend? Instead of kicking yourself in the ass for messing up a presentation or saying something silly or embarrassing to your partner, you could instead think, "Darling, it's ok if I mess up, I'll clean it up if I need to and do better next time. I still love, accept and forgive myself." Over time, you might not even think at all about messing up, you just prepare to do better next time.

Through healing your thoughts, you may even find that the gaps between your thoughts widen and you start feeling more calm and sense of harmony within.

From this place, you can do the deep work of healing your limiting beliefs and setting clear and powerful intentions. Moreover, you'll see that when you're happy, so are the people you attract into your life! Your thoughts are like radio signals and have the power to create and manifest. You can decide to start having a healthy mindset, starting today.

How to Begin to Release Your Negative Thinking

A wise man once said, *"Emptying your mind of your thoughts is like draining the ocean with a teacup."* In the beginning, the idea of letting go of our thoughts may seem daunting, due to the sheer volume and intensity of emotion behind them. We're so wrapped up in our mind (and we're surrounded by so much noise) that it's almost hard to detangle from them. The Buddha likened our thoughts to being pulled in four different directions by horses. In essence, dealing with our thoughts is the foundation of spiritual practice.

Here's a powerful exercise that will dramatically transform your life.

EXERCISE: LETTING GO OF SELF-JUDGMENT

Earmark an hour or two for this exercise. *Think of this as one of the most important exercises you will be doing in this book.*

In your journal, do a brain dump of all your negative thoughts. Go through each area of your life – your body image, your career, your relationships with your parents, siblings, friends, colleagues, your love life, your sense of self, your talents. Be as extensive as you can. Think about things that you say to yourself when you're feeling bad. Try to be as accurate as possible, noting your inner speech verbatim. What words do you use when you're self-critical? Are there key phrases that come up over and over again? You can use the below prompts.

I am so...

(E.g., *I am so underqualified. I am so fat.*)

I'll never...

(E.g., *I'll never get a man. I'll never get a better job – what's the point in trying. I'll never please my parents.*)

I can't...

(E.g., I can't believe how dumb I am. I can't stand how I look sometimes.)

I should/shouldn't...

(E.g., I should have been in a relationship by now. I shouldn't have let him go – am I stupid?)

I suck...

(E.g., I suck at giving presentations. My thighs suck.)

Now, for each of the above self-critical thoughts and beliefs, practice self-compassion and self-love.

Say to yourself, "Even though I think _____ (fill in the blank with sentences from above), I love, accept and forgive myself. I approve of myself." For example, *"Even though I think I should be in a relationship by now, I love, accept and forgive myself. I approve of myself."*

Keep doing this for <u>each and every thought.</u>

This will take time, maybe even hours, but I encourage you to go through it extensively, as each of those thoughts will get seen, heard and validated – and loved. Do it with intention and mindfulness. Allow yourself to feel the love and compassion for yourself, even if it feels foreign, or those thoughts somehow seem justified.

They are all judgments and toxic thoughts that have been percolating through your subconscious and have been sabotaging your life, over and over. You can train yourself to be self-loving and self-approving – which will make the thoughts disappear over time.

Make "Even though I think _____, I love, accept and forgive myself" a regular, daily practice in your life, and you will notice your negative thoughts starting to dissipate. You'll begin to feel a calmness and sense of harmony that you've never felt before.

This is my ultimate Jiu Jitsu trick in clearing self-critical, negative thoughts.

Another simple ninja trick for your thoughts: every time a negative thought arises, say, "Cancel!" This little magical trick will abruptly halt the thought before it turns into mind-venom and pollutes the air.

The 30-Day Mind Detox Plan

As you're on this journey of cleaning out your negative thinking, you want to create a nourishing environment that supports the detox process and promotes a healthy, happy mindset. The way we think is vital to what we attract in our life.

Contemplate what you read, listen to, watch, or whom you talk to – all of those are inputs into your senses, and inform what you think about. So, begin to have awareness of what you're exposing your mind to.

I would recommend that you do a thirty-day detox for your mind. In fact, if some of these are helpful, then I would urge you to consider doing them longer, or even making it a part of your daily life.

1. **Take a hiatus from news, television, podcasts, social media,** or any other type of entertainment. The goal is to allow yourself to be in silence, without any outside stimulation. Instead, on a highly selective basis, read something nurturing or spiritual, like inspiring interviews and talks. This may seem counterculture, but if you really want to heal your thinking, and allow for your mind to detox, it has to be given plenty of air and space, without too much external input so that negative thoughts and beliefs can percolate up to be healed and released. At the end of the day, the greatest service you can offer your mind is to be its gatekeeper, making sure that whatever your mind is exposed to is something you choose, consciously.

2. **Practice gratitude** when you wake up and when you go to bed. You'll notice that gratitude has a way of slowly transforming your "not-enoughness" into general positivity and a feeling of abundance. In fact, anytime you start getting into negative thoughts or a funk, think of things you are grateful for, and really feel the sense of gratefulness.

3. **As soon as you wake up, journal three pages in a notebook,** writing quickly whatever is arising in your stream of consciousness, even if it doesn't make any sense. This exercise, called Morning Pages, from the author of *The Artist's Way*, Julia Cameron, will transform your life by allowing you to do a brain dump of your thoughts even before you begin your day, which will feel like a purge. It will bring great clarity to you over time and make you feel more connected with yourself, as your thoughts are allowed to be seen and heard.

4. **Spend time in meditation every day.** It can be as simple as just focusing on your breath for twenty minutes. In fact, find ways of incorporating mindfulness when you're walking, doing your dishes or even showering. Silence and presence will greatly help you in your mental detox.

5. **Do yoga** and other forms of physical exercise while practicing mindfulness. Yoga helps stretch your body and your mind, creates energetic flow, and allows for toxicity to gently rise from your body. Be present for your discomfort, while offering yourself love and acceptance.

After the detox period, you can begin asking yourself about each thing you want to bring back in, "Does this energize me or drain me?" Bring each activity in your life in the quantity that makes you feel good and whole.

Shifting to a Language of Love and Abundance

As shared before, words and language are what create our reality and destroy possibility.

There was a powerful and eye-opening experiment done by a Japanese scientist, Dr. Masaru Emoto, which showed how molecular structures in water are transformed when exposed to human thoughts, sounds and intentions. In his book, *The Hidden Messages in Water*, he demonstrated how exposing water to words like "Love" and "Gratitude" resulted in aesthetically pleasing formations of the water crystals that looked like magical snowflakes, while water exposed to fearful and negative human language like "Die" or "Hate" resulted in disconnected, disfigured, and "unpleasant" formations.

Our body is made up of seventy percent of water – think about how our thoughts can change their formation, and what that might do to our energy field!

As you're continuing your Love Recovery journey, it's important to notice what words you're saying, because you are a masterful creator.

In the below chart, I share two different world views, and the words that they consist of.

TWO DIFFERENT WORLDS:
WHAT INNER / OUTER CONVERSATIONS ARE YOU HAVING…?

World of Survival: Mediocrity / Lack		World of Possibility: Extraordinary / Abundance	
Right/wrong	Being reasonable	Opportunity	Wonder
Good/bad	Lack	Love	Awe
Righteous/Evil	Worry	Togetherness	Kindness
Impossible	Future-oriented	Peace	Joy
Looking good	Safe	Listening	Celebration
Gossip	Separate	Miracle	Vulnerable
Sensation	Isolated	Self-expression	Power
Working hard	Rejection	Partnership	Sharing
Struggle	Alone	Inspiration	Collaboration
Fear	Victim	Gratitude	Acceptance
Blame	Denial	Understanding	Truth
Perfectionism	Goals	Being imperfect	Intention

As you can imagine, love has a hard time existing in the World of Survival. Fear thrives there. It's the reason why so many people experience depression and mental health issues. Speaking the language of love, whether it's through our thoughts or conversations that we're having, is important for creating a brand-new world that is extraordinary and fulfilling!

When you're having conversations, observe the language you use, and see if you can mindfully end a sentence before you blurt out anything negative. Begin to consciously use the words in the second bubble, like "miracle," "opportunity," etc. This may seem silly at first, given that we're used to having practical and sometimes pessimistic conversations. Be the one who shifts the dynamic! You'll begin to see your own miracles pop up in your life.

Reframing Your Life Events and Creating a New Story for Yourself

During this time of detoxing your mind, begin to observe the story or the narrative you are telling yourself about your life and the situations in it. Are you mostly disheartened, negative, or simply limiting in your thinking?

Historically, as women, we've been taught to downplay our desires or successes, and to make ourselves seem doomed, so as to not "get too big for one's britches" or cause jealousy amongst other women. I find myself naturally tending to do that, rather than singing my own praises or simply being proud of myself – and this is a hard narrative to shift, yet an important one. On the flip side, have you noticed that when you are around a woman who is genuinely appreciative and positive of herself, she radiates with a sense of possibility for not only herself, but also for those around her?

You have a choice as to how your own story is being told inside your head, and even how you share it with others.

A tool that's powerful is reframing. Take your current story, and

Share this type of thinking with others, so that they can also visualize your greatness unfolding.

EXERCISE: REFRAMING YOUR NARRATIVE

Take some time to write out some of your own disempowering narratives and write sentences to reframe them.

Here are some examples, especially as you're thinking or talking about your love life.

"I haven't met my soulmate." –> "*I haven't met my soulmate, yet, but I know he's on his way!*"

"I am doomed to be single." –> "*I am single and am creating the conditions for a healthy, loving partnership with myself and my future mate. The universe has my back and wants me to be happy. Plus, I choose to not settle in my love life.*"

"I can't believe the relationship's over." –> "*The relationship wasn't meant to work, and one or both of us were suffering. I'm open to a healthy relationship and am committed to doing the inner work to not recreate painful patterns.*"

"I am so mad at myself for what's going on in my love life." –> "*I love, accept and forgive myself for being single. Everything's flowing according to divine timing.*"

"There are no more good men out there." –> "*Just like me, there's a loving, kind, relationship-oriented man out there, who is the right partner for me. There is an abundance of kind-hearted men. Plus, all it takes is one!"*

Love Goddess, what's the new story of you that you want to share?

Spiritual Well-Being: Claiming Your Connection with the Divine

When I first started my Love Recovery journey, I really felt unworthy of love and felt skeptical that anything good could happen for me. I had grown up in a loving, religious home, but over time, due to my focus on education and work, by my twenties, my relationship with the divine had all but vanished. In fact, I thought being spiritual was cheesy, a way of life for eccentric people or something to be achieved after retirement. Ironically, I didn't realize that the lack of spiritual connection was causing my own spirit to decline, along with my sense of faith and trust for goodness in my life.

While working with Pat, she had me pray in a church, every single day, which I began to do to humor her. Still feeling a sense of bitterness around my love life, I questioned whether there was someone who loved me and what prayer had to offer. She asked me, "Were there moments in your life when you could have died, yet you were saved?" This question made me think of three very important experiences in my life, in which I could have very much been harmed, but through some miracle, I survived.

The first was when I was fourteen, and I was traveling by train in India, and I foolishly decided to get off the train in a small village. Somehow, after the train had left the station, my father had the intuition that I was missing and pulled the "emergency break" chain – and the train stopped. I ran almost a mile with broken flip-flops to reach the train, and there were dozens of people leaning out of the last caboose, holding out their hand to let me on. I made it! I shudder to think what could have happened to me had I been left behind, with no phone, money, or ability to speak the local language.

Another time, again in India, I was studying in my bedroom and felt a small piece of paint fall on me. I didn't think much of it, yet I had a notion to leave the room to investigate. Moments later, the ceiling came crashing through, crushing the bed I was laying on. What an unfortunate way to die, if there was one! I was dumbfounded by the sheer miracle of surviving.

Finally, there was an incident where someone had broken into my apartment in Philadelphia, in which I lived alone, and had strewn around my items in a violent manner. I could have been in there! I thank my lucky stars to this day for not facing that predicament, in which I wouldn't have had an escape.

Likewise, I could think of several instances where I was in precarious situations, and because of my intuition or good fortune I was saved or taken care of when I was vulnerable. Moreover, I could finally be in raw gratitude for my parents having birthed and taken care of me as a child, for without them I wouldn't be alive today, and the countless people and circumstances that had been orchestrated by the universe to keep me breathing, sheltered, fed and happy. I could finally see – being alive is simply a miracle!

I began my relationship with God from this place, of having renewed perspective and realizing that there were many unseen and seen forces that were guarding me, guiding me. I felt humbled. I was starting to feel incredibly loved for the first time in a very long time, and this time it felt unconditional and otherworldly.

As you're beginning your self-love journey, the first place to start is your spiritual health. Spirituality is and always has been the basis for understanding love – after all, why would our soul long for love so much, and why do we wish to experience the feeling of divine union and unconditional love? When you're connected to the divine in whatever unique way that resonates for you, you open up to the universe's love and abundance.

As your body needs food, rest and other nourishment, your spirit needs to be attended to the same, if not more. When your spiritual foundation is strong, it informs the rest of your body's health and your physical experience. It's from this place that you can build healthy spiritual connections with others – not just superficial or even toxic ones. You can heal your spiritual blocks as well as regenerate existing relationships from the place of spiritual well-being.

Whether you resonate with the word God, Jesus, Allah, Brahma, Sophia, Universe, the divine, Source, consciousness, your Higher Self, Mother, Father, Spirit, Love – the choice is yours in how you want to define this relationship and who you refer to for divine connection.

For simplicity's sake, I use God, because the word simply makes my heart flutter with a feeling of awe and humility.

"The rewards of life and devotion to God are love and inner rapture, and the capacity to receive the life of God." ~ Rumi

We each have shortcomings and we're vulnerable – that's the reality. However, we also have innumerable gifts, knowledge and experience that helps us make choices and fuels our actions.

What is that divine spark that helps us wake up every morning, open our hearts and love even when it hurts, and helps us roar with courage and strength when we face immeasurable loss? Where does the grace come from to forgive, have mercy or compassion for people we dislike, or to face storms in life in a calm, accepting way, knowing inherently that we're loved and safe inside? Where does the strength come from when we're facing the impossible, like giving birth or facing our own or a loved one's death? How do we heal and transform our spiritual blocks so that we can begin to live our true potential?

Simply put, all of this comes from God.

When a woman has a relationship with God, she doesn't need a man to fulfill that role that frankly only God could – of unconditionally loving her, protecting and providing for her, against all odds on the Earthly realm. This releases that aching neediness for security and comfort, because she has access to that wellspring of love within her. She also gains access to her God-given gifts and talents, whether it's her ability to heal herself, her intuition, her heart openness and ability to feel unconditional love. She's connected to her heart's wisdom and desires, her heart being the sacred portal for divine connection.

Sadly, women around the world have had a tumultuous relationship with God for a very long time. In many religions around the world, the feminine has been desecrated and deemed as inferior, and her body has been considered non-sacred and even profane. It is largely taught that women are inherently driven by desire and sexuality and cause men to "sin," cause wars or lose control over themselves through temptation. Yet, women are regularly sexually abused. Girls are taught early on not to do anything unholy, like getting pregnant or losing their virginity before marriage. In many places, menstrual flow is considered dirty.

From what I know now, the opposite is true! Women are actually more connected to the divine, *because* of our sexuality and the supernatural ability of giving birth, our innate wisdom and ability to bring beauty, life and healing to the world. Women make unbelievable lovers of the divine, which threatens the legitimacy and status quo of the powers that be. Unfortunately, there has been both an unconscious and conscious effort to control women, make women believe that they are less spiritual or less favored by God and *need* to depend on a patriarchal system for their survival.

The seed of unworthiness runs deep for women.

This is perhaps my biggest spiritual battle I fight nearly every day, and it shows up in layers. Even writing this book, and the prospect of others reading it is scary, and I'm woefully afraid of being mocked and rejected. At other times, I worry if I'll be provided for in my business, simply by being *me*. Or, in my romantic relationship, I become anxious that my man will leave me or lose his desire for me if I don't behave a certain way. My relationship with my sexuality has wounding and insecurity around whether I am sacred or profane. I rack my brain endlessly on whether I'm a "good enough" mother, wife, daughter, writer, businesswoman. This seed of unworthiness has a way of showing its ugly head when I'm depressed or facing a life-or-death situation.

Yet, I've found that the seed of unworthiness has led me to deepening my relationship with God and unraveling the magnificence of who I am. It's a wondrous exploration, one that requires a deepening of my faith and trust, and noticing my edges of vulnerability, whether it's in giving, asking or receiving. It has also led me back to myself – being my first soulmate, loving myself unconditionally, knowing that **to me,**

I am enough. I only need to love and validate myself, and seeking approval from others is at best, misguided and ultimately painful.

Unfortunately, humans are flawed, and the way we love is largely based on seeking safety and approval for who we are. There are very few people who can love unconditionally – they are probably sitting on a mountain, alone, meditating (but I guarantee, they're not free from their devilish, tormenting egos!). When we become parents, we bring our own limiting beliefs and wounds to how we take care of our children, which only perpetuates painful love patterns.

Having a relationship with a higher power is healing for our psyche on a psychological level because it's the only kind of love that's unwounded and unconditional. When you surrender to that kind of love, you can begin to emulate it in your own life.

How do you begin to have that spiritual connection? What does spiritual well-being look like? **The exercises I provided in the daily morning ritual – the gratitude exercise, the affirmations, meditation, mindfulness – are a powerful start, and you should be doing those every day.** This entire book will outline various ways of healing and releasing your spiritual blocks and reconnecting you with your divine feminine side.

Additionally, you have to create a spiritual life that feels rich and healing to you. Whether it's through daily prayer, joining a church group, a meditation circle, practicing mindfulness, being in nature, doing a Twelve-Step program, therapy, volunteering at a soup kitchen or being present with your loved ones, the choice of how to spend your time is yours – you'll be guided from your heart. There are numerous activities that support your innate sense of spiritual connection, restore the feeling of unconditional love and deepen your compassion and understanding of everyday life.

You can also begin to have a conversation with God, either verbally or by writing in your journal. Share what you're grateful for, vent or simply ask questions remaining open to receiving guidance. You're free – God will never judge you! You can pray for your well-being, and that of others. As a devotional practice, you can begin to treat each person and being as a reflection of God, and see every act of yours to be sacred, filled with love. When you walk around, you can practice gratitude, or send a smile to each person you pass by, thinking, "I see you, I love you, thank you for being in my life."

This is your personal inquiry and I invite you to explore it in a way that feels good to you, at any pace. This is a mystical, lifelong relationship and you will only keep growing.

A word of caution: If you feel skeptical or unsure about certain spiritual institutions, groups or activities, follow your intuition and maintain firm boundaries or even keep a distance. As in love, it's important to not simply give up your power to anyone outside of you, because it is "spiritual" or "right" for others.

Journal:

1. When are some moments that you can think of where you were saved or helped in a miraculous way?

2. List people you are grateful for, who have helped you along the way, whether it was during your childhood, teachers, mentors, friends or even strangers. If you're inspired, send them a note of appreciation.

3. How would you define your relationship with God right now? How do you see it evolving or possibly even transforming? What are some ways you can connect with God every day, in small or big ways?

4. What is your heart telling you to do right now in terms of your spiritual well-being?

5. If you could create a small daily prayer, what would it be?

> Meditate: When you close your eyes, how does it feel
> to be loved by God? Can you hold this feeling for five
> minutes while meditating? During the meditation,
> imagine all the times you were protected and cared for,
> and feel into a sense of gratefulness.

Emotional Well-Being: Building a Foundation of Empathy and Resilience

For a long time, I repressed my feelings. I didn't know what to do when I got excited, depressed, angry or insecure. No one had given me a template on how to manage my emotions, and the few times I cried in public, I felt silly and vulnerable. I'd gotten the message that being emotional was a woman's downfall. In relationships, when I was upset about something, I would just stay quiet and stifle my annoyance or finally blow up when it got too much. In general, though, I had an easy-going, fun demeanor – but inside I had other things brewing.

Interestingly, I would mostly lose my cool with a guy I was dating, yet hardly ever with friends or family. Isn't it fascinating that the person we covet the most – the person we're afraid of losing – is whom we feel safest to unleash our pain on? On the flipside, when things were going my way, a guy that I liked was texting me or I was out partying with my friends and traveling the world, I felt happy and excited. I was on this crazy adventure called life, and my emotions were just a part of me.

> I didn't give two thoughts about my feelings until after my breakup, when I was engulfed by my emotions and, for the very first time, I was forced to face them. After getting over my sadness and despair, I started feeling surges of indignation and anger that took over my being, making me blind to reality. I was a tigress on the prowl, ready to unleash my claws on someone! I felt unstable and couldn't really trust myself or the world around me.
>
> It is only now that I can see that I didn't have a strong emotional foundation, so there was nothing in me that truly felt safe and secure – I was a victim to the outside world. How could I reasonably be in a relationship if I had no control over my thoughts and feelings? Even though most people considered me as being calm, cool and collected, I was a magnet for drama because of my tumultuous emotional landscape.

Having spent years studying emotional health, I now understand how important emotional mastery is for men and women to be their most resilient, loving and passionate selves. This area is rarely covered in mental health education yet is what is critical to our well-being and happiness.

Emotions are powerful – they are the juice that fuel the human spirit, the power behind all that we do, the language of the heart and body. Whether you're happy and thrilled or down in the doldrums, there's a beauty and truth to be expressed and experienced. Emotions are what connect people to each other deeply and honestly, allowing us to live truly fulfilling lives.

Women have a unique role in relationships – we are the relationship experts, the emotional leaders – the ones who lead in vulnerability and emotional honesty, creating intimacy in the process. This unique gift is conferred upon us biologically, spiritually. We lead the way for our partners and children to know what it feels like to be emotionally honest and connected. Yet we flounder in this area because for all our lives, we've been living in a state of emotional shutdown and disapproval, along with not knowing how to deal with our own feelings.

The feeling of insecurity arises when you feel emotionally unsafe within yourself.

When you struggle with understanding and handling your feelings, you feel lost. You go through emotional ups and downs, from being a doormat to a bitch, and make embarrassing mistakes along the way. You piss someone off you didn't mean to, send explosive texts or become appeasing to a point of losing your sovereignty. How can you even begin to trust yourself if your emotions are haywire?

On top of that, you get hurt along the way and emotional wounds begin to pile up without ever being addressed. Experience enough wounds over a lifetime, and you begin to close down and develop a guardedness, leading to a fear of vulnerability and intimacy. This is how emotional blocks get formed and become lodged in our bodies, and we lose trust in love. *You don't want to be one of those wary women that can never trust, right?*

Here's the possibility for you, dear Love Goddess. You are at the perfect point of growing your emotional maturity and being a beacon of wholesome love and passion – where you can experience your entire emotional range from a place of groundedness and self-awareness.

When you feel emotionally connected to yourself and you're able to process your emotions, the sky is your limit. You can reach new levels of intimacy with your man because you feel safe to be vulnerable. Your actions come from a place of thoughtfulness rather than unconscious reactions from your wounds. You can have those difficult, edgy conversations that you normally feel shy about, yet you know matter to you. Men honor women who are in charge of their emotions, because they inherently feel a sense of safety, trust and freedom. *Women who are confident in their emotions are sexy and fiery!*

So how do you become a master in your emotions – and become a Love Goddess that draws in heart-opening experiences with people that matter to her?

The goal of this section is to give you the tools to begin to build that strong emotional foundation within yourself, and in the next chapter (Heal Your Heart and Close Your "Ex Files"), you'll go through the process of releasing old emotional wounds that no longer serve you.

An Overview of Emotions

Remember how I talked about thoughts being like energy packets? The same goes for emotions, which I see as:

Emotions = Energy in Motion

Emotions are like energetic patterns or information packets that reside in parts of you. They can have physical sensations in your body (for instance, anger can appear as a burning sensation around your heart or a heart quickening). Emotions are linked to thoughts, memories and beliefs.

Feelings are neither good nor bad. They just *are*. We shouldn't judge, suppress or deny them. By "trying" to feel good by avoiding our pain, we're being unfair and unkind to ourselves because our feelings are usually trying to tell us something. A great way to understand how important feelings are is by observing children. Kids don't cry unless they actually need something or are trying to communicate with their caregivers. When a baby is crying, we assume it's doing so because it's hungry, sleepy or has a poopy diaper and needs our help. We feel a sense of compassion and tenderness for the baby. Likewise, as adults, our feelings are communicating with us and we owe it to them to slow down and have compassion.

The trouble starts when you begin to push your feelings down or invalidate them. When they're suppressed, they live inside of you as trapped emotions. According to Chinese medicine, different organs hold on to certain emotions, like grief living in your lungs or anger in your liver. This goes on to fester as disease later on.

After a major traumatic event like a breakup, loss or a betrayal, if you harbor feelings of anger and resentment, an energetic wall gets created around your heart (called the "heart wall"). I estimate that nearly 85% of people have walls around their hearts to varying degrees, which prevents people from feeling open to vulnerability or even being connected to their hearts.

Self-Empathy: The Power Tool for Being with Your Emotions

As humans, we long to be understood and accepted for who we are. As you've probably guessed, I've found that the person who can truly, unequivocally offer that abundantly and freely to us is ourselves. A potent tool I've come across and use regularly is *self-empathy* which I learned through the Center for Nonviolent Communication. This practical, simple tool has changed my life and allows me to be honest with my feelings and needs in a mindful, self-compassionate way.

Self-empathy allows you to be there for your emotions and needs, naming and validating them, feeling them thoroughly without judgement. It's a self-awareness practice in which you're there as your own parent or best friend, asking yourself, "What am I feeling... am I feeling sad? Am I feeling nervous?" You sit with the emotions, allowing yourself to fully embody them and noticing the sensations that rise up. During this time, you don't go into the story or narrative, you simply stick to asking, "What am I feeling? What am I needing?"

Through practicing this regularly, you begin to feel like your own "empathy cup" is full, because your feelings, which are like little children, get to be felt, seen and heard and get the attention they need. You begin to understand what your needs are, based on your feelings.

It's from this place of your own cup being full that you can effectively be with someone else's emotions and connect with them deeply, without your own sense of emotional neediness getting in the way.

The life-changing benefits of this practice are countless. You start to feel a sense of stability and fulfillment in your life just by beginning to build your emotional layer. Your feelings become the pathway for accessing your inner compass and intuition. You become deeply connected to your body's consciousness and are operating at a heightened state of awareness. Moreover, you're able to get in touch with your truth, and can powerfully communicate your desires and feelings with your partner. As you go through your Love Recovery process, new and old emotions will come up to be healed, and through self-empathy, they begin to gently dissipate on their own as you bring your loving awareness to them.

Here's another magical outcome of practicing self-empathy regularly and focusing on your emotional well-being: **You become a magnet for an emotionally available man, because *you* are emotionally available.** This is not only an energetic principle, but a real, practical one – think of how many relationships you've sabotaged because of your emotional outbursts or inability to be there for your partner when he needed you.

Basics of Self-Empathy

So, what is this magical tool all about, anyways? There are two distinct parts – noticing your feelings and your accompanying needs, which I'll break down for you.

EXERCISE 1: BRING AWARENESS TO YOUR FEELINGS

- Get into a quiet, meditative state. Take a few deep breaths, scanning your body from head to toe, bringing attention to any sensations arising, as usually body sensations are connected with emotions.

- Open the list of feelings (*download and print the NVC Inventory of Feelings sheet from https://sarikajain.com/Soulmate-Plan-Resources/*)

- In a slow, mindful way, go through the list of "<u>feelings when your needs are **not** satisfied,</u>" section by section, asking yourself quietly, "What am I feeling? Am I feeling afraid? Am I feeling apprehensive?" You can affirm out loud, "I'm feeling dread. I'm feeling petrified. I'm feeling shaky." Say them out loud. Also, notice whether you feel them in your body and what the sensations are like. This lets you know whether you are "thinking" you're feeling something, versus actually feeling it. Do not go into any story or justification of why you feel the way you do. Try to go through it as comprehensively as you can, even if you list out all of the feelings. It doesn't matter if you only feel a tinge of a feeling, you can still name it.

- Now go through the list of "<u>feelings when your needs are satisfied,</u>" section by section. Which ones are you feeling now? Say them out loud. Also, notice where you feel them in your body.

There is no need to stay with any particular feeling. Simply notice it, allow yourself to feel it, acknowledge it and move on.

In the beginning you might not even know what you're feeling. Or perhaps you have intense feelings, and the intensity causes you discomfort or even fear. Just notice the emotions and end when you reach your edge.

At any one moment, you can feel so many feelings, even a hundred! This is surprising, given that we're used to identifying with a single feeling when someone asks us how we're doing. Moreover, our range of understanding of feelings is usually confined to a few: sad, frustrated, anxious, happy, excited. As you'll see, each emotion has its own nuance and vibration in your body. When a particular feeling is acknowledged, it feels like a string that's been plucked on a guitar. The feeling being seen and observed without judgement is the most important gift you can offer yourself. There are no negative or positive emotions – all are valid and important and deserve to be held with love.

Discovering Your Needs

Everyone in the world has a common set of needs. These are universal human needs, whether one is rich, poor, or from a different part of the world.

Here's a secret to understanding human psychology – at all times, we are being motivated to act to fulfill a need. *That is the basis for all of our actions.*

The way you connect to your needs is through your emotions.

EXERCISE 2: BRING AWARENESS TO YOUR NEEDS

- Get into a quiet, meditative state. Take a few deep breaths.

- Do a body scan, reconnecting with your body and going back to the feelings that you identified.

- Open the list of needs *(download and print the NVC Inventory of Needs from here: https://sarikajain.com/Soulmate-Plan-Resources/)*

- Go through the list and determine what needs of yours are currently **not being met** in the present moment. Go section by section, slowly. Say these words out loud. Do not go into any story or justification.

- Now, go through the list and determine what needs of yours *are* **being met.** Go section by section, slowly. Say these words out loud.

- See if you can just name these needs, without trying to solve for them for right now. Sometimes just knowing what you're needing right now is the most relevant form of wisdom.

> Journal: What have you learned about the nature of your needs, and of yourself? Isn't it interesting to note that most of your needs are probably already being met?

Needs are a powerful way to help us understand human behavior. It's almost like we are constantly motivated by our desire to fulfill our unmet needs.

In order to fulfill a need, we employ a *strategy*. A strategy is a set of actions that we take to help us fulfill our needs. There are many different ways of meeting a need, but often times we choose one on autopilot and that's unconscious.

For example, a person may use the *strategy* of cheating on her husband, because her needs for intimacy, partnership and connection aren't being fulfilled in her marriage. However, the other strategies she could have employed were to seek out a counselor, connect with her best friend, have an honest conversation with her husband or choose to form a deeper sense of connection and partnership with herself. No option is necessarily right or wrong, yet each one comes with its own set of consequences.

As another example, if you're single and feeling lonely or a sense of longing, you may sense that you have a need for intimacy and instinctively pick up your phone to look at your dating app. Or you wake up, needing a sense of connection and progress, and you quickly check your work e-mail.

It takes a lot of self-awareness and slowing down to really understand what your needs are and what actions you take to fulfill them. **The universe always *wants* to fulfill your needs, but since you're usually unclear about what they are, and don't take conscious action to fulfill them, you end up with a mixed bag of outcomes.**

You are likely spending all your time unconsciously trying to fulfill needs that you don't even know you have using strategies that you automatically use. No wonder life feels so out of control!

The way you learn about your needs is by accessing your feelings. For instance, if you identify that you're feeling shaky or insecure, you can ask yourself, "Am I needing support? Am I needing clarity?" Then, you can take a conscious action to fulfill that need.

Get to know these feelings and needs by doing this as often as you can, so that you can do this practice without looking at the sheets.

When and How to Practice Self-Empathy (Sarika's Version)

- Set a container for twenty minutes or however long you need at the moment. Setting a container is very important. In general, boundary setting in whatever you do is helpful as it allows you to "let go" and surrender during it.

- Close your eyes, take a few deep breaths and scan your body. Notice any body sensations.

- Then, begin to ask yourself what you're feeling with needs that *aren't* being met. In the beginning, I recommend you look at the feelings and needs lists (and be sure to keep a printout with you). If there's a sensation that's rising up, allow yourself to notice the sensation, like grief, or heartache. Breathe through it if needed.

- Ask what needs of yours aren't being met. Acknowledge them. *Do not go into any stories – stay with naming your feelings and needs.*

- As you contemplate your feelings and needs, think to yourself, "Even though I am feeling insecure, and needing comfort and support, **I love, accept and forgive myself.**"

- Now, go through the feelings of <u>fulfilled</u> needs. Notice them and allow yourself to really feel them – whether it's curiosity, openness, exhilaration, excitement. Breathe through these emotions, and let the emotions arise and take over your body.

- State the needs that *are* fulfilled for you, and feel a sense of gratitude for those needs that are met.

- At the end, thank yourself for giving yourself the of practicing self-empathy.

Do this practice at least once a day to allow for yourself to have true emotional connection with yourself.

Emotional Self-Care

At the end of the day, your emotional well-being is your greatest gift to yourself and your loved ones. Here are some tips to care for your emotional body, in addition to the regular practice of self-empathy (above):

1. **Rest is under-rated! As a Love Goddess, you deserve plenty of it.** I can't emphasize how important it is to sleep or lay down when you're feeling tired, especially when you're going through a spiritual growth or recovery process. Resting has a way of calming your nervous system and so much healing occurs while you're sleeping. I would recommend sleeping seven to eight hours a day, and if you have trouble sleeping, sleep earlier, and don't read or do anything stimulating before you go to bed, like sending an e-mail. Instead, when you're in bed, think of what you're grateful for, practice self-empathy, pray or simply meditate on your breath or the feeling of being loved.

2. **Move your body:** So much of our emotional energy gets pent up, and sometimes we get into depressive states if we don't move. Movement like yoga, exercise and dance helps get your energy moving, pumping your body with healthy hormones – all great for emotional health.

3. **Seek out professional support:** So many times, we go through life holding our own problems in our hearts, which becomes unbearable. Since being in Love Recovery, I've found it indispensable to have someone listen to me and help me move through my "stuckness" or overwhelming emotions. When you have someone holding your emotions, your emotional cup becomes bigger, and you can deal with even more. If you have experienced severe trauma, such as from an abusive relationship or a painful sexual experience, you might want to also consider pursuing psychosomatic bodywork and healing, such as "Rolfing" or trauma-informed yoga. I truly value the integration of mind-body approaches to healing our emotional bodies.

4. **Walk barefoot on the ground:** The earth has a powerful electromagnetic field, and when you walk on grass or soil for even five minutes a day, it grounds your emotional energy into the earth. Mother Earth is the ultimate healer.

5. **Hold space for intense emotions:** Let's face it, as humans we're meant to express ourselves by laughing hard and crying even harder, raging like a bull when we're mad! We've got all this emotional energy, and sometimes you need different tools to be with them. I'll share a few here:

a - Self-empathy on Fire:

When you're feeling deeply triggered, take time out from work or family, go into a quiet room, and sit, consciously focusing on your breath. Set a container for twenty minutes, or however long you like.

Then, scan your body, head to toe, noticing the sensations arising. If you feel burning or aching in your heart, spend time there, feeling these sensations. Name them, validate them *"I feel burning in my chest. I feel my heart pounding."* See if you can ask yourself how you feel: *"Am I feeling sad? Am I feeling angry?"* Try not to get lost in the story of why you feel this way. Just pay attention to the feelings and sensations, not judging them or wishing them to go away. As you feel the sensations, breathe. **If you have the time and courage, allow the emotion to well up inside of you, taking up your whole body. Be there for it, lovingly observing and accepting it.** If it's too much, take a break, and move to another body part, or simply focus on your breath. You can end with feeling a sense of love, acceptance and forgiveness for yourself.

"Anger is like a howling baby, suffering and crying. Your anger is your baby. The baby needs his mother to embrace him. You are the mother. Embrace your baby." ~ Thích Nhat Hanh

b - Swamping

This is a tool taught by Regena Thomasheuer, a feminine empowerment teacher. In this practice, you find a sacred, private space and play loud music. Make a playlist that has songs in the following order: anger, sadness, acceptance, openness, sensuality and ecstasy. Or simply choose a single emotion to be with. During this one-hour dance sequence, allow yourself to fully embody all your emotions and dance with abandon. Scream, shout, cry, wail, pound the floor, throw things.

Be theatrical and channel your inner two-year-old! Express all that wants to be without judgment or filters. End the session with sensual touching or caressing, connecting with your sensual desire within, your "turn on" so as to not be fueled by contempt, rather love and desire.

This practice will allow all your feelings to arise and you will transform it through the power of love and sensuality.

c - Dancing and Stomping

Playing music, such as drumming, or something else rhythmic, while dancing and stomping, will allow you to dissipate energy. Indigenous cultures understand the importance of channeling and transmuting energy through our bodies, and regularly use stomping on the earth (with intention) for a grounding effect. Exercise is a powerful way of moving adrenaline and cortisol through your body.

d - Laughter

After my breakup, I started taking part in laughter yoga. At first it seemed silly, yet I could see the therapeutic effect of it on my body. I intensely laughed at my situation and brought a sense of silliness and play into my life. Doing a practice like this allows the energy to move in your body, increases your capacity to deal with challenging emotions and ultimately transforms you energetically. Ultimately joy and pleasure, especially after detoxing difficult emotions, "turns on" your cells and genetic material, making you lighter and radiant.

e - Creativity

Perhaps the most powerful thing you can do during difficult times is to channel your energy into something creative, like journaling, painting, poetry or dance. The most heart-rending pieces of music were written by artists when they were going through some sort of loss, like a breakup. Many prominent historical moments, such as Nelson Mandela and Mahatma Gandhi's nonviolent disobedience, came from anger that was channeled in a compassionate way.

Your emotional health is the most fragile yet powerful part of your human experience. When you take care of it, you will feel connected not only to yourself, but to others in an openhearted way. During your Love Recovery, notice what triggers you, including people or certain activities, and see if you can minimize unnecessary outside stimulation, especially as you're building your emotional foundation. When you're around your family and friends, try to be compassionate with their problems, without getting absorbed into their drama. Practice self-empathy before having difficult conversations, and make a commitment to not try to control, fix or take on others' suffering in any way. Sometimes, just listening while practicing healthy boundary setting can be a powerful way to support someone else.

Physical Well-being: Designing a Lifestyle That Honors Your Body and Soul's Needs

I once dated a man whom I *really* had the hots for. Yet, there was a moment when things became clear to me about why we couldn't be together: when I looked down at his feet, the bottom of his feet had calluses and cuts – and he hadn't cut his toenails. I then visited his apartment and it felt half-lived in, with clothes strewn everywhere and his bathroom was dirty. He told me his mom and sisters lived down the street, and that he was so close with them that he basically ate his meals there.

This man, though smart, handsome and sweet, struggled with boundaries and self-care, and given that I was starting to spend a great deal of time loving myself and honoring my body's needs, we weren't on the same wavelength. In fact, I realized that **he likely couldn't really offer me anything substantive in a relationship, because he could barely take care of his own needs.** When we dated, it showed – he would flake on our dates or made it difficult to pin him down. I was growing into a radiant, healthy woman and I wasn't interested in another "project." I was proud of myself for not taking his behavior personally, and after a few dates, I ended it.

Think about the men you've dated in the past. Were they reliable, self-sufficient, had healthy boundaries or did they work insane hours and eat take out every day? Were they emotionally available, openhearted and could you imagine living a healthy, fulfilling life with them?

Love Goddess, here's the thing: if your lifestyle is healthy, balanced and full of self-care, then inevitably you will attract a man that's also focused on well-being. In fact, you will become a magnet for grounded, mature men who will honor and treat you like a goddess, because that's how you treat yourself. The way you live your life, with healthy boundaries and with people and activities that nourish you, will set the stage for greater love in your life. If you're living in survival mode, can you imagine thriving with someone else? You can't! You and your body deserve better.

So, what does it look like to have a lifestyle that promotes a loving, thriving relationship with yourself? How can you begin to form habits and rituals that release toxic patterns and promote your well-being, and for those around you?

By following the guidelines and exercises in this section, you will create a Goddessy lifestyle that energizes you and allows you to zap away toxicity. You'll find that you have more room for love because you'll be flowing with more grace and a sense of balance and ease. Moreover, you'll begin to align with a life that's more authentic, and you'll feel more connected with your inner compass and joyful spark.

Do you find yourself fixated on whether your boss likes your work, wondering whether you're doing enough for your parents or your job, or in general, feeling guilty, overwhelmed or exhausted? Are you in a draining relationship with a friend or an ex? When you're in a relationship, do you find yourself over-giving to the point of losing yourself or wondering what you really want anyways?

Boundary setting is a huge challenge for most people. In fact, you might find it a whole new concept that you were never introduced to. Both men and women struggle with it for different reasons. For millennia, women have been asked to give up everything of their own to take care of others. Women got married and became mothers at a young age, never getting a chance discover what kind of life keeps their spirits elevated and allows them to express their individuality.

Moreover, experiencing unhealthy boundaries begins when we're children. Most parents don't exhibit or honor their own boundaries, let alone each other's or their children's. Overgiving, fixing, controlling, emotional manipulation of a child because of one's own insecurities are commonly seen behaviors. If you have a strong, codependent relationship with a parent, you might not even realize it – but the symptoms include constantly worrying about a parent's well-being and happiness, and a sense of guilt or worry about winning their approval. I'll be addressing this in greater detail in the next chapter, but just know that if you are in an entangled relationship with your family, then this book will allow you to gently release the hold it has on you, so you can emerge as a healthy, independent person while promoting your family's health.

What if you could recreate your life so that you had plenty of time for fun and activities that light up your soul, and you could let go of people or activities that zap your energy? Wouldn't that feel rejuvenating and freeing?

The good news is that once you begin setting healthy boundaries, then the rest of your life begins to align with itself, easily. This means having a work-life balance that feels great and plenty of time for things that you value, including your own spiritual practices, love life, health, friends and pursuing your interests.

Dealing With Work

Most of us are workaholics to some degree because that is the culture that's been promoted. When you're single, your employer might expect you to work extra or put you on demanding projects. *What if, instead, you begin to take on attitude that you do have a family to take care of you – you!*

You must begin to assert your needs and you can do it in a gentle, kind way. Most of us get a deep sense of validation from work, but it can't be all that defines us. **In fact, our careers have a way of getting in the way of our love life, which is really the most vital part of our life.**

Here's a secret: the more relaxed, self-connected and aware you become, the more efficient and productive you will be. The choices you make will be wiser because you're coming from a place of awareness and calm. Things will flow, and you will be more magnetic, without needing to push and exert yourself!

So just trust that being self-nurturing and setting healthy boundaries with work will support you in making a big difference in every part of your life.

Start in small ways. Take a lunch break and go for a mindful walk. Take a few minutes break between intensive working sessions. Say no to projects that require you to do extra work or conversations with colleagues that aren't essential. Don't feel you have to respond to e-mails unless they're really urgent, and consider batching them – and don't respond to e-mails after work. Leave work at a reasonable time – imagine if you had kids or a parent to take care of? How do you envision your life beginning to look like, if you had a busy personal life? Begin to align with that, today. Communicate with your boss and colleagues about your needs and use humor if needed to dispel the tension. Come up with a schedule outside of work, so that you can commit to your said work hours. Set up fun events and hobbies after work – and stick to them!

Initially, your manager or colleagues may protest. You may have the urge to give in – after all, that's what most people do with their boundaries. Yet, **when you begin to respect yourself, your boundaries and your commitments to yourself, then other people will do the same.**

Be persistent. Work hard but play smart.

You're creating a sustainable life that will bring you fulfillment. Men are so much better at taking chances, then apologizing later – sometimes women get stuck in the "needing to please" mode and over-giving of themselves.

How to Let Go of People Who Don't Resonate with You

"You are the sum average of the five people you spend the most time" is a quote famously attributed to motivational speaker Jim Rohn.

Take a look at your friends and people you interact with. Who are the people who surround you – are they loving, kind and inspiring, or do they rile you up in some way? As you examine your circle, ask yourself for each one, "Does spending time with this person drain me, or energize me?"

In terms of letting go of people who don't serve you, there are two options, depending on the situation:

- Be gentle and allow the relationship to diffuse on its own. This doesn't mean you're being passive aggressive. Let your friend/

family member know that you're currently focusing on self-care, and you're taking a break from connecting for a while. You still love them, and you're there if they need you. *Over time, if a relationship doesn't resonate, it will slowly begin to dissipate on its own.* Or, if you want to continue to relate, then set healthy boundaries, like having a one-hour conversation with them every month.

- Be firm. If someone is truly being inconsiderate, aggressive or has hurt you in some way, let them know that their behavior is hurtful, and that you will be disconnecting for a while to focus on other things. Inside, you can practice Ho'oponopono (described below) or imagine releasing any cords that the person has with you (which I'll be sharing in the next chapter). You can think to yourself about the person, "I release you."

Trust in the process. You're not hurting anyone by being honest while owning your own feelings and needs and setting healthy boundaries.

Releasing Codependent or Toxic Relationships

According to the Merriam-Webster dictionary, codependency is defined as "a psychological condition or a relationship in which a person is controlled or manipulated by another who is affected with a pathological condition (such as an addiction to alcohol or heroin)."

I recently heard a disturbing statistic: we spend nearly 90% of our energy on our toxic relationships, according to Dr. Ramani Durvasala, psychologist and narcissism expert.

Which leaves 10% on our relationships that truly are worth our time, energy and love.

Coupled with the fact that our most important factor for health and fulfillment comes from our relationships, it is no surprise that most of us are drained, unhappy and constantly stuck in a cycle of suffering in our love life and relationships.

The reality is, we don't even realize that we're in codependent or toxic relationships, until it's too late and we're completely entangled.

Whether it's your boss, colleague, exes, a man you're seeing, an addict sibling, or a mother or father struggling with issues like low self-worth, narcissism or bipolar disorder, you'll be surprised how much time and energy you are spending to appease, fix or emotionally fill a void they have that can never be filled.

If you find yourself in such a situation, you do need to begin placing healthy boundaries. I would recommend that you receive professional help with a therapist who is an expert in toxic relationships. These relationships cause deep damage to your psyche and scar you permanently if you're not careful. I would also recommend that you read *The Language of Letting Go: Daily Meditations for Codependents*, by Melody Beattie.

On the positive side, I have seen that having a toxic parent or partner may be a part of your path to spiritual growth: it may point to important life lessons, spiritual blockages and skills you need to learn about your own style of relating. Some of the most compassionate, emotionally aware people I have met had a toxic parent!

In the next chapter, we'll talk about healing spiritual and emotional wounds with your loved ones and how you can release those relationships in a gentle way.

The Power of Ho'oponopono

I love using the Hawaiian practice called Ho'oponopono, which roughly translated into English, is "I'm sorry, thank you, I love you, please forgive me." This is a profound practice that can be used for anyone or any situation that triggers you. In Hawaii, a therapist, Dr.

Hew Len, cured an entire ward of criminally insane people using Ho'oponopono!

In your mind, think of people that trigger you (or someone you have hurt), and in your heart, begin to pray, *"I'm sorry, thank you, I love you, please forgive me,"* over and over. I do this with a lot of intention, recognizing that each person and interaction is a gift, and I can offer apology, gratitude and my love to transmute old wounds.

Alternatively, if someone has hurt you, you can think, "I accept you. I love you. I forgive you."

For instance, I once had a rude and aggressive boss. I felt hurt and wanted to quit. Before I did, I began to silently practice Ho'oponopono with him until I reached a place of peace within me. I could speak with him without getting all worked up. Slowly the charge around that relationship began to dissipate, and I found myself easily releasing that relationship and not carrying the pattern further. The next boss I had was much more compassionate and understanding.

This prayer has changed the course of my life, making me happier and more compassionate, while bringing me healthier relationships.

EXERCISE: INFUSING MY LIFE WITH HAPPINESS

Make a running list of activities that drain you or energize you. No need to actually begin doing these right away, just set an intention to start (or stop) activities when the right time arises to support you in creating a life that you love.

1. Things that make me unhappy or drain me – I want to less of...
(E.g. speak without thinking, spend time with negative people)
+ ...
+ ...
+ ...

2. Things that make me happy or energize me – I want to do more of... (E.g. travel the world, spend time in authentic relationships, read inspiring books, working out)

+ ...

+ ...

+ ...

By becoming in tune with your body and consciously choosing activities and people that align with your intentions, you'll begin to live a life that makes you feel like you're on cloud nine, no matter what your circumstances are. In fact, you'll even begin to enjoy your own company and want more and more of it!

The 5 As of Love:

Love is not merely felt, it is experienced and created through our actions. The question is, how do we love in a wise way? I found Thích Nhất Hạnh's teachings on the 4 As of love (from *True Love*, his book) to be poignant in learning how to share my love. I've adapted it to include a fifth one.

There are 5 As in which we show love to others: Affection, Attention, Appreciation, Acceptance and Approval.

Yet, how can you begin to offer these to yourself? What if you could perfect your self-love to such a level that it came naturally and bountifully, while addressing your core needs for love, safety and belonging? If it makes it easier, imagine offering the 5 As to a child.

These 5 As will help as a guide, while incorporating everything you've learned above about creating your emotional, mental and physical foundations.

I'll share some ideas around them, and then encourage you to continue the exploration.

Attention – Do you ever feel like you didn't get enough attention from your teachers, parents and other caretakers, friends, colleagues or lovers? Or do you find yourself denying your own wants and needs, because of some previous conditioning?

Well, now you have a chance to bridge that gap within yourself.

Take the time giving attention to your body, asking her for what she needs. As a mother would take care of her child, constantly asking herself (or her little one), "Darling, what are you needing? Do you need to sleep? Do you want to cry? Do you want to simply play? What kind of food will nourish your tiny, beautiful body?" She plays with her child, caresses her hair, and calls her sweetheart.

That's what your body wants from you. She doesn't want to be abandoned anymore. She wants to know that you're there for her, always. As her mother, father, lover, sister.

What foods does she like that will nourish her? What kind of rest and exercise is soothing for her nervous system? What relationships and activities energize versus drain her? What stimulation does she need, or does she just need quiet and stillness? What kind of spiritual or self-care practices make her feel whole and grounded?

Be in tune with your body, taking all the time in the world, as if nothing else matters.

In what other ways can you practice attention to yourself?

Acceptance – One of our deepest pains is that we feel like we're not accepted for who we are. Yet, the biggest challenge and roadblock to love that we face is our own lack of self-acceptance. It's like we're in constant denial of our needs, choices, appearance and our situation.

What if you were to radically accept yourself for who you are? What your life choices have been, and what they will be going forward? Can you find gentle acceptance in your body and appearance, emotions, your financial situation, your parents, siblings, job, home and relationship situation? Can you accept the world around you, seeing all is perfect as is?

Find acceptance in all these things about yourself, and others that come up in your day. You can think, "I accept my job, I accept my parents, I accept my looks, I accept my breakup …" It may not be easy if you're normally self-critical or struggle with self-doubt and low self-esteem. Yet, this is the greatest medicine you can offer yourself, and you can slowly begin to rewire your thinking into one of self-acceptance.

Just because you are accepting yourself and your life doesn't mean that you are simply content with mediocrity. *It sounds paradoxical but change and transformation can only happen when you first accept yourself and everything in your life, as is.* You can hold space within yourself for both acceptance in your life, *and* a deep desire for something bigger and better.

Appreciation – "Whatever you appreciate, appreciates." Sometimes it's easy to appreciate others, but not yourself. Yet, you are a being with amazing qualities! When you appreciate things about yourself, you can become your own greatest cheerleader and you'll begin to see your whole self, versus what you feel you're lacking.

Appreciate everything in your life, the good and the bad. Appreciate your body. Appreciate yourself for taking steps in your life to be happier, or simply for being your true self. Say words of appreciation to yourself.

See if you can list all your great qualities, such as your intelligence, wit, humor, kindness. In fact, make a list of all your capabilities and strengths (rather than simply your achievements) especially the ones that are related to your personality.

For instance:

"I appreciate that I am a gourmet cook."

"I appreciate that I am kindhearted and generous."

"I appreciate my body and health, and my healthy habits."

"I appreciate that I am always seeking ways to be a better person,
and that I am a curious, wise soul."

The list could go on and on. In fact, you can take a whole day doing this exercise! See if you can shift your mind into one of self-appreciation in general, and feel free to express your greatness with others, in a genuine way.

Affection – The inner child in you craves for love and affection. Studies have shown that newborns need to be held in order to survive, and that on average, a person needs seven hugs a day to thrive. How can you offer yourself affection, the way a parent or grandparent does with a child?

This is possibly the most fun of the Five As! Treating yourself to ice cream, hugging yourself and caressing your arms, stroking your hair … Take yourself on dates and shift your inner language to one of love and affection, like calling yourself sweetheart and darling. Let yourself know that you are there for her, all the time, saying, "Darling Sarika, all is well. You are safe. I am here for you ." When you look in the mirror to brush or do your makeup, lovingly gaze at yourself and marvel at your beauty. Say, "Good morning goddess! You are so cute, funny and beautiful!" Put on your makeup joyfully, like a beauty ritual. If you are feeling sexually aroused, pleasure yourself and revel in the sweetness and lusciousness of your body. Ask yourself, what else do you crave for? A spa day, a romantic dinner, writing a love letter to yourself?

Affection adds the sweetness and joy in any relationship, so consciously offer that to yourself.

Approval – When you were born, you needed the approval of your parents to survive. Over time, the love you received may have seemed conditional from them, because your parents might not have approved of all your actions. You learned to behave in a way as to seek approval in order to survive. Over time, you've become conditioned to seek approval from your teachers, friends, lovers, to the point of it becoming normal.

It is human nature to seek approval, like a flower seeking sunlight from the sun.

The danger is that you begin to lose connection to your own inner compass and truth. You bend into a pretzel to appease your lover and aren't able to discern and communicate your own desires. You follow a path that's set out for you and aren't able to trust yourself. You become paralyzed by self-doubt and depend on others for their opinion and validation.

You must begin to move that voice of approval within and take over the place of the inner critic.

Begin to approve of everything in your life. The choices you've made till now, your style of clothing, your relationship status and past relationships, your creativity and art. Approve of your choice in parents (which you made before you were born), of your body and appearance, of your age. Approve of your education and intelligence, your career choices.

When you make a choice going forward, approve of it! Don't seek out others' validation or opinions, unless it is life or death. Learn to trust in your inner intuition and what feels right. Trust that when you're truly self-connected, you will be making choices based on your inner knowing. Take a break from social media and seeking likes for your posts (take a full hiatus from it).

There are no wrong choices. Your path is self-correcting, always. You can trust that if your intention is clear and pure, and no matter what choice you make, you will reach where you need to. There are no coincidences, and we shape our reality through our intentions. Yet, we're here to discover new truths, experience adventure, and have experiences of all types, ranging from heartbreak to ecstasy. Approve of all your zany choices, even if they don't make sense.

This doesn't mean to become reckless – rather, it means to honor your deep-rooted, "unreasonable" desires and the situations you find yourself in.

If you Appreciate, Accept and Approve of yourself, and give Attention and Affection to yourself, then you will attract people who will love you in the same way. You will energetically "train" others around you on how to love you, by the way you love yourself. It's like creating your own "How to love me manual" that you will share with your soulmate.

EXERCISE: THE 5 A'S OF LOVE

Set aside a few hours. Play some beautiful, uplifting, sensual music. Light a candle. Then, begin journaling on the following:

Imagine that you are your own beloved soulmate. You want to be showered with these 5 A's. What do each of the 5 A's mean to you and how can you practice these in your life for yourself?

Going forward, you can pick one of the 5 A's to practice for the day.

This final step of Becoming a Love Magnet is about opening your heart to love. Love comes in many forms – a smile from a stranger, compliments, gifts, the sun shining down on you, an act of kindness, or a call from your mother.

There is so much love flowing to you every day, but the issue is that you're not ready to receive it – even the healthy love. You have been so conditioned to think of love in a specific way – romantic love with a desirable partner. You find it hard to receive love unless it's OK'd by your ego. You want to be loved in a certain way, and when you don't get that, you shut down or become defensive.

The thing is, it's not your fault. There's been thousands of years of conditioning that's prevented women from seeking pleasure and receiving love. How many times have you seen your mother or grandmother simply receive with grace and ease, or bask in pleasure? Very few women till now have allowed themselves to ask and receive, and instead, find themselves overworked and constantly caring for others, while fighting for validation and approval.

Sadly, deep down, a majority of women and girls feel undeserving and unworthy of love, which creates a barrier to receiving love, because they doubt it.

Meditate: Take a moment to close your eyes and feel into the question, "What do I feel when I receive?" Do you feel embarrassed, self-conscious or afraid? Do you feel a burning sensation in your heart, or a twist in your gut? Does your body shut down? Do you feel hurt or angry? Or do you feel a sense of ease and pleasure? Be with whatever sensations arise, and breathe through it, honoring it.

If receiving doesn't come easily for you, take it one day at a time, and be easy on yourself. When someone pays you a compliment, say, "Thank you" and smile. If you're ballsy, you can even add, "That's true." That's it! For instance, if someone says, "Wow, you have a way with words," you answer, "Thank you. It's true." It may feel incredibly hard in the beginning, and you may find yourself doubting whether it's true or not. It doesn't matter, fake it till you make it.

Allow people to open the door for you or congratulate you on an achievement. When people smile at you, smile and graciously accept it, without trying to change or alter anything. Sometimes, when men pass me and say, "Damn, you're fine! Have a blessed day," I actually feel quite grateful, and respond with, "Thank you, you too." I sometimes smile at the person, wishing in my heart for them to be well, "May you be happy, may you be peace, may you be free from suffering." Of course, I exercise caution with whom I interact with, but I know that most people are fundamentally good.

See if you can enjoy something you receive – a gift, the sunshine and nature, a delicious meal cooked for you – without trying to change *anything*. Try to receive without expectations and be open to how the gift is being given to you.

Whenever you find yourself stumbling for a response, just stick to "Thank you" and smile – this might be the biggest challenge for you!

Of course, this doesn't mean that you need to put up with toxic relationships, manipulative flattery and heavy patterns of giving loaded with expectations. In those cases, you can simply receive the compliment or the item, and graciously thank them. You can still receive, without creating a story or sense of heaviness. Over time, you can distance yourself from the person, set healthy boundaries and release your own patterns of feeling a sense of obligation.

Being in the flow of love is a key part of awakening your feminine side – the gracious, pleasure-filled goddess who receives and bestows people with her kindness, gratitude and love. As a Love Magnet, you will bring back some level of joy in a crazed, imbalanced world.

STEP 2: HEAL YOUR HEART

and Close your "Ex Files"

"Love sometimes wants to do us a great favor: hold us upside down and shake all the nonsense out." ~ Hafiz

Remember that time you cried for months on end, downing bottles of alcohol and God knows what else to numb the pain from that devastating breakup from which you never fully recovered? Or when your first true love pretended to never notice you in high school? When your parents fought when you were a child, or now, when your mom laments about how you'll ever land a man or that you're being too picky? The pains add up and hurt like *hell*.

When your heart has experienced physical pain, or is heavy with emotional wounds from the past, you become afraid of reliving that pain. You put up an energetic wall around it because you're afraid of being vulnerable, sending signals like *"I don't trust you. I don't need you. Stay away!"* On top of that, you may have unresolved energetic and spiritual cords with exes and family members that continue to tug at you or close you off from other healthy relationships.

All of these things form blocks in your heart, leading to you repeating all sorts of sabotage patterns to keep you single or in failing relationships. The pain lives in different parts of your body, too, and **yet the heart is the entryway because of its connection with divinity and being able to access the healing power of love.**

"The wound is the place that the light enters you." ~ Rumi

Girl, I know you *want* to love with a full, open heart that's bursting at its seams! You know you are capable of loving from this place of unconditionality and generosity – and your body *craves* for experiencing this kind of love that defies all norms and limitations. You're worthy of finding a partner who wants this too – a love that's free of drama, and one that inspires commitment and courage from both of you. Yet, the blocks in your heart are preventing you from this kind of love.

The heart is waiting to be excavated by your inner archeologist so that your truth can finally shine through and illuminate the path to love. **You are gifted with the Power of Love, which will take you through this very process of heart healing.** Your heart's desire to experience such love and your feeling of love for yourself and the world around you is what keeps propelling you forward on your path to recovery.

The Power of the Heart

Living in a head-based society, where one's mind and intelligence are considered most important (and are financially rewarded), we are unaware of the potency and the true power of the heart. The mind can only love from ego, and that kind of love ultimately falls apart because of its constant rationalizing, measuring and filtering mechanisms.

The heart is the connection to higher wisdom and unconditional love. It's the best inner compass: it *feels* what is true and resonant with it, and simply *knows* what's right and wrong for you. Your heart is more than just an organ that pumps blood and life force into the rest of the body (already a miraculous achievement). It is also the portal to the divine, your connection with God, the infinite mystery and intelligence of life.

The heart is a powerful energy center in your body. No doubt, the brain has its own electromagnetic field, but it is relatively weak compared with the heart's that is 5,000 times stronger magnetically! Your thoughts and emotions affect the heart's electromagnetic field, which sends out a certain vibration and affects those in your environment, whether or not you are conscious of it. Your heart can be felt from several feet away – even in the next room!

You may, at first, feel distrustful of your heart because of all the painful mistakes you've made, whether it was to pursue unrequited or abusive love or a career that fell apart. Alternatively, you might be so disconnected with your heart that you aren't aware of it; or if you do bring attention to it, a part of it feels heavy and achy which is uncomfortable to turn towards.

Have you ever heard of someone who died of a broken heart? It's actually real. Broken heart syndrome is also called stress-induced cardiomyopathy or "takotsubo cardiomyopathy." Women are more likely than men to experience the sudden, intense chest pain — the reaction to a surge of stress hormones — that can be caused by an emotionally stressful event. It could be the death of a loved one or even a divorce, breakup or physical separation, betrayal or romantic rejection. The feeling in your heart can be of stretching, shortness of breath and actual, physical pain. So, on a physical level, heartbreak is real.

When your heart is heavy with guilt, shame, regret and searing pain from your heartache, it becomes almost lifeless. You feel like you're in survival mode, living on very little hope and life force.

When you begin the process of clearing your heart of spiritual blocks and painful memories, you'll feel a lifting of the heaviness and burden you've been carrying and begin mending your broken heart. You'll access an indescribable sense of peace that already resides within you. You will see things more clearly and make better decisions that are healthy for you and your loved ones. Moreover, you will begin vibrating with a higher, more coherent frequency which will align you with the innate abundance and love you were born with. An open heart has the ability to magnetically draw people and opportunities to you.

When your heart heals, you will feel an irresistible sense of happiness and freedom from within.

"Only from the heart, can you touch the sky." ~ Rumi

EXERCISE: TUNING INTO YOUR HEART

Sit in a quiet space, close your eyes, take a couple of breaths and tune into your body. Tune into what your greatest, deepest desire or intention is right now. Then say out loud, "I really desire [fill in the blanks] but something is blocking me."

For instance, "I really, truly desire a juicy, meaningful, intimate relationship with my soulmate and to experience lasting love, but something is blocking me."

Keeping your eyes closed, drop your attention to your heart, and notice the sensations arising. What does it feel like? A flutter, burning, twists, a wave of energy moving through? What feelings arise? Simply be there for the sensations, breathing through it, naming the sensations and feelings. Now, scan your body, slowly, from head to toe. What other sensations are arising for you? If you feel numbness, that's ok too.

Journal on what you felt, and anything else that has come up for you from this exercise.

This exercise helps shine light on where your love block lives in your body, what it looks like and how it feels. If you didn't feel or notice anything, that's ok too. Practice love, acceptance and forgiveness for whatever is arising for you.

Three Steps to Heart-Freedom

In my work, I've found that there are three primary sources of pain that are preventing you from living a life of love:

1. Yourself: The pain, shame and guilt that you've been carrying for mistakes you've made, intentionally or otherwise (which promotes the sense that there's something inherently wrong, bad or unworthy about you)

2. Your childhood experiences: The aching sense of hurt and helplessness that you encountered with your parents and care-givers while you were a child

3. Your exes/past relationships: The anger, pain and regret from your past relationships (which I call the "Ex Files").

Of course, there are other types and levels of hurt, but **these are the main ones that specifically impact your love life.**

In this step, you will learn what it means to lift the baggage from your heart that has accumulated since your childhood. You will examine your own self-created blocks, as well as that from your childhood and family blueprint. You'll discover and release "stuckness" or unresolved pain from your past relationships in a process that I call "Close Your Ex Files."

Rather than avoiding the wounds as and continuing with the same relationship patterns as you may have in the past, choose to face them now with love and compassion! You will let light into your heart. Your pain is a gift – it's a special package created for you to learn about life, release your limitations and old stories, and how to experience love and loss with resilience and joy.

Allow your heart to be broken open. It may hurt, but know that, in the end, there will be greater flow of love and grace possible than before.

You'll feel a sense of completion from your past, and find meaning, forgiveness and release with exes, parents and others whom you loved. In doing so, you'll begin to restore your faith, love and trust in others, including men, and you'll open up your heart to new, healthy relationships.

Note: This is the time to use all the self-love tools from the previous chapter, "Be a Love Magnet," to support your heart-healing.

EXERCISE: IS MY HEART BLOCKED? SELF-ASSESSMENT:

Answer True/False for the below statements. There is no right answer – we are all in the process of clearing our heart blocks. This is a lifelong journey! The main thing is to gently bring awareness and set an intention to release the blocks naturally when they come up to be cleared.

1. When I bring my attention to my heart, I feel painful sensations of heartache, longing, sadness or grief. _____

2. I tend to avoid feelings altogether, try to hide them or shift to "positive" emotions quickly. _____

3. I attract people who drain my energy, or who don't love and respect me. _____

4. I was molested or sexually abused as a child. _____

5. I find it hard to let go of control in relationships. _____

6. I experienced a major betrayal and have difficulty trusting men. _____

7. I experience painful dating patterns, like attracting men who are emotionally unavailable or aggressive. _____

8. I had a major breakup which I still haven't healed from or still wonder why it ended. _____

9. I had a codependent relationship with a parent or another loved one (someone who thwarted my growth and healthy independence, or was abusive to me), or I experienced rejection from a parent. _____

10. My parents' relationship was painful, and I still feel grief about it. _____

Count how many "Trues" you have. The more you have, the more it indicates that your heart is blocked and needs to release baggage to move into a healthier, happier place to receive love.

Allow yourself to fully feel all the emotions and fears, accept them, and let them go. Find the tools from "Be a Love Magnet," such as self-empathy, to be with these emotions, and accept where you are in your Love Recovery journey.

Have faith that shining light on your fears and pain is the first and most important step to healing your heart.

What is reparenting and why is it so important?

Reparenting is the process of giving yourself what you didn't (ideally) receive from your parents or others when you were a child. When you were young, there were many moments in which your needs weren't met, or you were hurt by your parents and caregivers. They were missed opportunities for connection in which you interpreted the action as a lack of love. Moreover, you may be carrying guilt or shame from your past. You may have done hurtful or silly things like steal a book from the library, say something insensitive to your sibling (or physically hurt them), or have a fight with a childhood friend that caused you two to fall apart.

Here comes another superpower of yours – time travel! You now have the chance to go back in time and be there for that little girl and repair that hurt that you felt, re-patching those missing connections in your psyche. You can also raise your consciousness to understand why your parents or others behaved in a certain way and have compassion for their actions. You can release that "evidence" that you are unlovable by the sheer action of loving yourself in that moment, right now. Each connection you heal will help you feel more and more whole.

When you can begin to love, accept and nourish yourself as a parent ideally would, and heal those moments you lost connection, then you begin the process of reparenting yourself. Your psyche and nervous system don't know the difference between you or anyone else – they just know how they are treated and what is being said. They react in a certain way, based on what's familiar, but are also capable of being conditioned differently through mindfulness and love.

By the end of the chapter, you'll feel like a whole new woman who's embraced your past, learned the lessons you needed to and feel a sense of freedom and abundance about the opportunities yet to come.

One thing you might be surprised to see are the different people and situations that will pop up that feel coincidental to what you are healing. For instance, while clearing your "Ex Files," you may get a message from an ex, or while healing your childhood wounds, you might have an enlightening conversation with your mom where she may even gain healing and clarity. With my clients, I've seen so many miracles happen during their heart healing journey – old friends coming out of the woodwork or even someone declaring their love for them!

This is perhaps the most important chapter in the book, so I would recommend you commit to doing all the exercises and set an intention to truly, once and for all, heal and release these different parts of your past.

Keeping Your Heart Nourished and Open

As you're detoxing and healing your heart, you will be entering a period of time of deep vulnerability, where you may bring back feelings of helplessness, grief, anger and so much more.

This is not to scare you. I know and believe that you are strong and capable of facing and healing all of this – and you are more ready than ever. If you're here, it's no coincidence. You have the willpower and inner strength to heal your past, finally, so you can get on to your new, exciting life ahead! Moreover, you have created a foundation of self-love which will support you like a sturdy boat going through choppy waters as you reach the shores where your best life is waiting.

There is no right or wrong way to do this chapter, and if you're a perfectionist, you may believe that what you're doing isn't enough. Yet, just know that doing these exercises prescribed with the intention of love and healing will get you there.

As you're going through the Heal Your Heart process, you will need to nourish your heart and soul. Be kind and gentle with yourself.

Here are some ideas and tips to support your heart healing and opening:

1. Create a sacred container for yourself, where you're away from the outside world or stimulation, unless it's healthy and natural – like being in nature or dinner with spiritually-minded friends. Get plenty of rest, meditate, eat heart-healthy food (like leafy greens and salads) or foods that lift your spirit. Let your friends and family know that you're taking some space for yourself.

2. Continue to use the self-love tools you learned about in the last chapter, such as the morning ritual, the 5 As of love, mindfulness, practicing self-forgiveness for your self-critical thinking and setting boundaries. This is the time to foster and strengthen your inner spiritual, mental, physical and emotional foundation. You deserve all the love and care in these times! As heavy emotions come up, practice self-empathy, swamping, journaling, dancing, breathing, creativity or working with a professional.

3. Surround yourself with beauty, like soothing music (there are many high-frequency and healing music tracks and affirmations on YouTube), diffusers, candles, artwork, nature – whatever keeps you inspired and connected.

Whatever you choose to support in your heart healing is perfect, even if it's to do nothing, laze around or simply be in silence.

Heart-Freedom: Free Yourself, From Yourself

I couldn't speak up for myself.

I took abuse.

I lost my childhood.

My brother is and was better than me.

I regret that I failed in 3 subjects in 9th grade, my dad slapped me.

I regret that I have ADD.

I regret learning about sex way before other children my age did.

I treated other kids badly, especially when I had power.

I regret that I hit my sisters so many times when we were kids.

I regret my bossy, controlling ways in my family.

I am ashamed that my panty fell off in front of so many people and they laughed at me.

I am ashamed of getting my period in a busy train, with everyone seeing blood all over my clothing.

I regret my dysfunctional family.

I regret not having learned how to be affectionate. My parents never hugged me.

I regret having studied the wrong major in college.

I regret not being as personable or outgoing as a lot of other people.

I regret being in relationships even when I knew deep inside that they were not right for me. I am ashamed of letting those men in my life.

I regret being less aggressive and not understanding boundaries in my 20s.

I regret I didn't save enough money.

I regret that I can't take my mother out of her trap.

I regret not living close to my family. I didn't get to see my adorable, cute nephews grow up.

I regret not meeting someone with whom everything happened easily – something like love at first sight/time.

I regret love not happening as it supposedly happens on the streets of Paris, with me being young and full of bohemia.

I regret things not having had worked out with Devin, the first person I was with.

I regret being over forty and single.

I regret not having had done my MBA from a top business school.

I regret feeling mediocre in my schooling and background.

I regret not having had discipline and patience to do well in school early in life.

I regret that I say more than I do. I have dreams but never follow through, and when I start, I feel inertia. I lose my patience quickly.

I regret not being married at this point and have to deal with the worst and lowest of the barrel. I can't believe how much desperate energy I am attracting.

I regret not having a super intelligent boyfriend/partner.

Wow, don't you feel the heaviness just reading about someone's regrets! This is just an iota of what an average person carries around with them. Take a moment to reflect on what you've been carrying around. It's like we're backpackers with a lifetime's load of painful stories on our backs, traveling from place to place, unable to put the bag down. Think of how this sense of guilt, shame and resentment is blocking you from feeling a sense of love and possibility in your world.

As you can see, so many of these regrets aren't valid anymore. Your ego is collecting evidence of how unlovable you are (which isn't true), and that is something you can do without! Whether you made certain choices you regret or were in situations that you had no control over, you handled things the best way you could, and sometimes even made some miscalculations.

This is life, dear Love Goddess – there is no "right protocol," failures or mistakes. Every life incident is simply a step to the next, a learning opportunity. Whoever said that you had to be perfect? The universe is built on imperfections (think about all the people you love – aren't they imperfect?). That's what makes the world perfect.

At this juncture, you can set an intention to free yourself from your self-created heavy shackles, and step into a guilt-free life!

The below exercises will help you do so.

EXERCISE: LETTING GO OF MY REGRETS

This exercise is an experiential journey of practicing radical self-love and self-acceptance throughout your life. Your psyche is a conglomeration of all of your old selves from conception till now - the different iterations of who you were, choices you made and your reactions to situations. You will go through a process of releasing all the related guilt and stories you've been holding onto.

1. Create a list of all your regrets, starting from childhood, all the way till now. Get as many down on a piece of paper and be as exhaustive as you can. Feel free to pour your heart out. You can even take days to create it to be thorough. Share it with a friend or coach.

2. One evening, set aside 45 minutes for a meditative exercise. If it goes longer, that's ok.

Sit in a dark room, with a candle.

Then, imagine yourself at each age, starting from the day you were conceived. Go year by year. Imagine this little version of you, in front of you. How is she doing/feeling? Who is she? What is she going through? What are her regrets/sadness at that moment?

Observe her and tell her, "Dear one, even though [regret], I still love, accept and forgive you. I approve of you." Imagine you giving that version of yourself a hug, a caress, or simply a look of utter kindness and compassion. Imagine you are your own mother, father, older sister. Have that tone/intention. Understand what is going on, and know that each age you are, you are simply doing your best.

Keep going, year by year, until the present moment. Observe the memories that come up.

Then burn the paper with the intention of healing your past. You can do a prayer of release, burn some sage in the house, as you set an intention to release yourself from your own imperfections.

As new (or old) regrets arise, practice "I love, accept and forgive myself," and make a resolution to do better next time. Lady, no more regrets for you!

Prayer For a New Life

Dear God,

Thank you for this opportunity to be on this beautiful earth.

Thank you for my life.

Today, I begin anew.

I am ready to give up my darkness and heaviness, and step into freedom.

I know that each mistake I've made in my life was a chance for me to learn.

I release my hurts, guilt, and shame which I have carried with me.

I realize that they were essential for me to learn, grow and heal.

Please grant me the wisdom to heal these wounds.

I forgive myself and others who have hurt me, and I seek forgiveness from those I've hurt.

I vow to love, accept and forgive myself, for exactly who and where I am.

I am ready to stand in my own light,

To embrace the fullness of who I am –

A well-intentioned, kind human being, becoming more and more aware.

I embrace my joyful, innocent, free-spirited inner child.

I open to the mystery of all of who I am, and vow to lead a life of openheartedness and love.

I am ready to trust myself and Life,

and make the best choices possible in every moment.

I stand for my own happiness, peace and liberation,

which in turn empowers others to do the same.

May I wake up each day with a sense of freedom, a new beginning, for a new life.

Amen.

Heart-Freedom: Heal Yourself from Your Family Blueprint

We all dread the moment when we finally admit, "Oh gosh, I'm beginning to sound like my mother…" So much of our lives, we try not to become like them - and yet, we surreptitiously fall into saying some of their infamous phrases and even begin thinking their thoughts! In our romantic relationships, we find ourselves repeating some of their patterns, or working hard to do the opposite, because of the fear of becoming them.

Why does this happen, even though we're distinctly different people from them? Our life experiences and education are markedly different. Yet, we find ourselves subconsciously drawing in romantic relationships that mimic our parents', or experience drama due to some unhealed trauma with a parent. The unprocessed pain lives in our heart, creating blocks and barriers to love.

Your parents and caretakers were the first role models and educators for you. Between the ages of one through seven, you were living in a dream state and were heavily influenced by the world around you. You picked up your caregivers' thoughts, beliefs, and observed how they handle life situations, which affect you till this day.

For instance, if your mother fell into victim mode frequently, doted heavily on your father to keep him happy or criticized him often, then you may find yourself doing one of two things – either subconsciously copying her, or doing the opposite. If your father left the family, was abusive, or emotionally unavailable because he was at work most of the time, you might subconsciously be attracted to a similar man or are unable to trust men. You have adopted many of your parents' traits, like it or not! On top of all this, you may hold pain from specific moments of your childhood when you witnessed a fight or are still reeling from betrayal.

When you encounter something painful, like a date ghosting you, or your lover shutting down or withdrawing when you bring up something that is bothering you, it triggers old wounds and you emotionally get drawn into the drama you once witnessed as a child. If someone raises their voice at you or you're criticized, it may remind you of your mother who did the same, and you go into fight, flight or flee mode. (Note: A new type of coping mechanism, "fawning" was recently discovered, wherein if your parent was narcissistic, controlling or abusive, you would simply do as they say so as to appease them and survive. As it turns out, more women than men struggle with this.)

Children are innocent, aware beings, absorbing everything their parents feel, say or do. Parents' emotional health directly affects their children. Children also feel a sense of responsibility for caring for their parents' happiness, because, in their young minds, they think their pain is due to them.

In an ideal world, your parents were supposed to provide for you in many ways – paying attention to you, validating your emotions, bathing, feeding and clothing you, teaching you about personal safety and finances, giving you a sense of faith and trust in the world ... and so much more! They were supposed to love and cherish each other and honor and respect themselves. Unfortunately, because most parents struggle with the overwhelming nature of parenting, drama in their own lives and replaying their own unconscious patterns, they aren't able to provide much of this for their children or for each other.

As you can see, the connection between your love life and that of your relationship with your parents is strongly connected. This is called the Family Blueprint, and determines your mental model around love, which is unconsciously affecting your life in every possible way.

On a deeper level, you are connected to your parents through energetic and spiritual cords, which are needed until you are eighteen because they are your caretakers. You can have cords with each of your chakras (energy centers) with each of your parents. Now, as an adult, you can release these cords.

There are many psychological theories that can help you understand the way you love, and I'll share two below.

Attachment Theory:[1] Starting from the day you were conceived, your nervous system is directly connected to your mother's. In fact,

1 - Originally formulated by psychiatrist and psychoanalyst, John Bowlby

after birth, you were practically one body with both your parents, as they fulfilled your needs and gave you the love to survive and grow. Sometimes, however, as explained above, those needs may not have been met, most importantly on physical and emotional levels.

Depending on the ways that you received this love, and the level of emotional and social attachment you have with at least one of your parents, you may have developed a sense of secure attachment, anxious attachment, or being avoidant altogether. If you're secure, you find it relatively easy to get close to others and are comfortable depending on them and them on you. You don't worry about being abandoned or about someone getting too close to you. If you're anxious, you feel insecure and worry that your partner doesn't really love you or won't stay with you. You want to merge completely with another person, and this desire scares people away.

Imago Theory: According to Dr. Harville Hendrix and Dr. Helen Hunt who developed this theory, we become wounded during the early nurturing and socialization stages of childhood by our primary caretakers. We have a composite image of all the positive and negative traits of our primary caretakers deep in our unconscious mind. This is called the Imago. We look for someone who is an "Imago Match" that is, someone who matches up with the composite image of all of the positive (and negative) qualities of our primary caretakers. This becomes a template for the romantic partner we look for down the road. The trouble that occurs is that if you have an unconscious wound that hasn't been resolved with a parent, then you invariably continue to struggle with trying to heal that wound in your love life.

The study of our parents' relationships, and how it affects our romantic life is rich and interesting. Without getting into too much more around this and not to complicate it further, simply know that no matter what your relationship was with your parents, or however much you believe they influenced you, you can now take the right steps to heal and create a new, rock solid foundation within you to attract a healthy, joyful relationship that's resonant with your soul.

In my work, I've seen three aspects deeply support in clearing past wounds from your parents – the Mother Wound, the Father Wound, and ancestral wounds. Doing all three of these will unravel you from your past conditioning and spiritual blocks that are keeping you stuck in a holding pattern and rewire you for a new type of relationship than the ones your parents had, or the one you might still have with them.

Healing one's Father Wound and Mother Wound is some of the most profound work that anyone can undertake. Even when you attract your life partner, you may find that you have room to grow and heal in these areas – and you and your partner will continue to support each other in that.

Ultimately, you will find that you have an inner mother and father within you – and developing the wisdom and capacity to be that for yourself is truly a miracle. **This is the essence of reparenting – feeling a sense of completion about the upbringing you had and learning to love and care for yourself as a parent would.**

Healing the Mother Wound

Lara, a twenty-eight-year-old, elegant, articulate accountant, was exhausted chasing down her man halfway across the world in Europe. In the six months that they had been dating, she had visited him three times, yet he hadn't come to visit. Even though he was the perfect man on paper and was kind and doting while she was with him, she was tired of his unavailability and the anxiety of what would happen in their relationship.

As we began the work around heart healing and exploring her blocks, it turned out that she still hadn't overcome the tremendous grief of losing her mother just a few years prior. Her mother had died of cancer, and Lara had been there caring for her until her last days. However, the trauma started earlier, with her mom's bipolar disorder, and Lara's constant, painful push-pull relationship with her. Her mother was depressive, and her reactions ranged from loving and supportive to outright anger and contempt. She loved her mother a lot, but also felt sorry for her situation of being a daughter-in-law in a culturally traditional Middle Eastern household. Deep down inside, she felt betrayed by her mother due to her untimely death, leading to a loss of trust in love, and even a sense of unworthiness. Due to this fear of betrayal, unconsciously, she kept attracting men with whom a relationship wouldn't last. The last few men she dated were long distance, in which she had to keep working to keep the relationship alive – like that with her mother. Her mother also had strong contempt for her father, seeing him as incapable, constantly criticizing and emasculating him. Lara noticed that she had a tendency towards doing the same. She felt both longing and disgust with men. Lastly, her mother came from a rich family, while her father was from a more "earthy" family, and the financial struggles were part of the reason that her mother held contempt for her father.

As Lara looked deeply into her mother's life, she saw her childhood was troubled and painful. As she gained compassion for her mother, she could release her spiritual cords with her, as well as the burden of her beliefs and conditioning. She realized she could be her own woman, while honoring her mother's influence and also embracing the deeply spiritual and powerful

146

maternal lineage passed down from her mother. She had a chance to finally grieve and express all her emotions about her mother, release the blocks in her body, and began to mother herself consciously.

Within a few months, as a new woman, she met her soulmate – a deeply kind, handsome spiritual man. They married each other and created their own life together based on compassion, understanding and loads of adventure – vastly different from the one she witnessed while growing up.

You were conceived in this world through a divine spark, in a magical space that was your mother's womb. The process of going from a bunch of cells, into a full-fledged fetus is hard to fathom! The intelligence of your mother's body and the protectiveness of your father's energy helped nurture you in the womb.

Whether or not on an egoic level your parents loved each other – on a subconscious and spiritual level, they loved each other deeply and created you through their love.

The moment you were born, you were bathed, fed, taken care of. Your cries would keep your mother awake at night, and she would nurse you, play with you, and do her very best to keep you safe and healthy. She likely saw you as a part of her, an extension of her, given that your cells are made up of hers – everything from your hair down to your toenails.

However, as a person, her sense of happiness and ideas around parenting was subject to her own life circumstances, thoughts, beliefs and trauma. Her own mother likely formed the foundation of what a woman should and could be. If she got married young or had children before she even had a chance to form her own identity, she likely never even had a chance to self-actualize as an independent woman.

The Mother Wound arises when a mother's way of being and loving hinders the child's sense of self in some way. From the moment a child is conceived, she begins to learn about the world and form her initial beliefs through her mother's womb. She hears the environment, the mother's words and thoughts, and it forms her foundation. Her nervous system is tied with her mother's, and whatever the mother feels, the baby does. Once the baby is born, she is dependent on her mother for survival, and learns how to communicate and behave in order to get her needs met.

Being a baby is inherently vulnerable, where you're in the position of depending on someone completely for your survival and care. If that caretaker is present and loving, then you may develop a sense of emotional security and safety within. On the flipside, if she's distracted, judgmental or disapproving, then you'll begin to seek different ways of seeking out her attention and winning her approval. Her love for you is paramount for your own sense of safety.

A mother may struggle with the new role of parenting. In a patriarchal world where women are given very little support, and childcare is largely seen as a woman's role, she is often alone, toiling away for hours on end, to care for her children. In certain cultures, there are entire families and villages that help take care of children – but in today's world, most of it is left to the woman. Even if she's working and has childcare support, she still has a great deal of responsibility. The feelings of resentment, contempt, exhaustion and overwhelm are common.

In many cases, mothers may struggle mentally and emotionally to take care of themselves, let alone a child. As you've learned from the chapter on self-love, a great deal goes into taking care of oneself, let alone others! If your mother didn't know how to take care of her needs, then she more than likely failed on many levels to provide for yours –

especially when you were young and helpless, and needed her assistance.

Your mother's beliefs and the way she thinks of being a woman unconsciously become the map inside of you. Whatever her beliefs around money, sex, relationships, men and career, to a great degree become the basis of your own values and thoughts.

According to clinical psychologist Dr. Stephen Poulter, there are five types of mothers:

1. Perfectionist mother: She tends to be hyper-critical, controlling and anxious, and focused on her and her family's appearance. She compares her children to others or to each other, creating complexes. Her children end up having low self-esteem and feel self-conscious and "not good enough," not receiving the approval from their mother.

2. Unpredictable mother: She has mood swings, feels anxious and insecure, and can lash out at her children when she has emotional outbursts. She's the epitome of drama. This is the most unsteady of the five. Her children may end up having co-dependent relationships with their moms, feeling responsible for her sense of self and happiness, and also struggle with emotional volatility of their own.

3. Best friend mother: She sees her children as her equals, and she somewhat avoids the "official" role of being a mother, because she eschews that level of responsibility and inherent expectations. She's a great friend to her kids but struggles with boundaries and sometimes relies on her kids as her confidantes. Children who grow up in this setting miss out on healthy boundary setting and the benefits of maternal care,

and they find themselves sometimes becoming the parent figure.

4. Me-first mother: Emotionally insecure and self-absorbed, she sees her children as extensions of her. This happens to be the most common type of mother. Her children end up being people pleasers and toe the line of their mother.

5. Complete mother: This one sounds perfect! Yet less than ten percent of moms fall into this category. She is emotionally and mentally balanced for the most part and sees her children as their own individuals. She's not perfect by any means, but is still committed to healthy motherhood, as much as she's capable of providing. Her kids feel emotionally secure and have a loving, trusting relationship with themselves and others.

Your own mother may have been one of these, or a combination. You can use this list to get a broad idea of how you were impacted by her. The great thing is that you can not only heal from this and create the Complete Mother within you, but you are also stepping into becoming a more conscious, grounded mother yourself, if you do have kids of your own.

All this isn't to validate a mother's behaviors or beliefs, or to justify as to why she wasn't a good enough mother for you. The hurt you felt as a child from your mother is real and needs to be seen and loved. Even if you've done years of therapy, there might still be spiritual and emotional blocks that need to be healed, and issues that you still haven't resolved.

I know, in your heart, your greatest intention is to love your mother for who she was and have gratitude for her, while holding your own as a woman, creating a life that's definitively yours – a more evolved, happier, holistic version than the life that our parents led (no offense to them! Yet, they helped set us up for this, and it is because of them that we are able to do so in our lifetime). When you can reach a place where you don't feel so triggered by your mother, have genuine gratitude for her giving birth to you (which is perhaps her greatest gift to you), and reach a place of appreciation for who she is, then you will feel a sense of heart freedom.

Below are the exercises to heal the Mother Wound:

EXERCISE 1: JOURNAL ON YOUR RELATIONSHIP WITH YOUR MOTHER:

1. *Describe your mother's qualities that you love and appreciate.*
2. *What was your relationship like with her?*
3. *When did you feel a sense of love and connection with her? When did you not?*
4. *What gifts and talents has she given you, and what life lessons have you learned from her?*

EXERCISE 2: JOURNAL ON YOUR MOTHER'S LIFE AND HOW IT IMPACTS YOU:

1. *In your journal, make an inventory of your mother's beliefs – partnership, sex, money, relationships, career – list them all out. Be as comprehensive as possible.*
2. *Describe how these beliefs are relevant to you.*
3. *Journal about other elements of her childhood and development patterns. Describe your mom as a child. Who was she, what were her parents like? When she was born, what were the circumstances? What were likely some inflection points/experiences in her life (i.e.,*

starting school, getting married, etc.) in which she may have changed as a person? What were her siblings like? In what ways was she happy? In what ways was she hurt? What led her to meet your father, and how has their life been together?

Practice self-empathy on any of the wounds, revelations or limiting beliefs that come up from the above exercise. Allow yourself to grieve. We can't change our parents, but we do have a right to feel sad about things that we missed. As it relates to any limitations that you may have picked up, meditate on it, and tell yourself, "Even if I subconsciously believe ___, I still love, accept and forgive myself."

EXERCISE 3: ACKNOWLEDGE YOUR NEEDS FROM YOUR MOTHER AND CLAIM THEM FOR YOURSELF.

Write a list of what was missing from your childhood from your mom. Use the following examples to help identify what was missing:

- Protecting you from others
- Cherishing you, seeing your beauty and sacredness
- Honoring your boundaries and privacy
- Making you feel connected, attended to and nurtured
- Loving you unconditionally, without expecting anything in return
- Taking care of your physical needs
- Teaching you basic life skills
- Having integrity and was reliable
- Being your cheerleader and supporting you in your talents

When you have written your list, write out and say the following regarding each quality that was missing for you:

I forgive my mother for not _____. I release her from the responsibility and will offer it to myself. I promise to do my best to begin _____ myself from this day forward.

Print out this list and, on a daily basis, begin to mother yourself in these ways. Begin to speak to yourself as a kind mother, one that is loving and supportive of you. Recognize that the mother in you is eternally loving and present for you.

EXERCISE 4: CUTTING SPIRITUAL AND ENERGETIC CORDS WITH YOUR MOTHER

Meditation:

Set aside one evening to do this meditation.

- Light a candle and sit in a dark room.

- Invite your mother (spiritually) into your space, and also your Higher Self.

- Envision your mother throughout her life – her childhood, adolescence, teenage years, college years, late twenties, to the present day, based on what you journaled. Imagine seeing her sitting in front of you at each age. Who is she? What is she going through? Listen deeply, observe, and say "I love you, accept you, I forgive you." Hug/caress her. Ask her for her forgiveness; you can say, "Mom, I'm sorry, thank you, I love you."

- Now, set the intention to tell your mom that you are ready to cut the cords with her.

- Go into your body and feel where the sensations arise when you think of her. Which part of your body do you feel her presence? Which chakras?

- State how you feel, and what you need/needed. Take as long as you need. Be assertive and honest.

- You may cry, grieve while doing this. Allow your emotions to let loose, and be completely naked, vulnerable. You have nothing to lose!

- Then say, with the intention of seeking forgiveness for your own mistakes in the relationship, "I am sorry, thank you, I love you..." over and over till you really mean it. You can even add the mantra, "I love you, accept you, I forgive you."

- Say, "I am now removing these energetic cords with you. I release all unhealthy connections to me."

- Then, imagine removing that cord from your body. You can use your hands to unhook the cord to you, like taking a hose out of the fire hydrant. Or you can imagine cutting that cord with a strong swipe of your hand like a karate swipe.

- Take the end of the cord that was connected with you and put it into the ground (i.e., "ground" the cord) so that instead of being connected with you, her cord is connected to the earth. This is absolutely healthy.

- Repeat if there are multiple cords.

- Imagine healing the "open wounds" with golden light emanating from the center of your heart.

- Now, imagine a golden bridge of unconditional love between you and your mom.

- Use sage to clear your place.

- Allow whatever time you need to, to do this exercise completely.

I've included a recording on performing the cord-cutting ritual which you can download here *(note – the meditation asks that you write a letter many days prior, please feel free to ignore)*: *https://sarikajain.com/Soulmate-Plan-Resources/*

End with this prayer:

Dear God,
I pray for love, healing and grace for my mother.
I am thankful for the life she gave me.
For the ways she nourished and supported me, I give gratitude.
For the ways she acted from her wounds and unintentionally hurt me, please help me to forgive her and receive your healing.
May her soul be blessed, her way forward be paved with grace and ease.
Please help us release each other and any psychic cords that no longer serve.
Please also help me heal any bitterness or anger I still hold.
I recognize the role she played in helping me be where I am, for which I am grateful. I would not be here without her.
Thank you, dear mother, for your service to me, for bringing me into this world.

May you be happy, may you be at peace, may you be free from suffering.

May we enter into a relationship that's in alignment with God's plan for us.

I vow to step into each day, in greater understanding and compassion for my mother and our relationship, to the best of my abilities.

Thank you, God, for I am free now.

Amen.

Healing the Father Wound

While growing up, Grace's father had his sweet and caring sides. He would make her laugh and she felt like she could confide in him, given that she had a somewhat estranged relationship with her mother who struggled with unpredictable mood swings and addiction. Since he was the reliable parent, Grace did whatever she could to stay on his good side.

However, things were not always rosy with her father. He often criticized Grace's choices, including condemning her for her love for playing the violin, saying that music wasn't a worthwhile activity. He pushed her to become an engineer, which she ultimately did. Oftentimes, when she was a child, he left her with his own father, who was domineering and unempathetic. One time, she remembers being locked in a room with a giant spider and her grandfather refused to open the door, punishing her for something. She felt deeply afraid and helpless in that moment. She told her father, but he didn't do anything, making her believe he couldn't protect her. Her father was also away for most of the year, ironically as a traveling musician himself –

and she felt alone with her emotionally unavailable and abusive mother, with no one to protect her.

Because of this complicated relationship with her parents, as an adult Grace struggled to find a sense of "home." She mostly ate out, her home was unkempt, and she disliked her body. No amount of working out made her feel beautiful or healthy, even though she was a stunning, deeply caring woman. She kept losing herself in relationships with non-committal men, appeasing them, as was her coping mechanism she developed with her father. She had never been in a serious relationship with a man who cherished and adored her.

In the process of healing her Father Wound, Grace explored his life and childhood and began to have more compassion for him. Her father was an immigrant from China, having experienced atrocities during the Cultural Revolution which had left him and has family in poverty and deep-set psychological trauma. He also was influenced by traditional patriarchal views of women, although he wanted the best for his daughter and loved her deeply. He struggled with his own relationships with his past, integrating in the West speaking very little English and making a living a musician.

Of course, all of this didn't make up for the painful and disorganized childhood she had, and the loss of a dependable, loving fatherly figure in her life. When we tapped into her heart and body, she felt strong blocks about men with a deep sense of distrust for them. She felt trapped by her patriarchal upbringing, troubled about her femininity and sexuality, and didn't have a strong connection with her masculine within.

Through healing her Father Wound, Grace could finally forgive him and herself and release her father's influence while embracing his positive qualities. She started getting in touch with her strong feminine side and began to open up to healthy relationships with men. Through a process of reparenting herself and cutting cords with her father, she felt a new lease on life with her past behind her – and began brimming with love and confidence, attracting men who respect and adore her!

What was your relationship with your father like? Was he mostly loving and supportive, or distant and moody? Maybe he was somewhere in between. Whatever your relationship was with your father forms a big part of your psyche about men, love, career, and so much more. As I shared before, we have masculine and feminine energies running through us, and our understanding of the masculine and the resultant beliefs and coping mechanisms we've picked up impacts our masculine side and the men we continue to attract into our lives.

If you're one of the lucky women who had an unequivocally great relationship with your father – what a tremendous boon and blessing. You should be on cloud nine, thanking your lucky stars to the highest of heavens, celebrating till you practically pass out! I know I'm sounding uncanny or ironic – but it's true – having a perfect father (or perfect mother) is truly a rare occurrence, like winning the lottery.

On the flip side, if your relationship with your father is either pretty good, complicated or downright painful, then you're in the majority. Yes – having "Daddy Issues" is a real thing. Most women struggle with it to varying degrees. However, all is not lost. In fact, you have so much more to gain if you approach the situation with the lens of healing and understanding. Women who have had difficult relationships with their fathers have overcome their misgivings and turned into more powerful, loving, wise versions of themselves, manifesting tremendous relationships with men. As I mentioned before, life gives us certain lessons to learn and grow from, and choosing our parents before we're born is perhaps the most foundational of all our life's teachings.

Your relationship with your father, however loving or challenging, is your pathway to understanding the masculine and creating a whole new relationship with men. Sometimes, through our own trauma, we get a chance to unlearn things in order look at the world with fresh possibility. God knows, our world needs a new perspective on how we women relate with men!

The way your father related to your mother is vital. If he was a consistent provider and protector, then your family likely felt safe and secure. On top of that, if he was loving, attentive and appreciative, your mother probably felt emotionally stable enough to be able to shine and be the best version of herself. Yet, if he was abusive or emotionally unavailable, then your mother may have suffered, and you might have taken on feelings of protectiveness, resentment and distrust, amongst many other difficult emotions.

Your father also played a key role in your psychological development, starting from the very moment you were born. In fact, I once heard that a man's response to seeing his daughter for the first time after birth is imprinted on her brain – whether he was afraid, protective or wonderfully delighted and excited. The difference between a loving father and an absent father makes a huge difference in how the child grows up. A father plays an important role in how a woman develops her self-esteem, perceives her body image, how she does academically, and how a woman should be treated by a man. In fact, he plays a direct role in the kind of partner she ultimately attracts. While the mother's role is to help her child feel safe and nurtured, a father helps a daughter understand the world and how to be self-expressed. He teaches many qualities about how to be resilient, financially stable, and how to have trusting, healthy relationships. He protects his daughter, is a good provider, and helps her assert her boundaries. Sometimes, the role of a father is downplayed compared to a mother's, yet it's equally important. Sadly, fathers sometimes struggle with finding their role at home.

Over the years, I've developed deep compassion for the masculine and everything that men have been through. Being in a patriarchal system *seems* beneficial to men, but it isn't. It's emasculating, and starting from a young age, boys learn to hide or bury their emotions, and compete in alpha male, success-oriented settings. Parents from older generations have placed a lot of expectations on their sons to carry the success of their lineage and be providers for their families. Young men aren't taught anything about raising children or being in nurturing relationships, and in previous generations, got married early as well. In fact, they are taught grossly unhealthy things about sex and women's psychology (think of all the men's magazines!), many a time through porn or their peers, and struggle with their self-expression, in general. On top of this, we've been living in a war culture, where men have been drafted or served in military, or engaged in working within corrupt institutions, leading to varying levels of unresolved Post Traumatic Stress Disorder (PTSD). Men have to make a living no matter how economically difficult times are, taking on jobs they don't necessarily feel passionate about and feel ashamed if they can't provide for their families. In recent years, men are becoming even more confused about their roles, due to the blurring of gender lines between men and women, economic uncertainty and the feminine justice movement which has laid a strong, judgmental gaze on men's behavior with women.

As a result of all of this, most men struggle with their sexuality, emotions, communication skills and have unhealthy conditioning that they are unraveling just as we women are.

It's important to have compassion for men and our own fathers, who no doubt led difficult lives. I haven't met a single father who doesn't truly care for his family yet is constantly beset by his own inner demons. I share all of this to give a context to understand your father on a broader level than your interpersonal experience with him.

To help you begin to heal from the Father Wound, it's helpful to understand what kind of relationship you might have had and what impact it's had on you. I'm sharing below five types of fathers and potential trauma (note: these are provided as examples). Your own father might be some or a combination of these, as not one shoe fits all.

1. Angry tyrant: He's aggressive, always right, critical, and can suddenly erupt out of the blue. He can be hurtful through his silences, words and actions. The family is afraid and they walk around on eggshells around him. In rare cases, he may suffer from narcissism. A daughter growing up in this setting is afraid of making men angry and feels a sense of helplessness and powerlessness with men. She may even disassociate from her body in times of stress. Her needs are denied, and she may feel low self-worth.

2. Far and away: This type of father spends most of his time away from home or has moved out completely, and at some point, may feel too ashamed to come back. Growing up without a father figure, the daughter suffers from an array of issues, ranging from lack of discipline, structure, self-expression and feeling safe and protected. The sense of betrayal and lack of trust is deep.

3. Here but not present: This type of father is at home but he's not emotionally present. He may be struggling with his own pent-up emotions of depression, guilt, shame or regret and can't seem to connect or communicate with his close ones. He feels detached from his family, and his children pine for his atten-

tion, but also suffer in silence. The effect on his daughter can run deep. She may not be able to express herself emotionally, as she has learned that it's unsafe. She feels unloved by her father and may struggle from low self-worth. She may take on the responsibility to make him happy, as children sometimes do. Later on in life, she may subconsciously attract emotionally unavailable men to heal that wound.

4. Part-time dad: This type of father is busy most of the time but carves out time for his family and children during evenings or weekends. He assumes that most of the parenting role will be done by the mother or others in his household. He may be this way because of societal or cultural norms, or because he is busy with work and assumes that his primary (and main) responsibility is to provide for the household and be a good role model for his children in terms of hard work and success. In some cases, he may also simply not be an engaged or emotionally available parent (or partner). His daughter doesn't feel as attached to him and may appease him to get his attention. She misses out on his wisdom and love, and witnessing a deep, intimate relationship between her parents. While growing up, she strives to be independent, strong and successful in her career. She struggles with emotional expression and intimacy, and possibly even low self-esteem.

5. Mr. Perfect: This type of dad is rare. He's emotionally available and expressive and is present for his family. He strives to be an engaged parent. He's aware of his flaws and strengths and isn't afraid of being wrong. This type of dad shows up for his children's education, activities and day-to-day care where possible, on top of his work responsibilities. He loves, protects, serves, and provides for their physical, emotional, and spiri-

tual needs. He's not afraid to affirm his love for his children, and when they're in his presence, they feel emotionally and physically safe and secure. His daughter grows up with a healthy expectation of men and relationships and has high self-esteem. On the flip side, she may even subconsciously pedestalize her father, making it hard to find a partner who would live up to her standards.

At the end of the day, your father played a vital role in your life, and taking the time to unravel and release anything that doesn't serve you anymore is your birthright and prerogative. You get to be the captain of your ship, determining what beliefs and stories you want to hold from your childhood going forward, and what beautiful jewels you want to unearth through your relationship with your father. Coming from a place of compassion and forgiveness for your father, yet being honest with yourself, is the path to recovery. Moreover, you can reparent yourself from the missed connections with your father, creating a strong father within you that will always love you, protect you and provide for you, no matter what.

Below are some exercises to heal the Father Wound.

EXERCISE 1: JOURNAL ON YOUR RELATIONSHIP WITH YOUR FATHER:

1. *Describe your father's qualities that you love and appreciate.*
2. *What was your relationship like with him?*
3. *When did you feel a sense of love and connection with him? When did you not?*

4. *What gifts and talents has he given you, and what life lessons have you learned from him?*

Take some time to practice self-empathy and acceptance of this list. Grieve if you need to or come into appreciation for all the positive qualities in your relationship.

EXERCISE 2: JOURNAL ON YOUR FATHER'S LIFE AND BELIEFS:

1. *In your journal, make an inventory of your father's beliefs: partnership, sex, money, relationships, career – list them all out. Be as comprehensive as possible.*
2. *Describe how these beliefs are relevant to you. Which beliefs have you picked up?*
3. *Journal about other elements of his childhood and development patterns. Describe your father as a child. Who was he, what were his parents like? When he was born, what were the circumstances? What were likely some inflection points/experiences in his life (e.g., starting school, getting married, etc.) in which he may have changed as a person? What were his siblings like? In what ways was he happy? In what ways was he hurt? How has his life been with your mother?*

Practice self-empathy on any of the wounds, revelations or limiting beliefs that come up from the above exercise. Allow yourself to feel whatever arises. We can't change our parents, but we do have a right to feel sad about things that we missed! As it relates to any limitations that you may have picked up, meditate on it, and tell yourself, "Even if I subconsciously believe xxx, I still love, accept and forgive myself." By practicing this, you are letting go of the hold of the belief, simply by bringing awareness.

EXERCISE 3: ACKNOWLEDGE YOUR NEEDS FROM YOUR FATHER AND CLAIM THEM FOR YOURSELF

Write a list of what was missing from your childhood from your father. Use the following examples to help identify what was missing:

- Protecting you from others
- Cherishing you, seeing your beauty and sacredness
- Honoring your boundaries and privacy
- Making you feel connected, attended to and nurtured
- Loving you unconditionally, without expecting anything in return
- Taking care of your physical needs
- Teaching you basic life skills
- Having integrity and was reliable
- Being your cheerleader and supporting you in your talents.

When you have written your list, write out and say the following regarding each quality that was missing for you:

I forgive my father for not _____. I release him from the responsibility and will offer it to myself. I promise to do my best to begin _____ myself from this day forward.

Print out this list and, on a daily basis, begin to father yourself in these ways. Begin to speak to yourself as a kind father, one that is loving and supportive of you. Recognize that the father in you is eternally loving and present for you.

EXERCISE 4: CUTTING SPIRITUAL AND ENERGETIC CORDS WITH YOUR FATHER

Meditation:

Set aside one evening to do this meditation.

- Light a candle and sit in a dark room.

- Invite your father (spiritually) into your space, and also your Higher Self.

- Envision your father throughout his life - his childhood, adolescence, teenage years, college years, late twenties, to the present day, based on what you journaled. Imagine seeing him sitting in front of you at each age. Who is he? What is he going through? Listen deeply, observe, and say, "I love you, accept you, I forgive you." Hug/caress him. Ask him for his forgiveness; you can say, "Dad, I'm sorry, thank you, I love you."

- Now, set the intention to tell your father that you are ready to cut the cords with him.

- Go into your body and feel where the sensations arise when you think of him. Which part of your body do you feel his presence? Which chakras?

- State how you feel, and what you need/needed. Take as long as you need. Be assertive and honest.

- You may cry or grieve while doing this. Allow your emotions to be let loose, and be completely naked, vulnerable. You have nothing to lose.

- Then say, with the intention of seeking forgiveness for your own mistakes in the relationship, "I am sorry, thank you, I love you..." over and over until you really mean it. You can even add the mantra, "I love you, accept you, I forgive you."

- Say, "I am now removing these energetic cords with you. I release all unhealthy connections to me."

- Then, imagine removing that cord from your body – physically make the removal happen with your hands. Alternatively, you can imagine cutting that cord with a strong swipe of your hand like a karate swipe.

- Take the end of the cord that was connected with you and put it into the ground (i.e., "ground" the cord) so that instead of being connected with you, his cord is connected to the earth. This is absolutely healthy.

- Repeat if multiple cords.

- Imagine healing the "open wounds" with golden light emanating from the center of your heart.

- Now, imagine a golden bridge of unconditional love between you and your father.

- Use sage to clear your place.

- Allow whatever time you need to, to do this exercise completely.

As mentioned earlier, I've included a recording on performing the cord-cutting ritual which you can download here (note: the meditation asks that you write a letter many days prior, please feel free to ignore): https://sarikajain.com/Soulmate-Plan-Resources/

End with this prayer:

Dear God,
I pray for love, healing and grace for my father.
I am thankful for the life he gave me.
For the ways he nourished and supported me, I give gratitude.
For the ways he acted from his wounds and unintentionally hurt me, please help me to forgive him and receive your healing.
May his soul be blessed, his way forward be paved with grace and ease.
Please help us release each other and any psychic cords that no longer serve.
Please also help me heal any bitterness or anger I still hold.
I recognize the role he played in helping me be where I am, for which I am grateful. I would not be here without him.
Thank you, dear father, for your service to me, for bringing me into this world.
May you be happy, may you be at peace, may you be free from suffering.
May we enter into a relationship that's in alignment with God's plan for us.
I vow to step into each day, in greater understanding and compassion for my father and our relationship, to the best of my abilities.
Thank you, God, for I am free now.
Amen.

Releasing Any Remaining Charge and Finding Forgiveness and Acceptance of Your Parents

If you're still feeling charged emotions about your mother or father, it's ok! Your parents played a huge role in your psyche, and depending on your trauma, there may still be some pain that comes up over time, especially if you are connected with them.

I shared tools around emotional self-care. In the privacy of your home, you can grieve and get angry all you want. At some point, see if you can reach a point of acceptance and even appreciation for your parent. You can start to think of a few things that you appreciate about your parent. "I appreciate that you did ___" or "I appreciate how mom / dad does ___". And if more starts arising – keep going! It may be more than you realize. Take as much as time as you need. Finally, start to practice love for your parent. Feel the love glowing from your heart, permeating and enveloping them.

As you begin transforming your relationship with both your parents, and the mother and father within, you will start to notice a newfound lease on life, a sense of compassion and openness to new possibilities. At the end of the day, your parents represent your relationship with God because they brought us to Earth. When you release your inner limitations created by the Mother and Father Wounds, you begin expanding into new pleasures and a sense of spaciousness in your exploration as a woman. Your heart gets shattered and broken open to the real potential of the inner mother and inner father – the tremendous capacity to hold both immeasurable joy and suffering from a place of compassion and wisdom. Healing the Mother and Father Wounds may be a lifelong journey for you, and that's perfect too! We heal in layers, and new levels of healing appear as you keep expanding your love consciousness.

Over time, as you learn to accept your parents more for who they are, and have greater compassion for their life and choices, you may reach a point of true forgiveness and even appreciation. It's a step-by-step journey; and for many women, healing their relationship with their parents is a big part of learning to be vulnerable and trusting with men and life in general. On a spiritual level, you may even begin to truly realize that you chose your parents in this lifetime for aligning with your purpose of stepping into becoming the most loving version of yourself, and this can feel empowering.

Forgiveness is possible even for the most difficult of childhood situations. True story, and this may seem impossible to believe: I have a friend whose mother was killed by her father. Yes, sometimes very disturbed people do things when they're angry. What I'm amazed by is my friend's relentless pursuit of truth and healing, and through a process of reconciliation she was able to forgive her father. She is one of the most courageous, openhearted women I know!

Your parents did their level best in how they raised you, given their own conditioning and what they had capacity for at their level of consciousness. They probably dealt with way worse when they were children from their own parents. No one has taught our parents how to be a good spouse or parent – they never had a Love Coach or relationship teacher. They will also likely never reach your level of consciousness, and expecting your parents to change is unfair.

Here's some good news – when you do the work of healing your Mother and Father Wounds, you change your own DNA and the impacts on your children and future generations (this is studied in a fascinating field known as epigenetics). I truly believe the healing also moves backwards in your lineage as well. We're all connected through consciousness, especially to our family – it's not called a family tree for nothing!

The more you are able to let go of your emotional blocks from your childhood, the more freedom you will feel in your dating life. You will attract healthier, stronger, longer lasting relationships.

Note: Don't feel the need to fix your parents or heal your wounds quickly – just taking a first step through these exercises is enough. You can always come back to this chapter at a later time. Continue to try to have a compassionate, yet healthy relationship with your parents. Set boundaries yet show up for them at least once a week if you can. Working hard to create a healthy relationship with your parents, while honoring your own needs and speaking with honesty is, in itself, a tall task.

Remember to practice self-love and self-compassion throughout this process.

Releasing Ancestral Blocks

"If you look deeply into the palm of your hand, you will see your parents and all the generations of your ancestors. All of them are alive in this moment. Each is present in your body. You are the continuation of each of these people."
~ Thích Nhat Hanh

Who would have thought that your great, great, great grand-mother could be having an impact on your love life! In our modern world, most of us hardly consider our past relatives except through memories. Yet, we're living the outcome of all of their actions, feelings and situations they've been through. Whether it's through DNA, or through spiritual transmission, their beliefs and stories passed down the lineage all the way to you. They say that we are affected most by the seven previous generations, and we affect our progeny, seven generations down – that's how important the actions you're taking today are.

Life hasn't been easy for our ancestors: people died relatively young and lost children to diseases. Alcoholism, abuse, oppression, poverty, disease and societal trauma were rampant, depending on the country and religion they grew up in.

Yet, your ancestors did the best they could, with the wisdom and resources they had. All of their actions, over time, helped raise your family's consciousness, and each generation laid the groundwork for the next. Their faith, whatever religion they followed, helped build your spiritual foundation. Your life right now is so much more abundant and opportunity-filled, due to their love and sacrifices.

Take a moment to think about your ancestors. Who were they, where did they live, what might have their lives been like? If you need to ask your parents, this is a great time. What were their merits and stories of greatness? What hardships did women and men face? Were there any major ups and downs – like a famine, oppression, business failures, domestic abuse, divorces? Did any of them suffer from depression, anxiety, addiction or other mental or emotional issues? Did the women in your family feel disempowered, overwhelmed, resentful? Did they work? Did they have loving family and a support system around them? What was their relationship like with their husbands and children? What were the traditional customs for women which may have held them back in some way? Were the men in engaged in family life, or largely aloof? Are there any family members who have been excluded or disgraced? Are there ancestral patterns of violence – either to or from a family member? Any of these can create heart blocks or walls around the heart, and impact a person's way of loving, which gets passed down as relationship trauma.

A lot of the issues raised above end up being unresolved and fester for the next few generations in different ways, by showing up as heart blockages, limiting beliefs or sabotage patterns. For instance, if your grandmother felt contempt for your grandfather, then you may carry that same feeling or hurt, and may hold a belief that "women are better than men" or "men can't be trusted". Or, your grandparents on your father's side may have carried a sense of heavy burden due to economic hardships they faced, and now you're feeling that sense of burden on you.

Whatever your family's history has been – it's time to gently release any blocks that are holding you back from your ancestry.

Although this may seem like a really dense topic for which many different types of therapies are available, for the purposes of your love life, just doing the exercises below will support you in releasing any heaviness or beliefs you might be clinging on to, subconsciously.

EXERCISE 1: HONORING YOUR ANCESTORS:

Create an altar with your ancestors' pictures, belongings or other memorabilia. Every day, for a week, light a candle and give your thanks for the many gifts that you've received. You can practice gratitude, or even speak to certain ancestors, honoring them, thinking of heartwarming stories. Imagine them as children themselves, playing and being their innocent selves. When you're conducting your day-to-day activities, think about your ancestors, who they were, imagining even mindfully walking and breathing with them, hand in hand. Visualize them surrounding you, smiling at you with deep pride; feel their love shining through, enveloping you like a golden, healing bubble.

EXERCISE 2: RELEASING BELIEFS OR WOUNDS
THAT NO LONGER SERVE

1. Write down any beliefs, thoughts, habits, heavy emotions or fears that continually block you from getting what you desire in life that you believe come from your ancestors.

2. Sit in a dark room with a candle. Invite your ancestor(s) into the space (you can do it one ancestor at a time, or invite several, whatever feels right to you).

3. Give thanks to your ancestor(s) for the gifts they have given you, and honor those thoughts/beliefs/habits and fears from the past. Thank your ancestor, practicing "I'm sorry, thank you, I love you." Tell your ancestor(s) that you are no longer going to carry these with you, and that you are releasing that which doesn't serve you anymore. Physically hand back the emotions/beliefs that you no longer want (imagine giving it to them, thanking them).

4. At this time, you may practice cord cutting with any of your ancestor(s), as you see appropriate.

5. When you are done, you can burn the piece of paper. As the paper turns to ashes, set your intention that you are releasing and purging those thoughts/beliefs/fears/habits from your subconscious mind.

6. Envision a golden light surrounding you, filling the new empty space with healing energy. Pray for love, healing, forgiveness and grace in your life.

7.   You can end with a prayer, such as this one (feel free to modify, or make it your own), or look up another that resonates with you. Sage your place afterwards.

"My dearest ancestors, especially those from the past seven generations, including my parents, grandparents, great grandparents etc., I am eternally grateful to you. Thank you for everything you have done for me. Thank you for your vision and insight, your hard work and commitment to do your best in times that were so different to what we are experiencing now. It is because of you that I am experiencing the conditions of my life. If I have hurt or harmed you in any way, I ask for forgiveness.

On behalf of my ancestors, may we forgive those we have hurt, unintentionally or intentionally, and ask for forgiveness from those who have hurt my lineage, throughout all of time. May we be blessed by God, and live in peace, grace, abundance and harmony with all living beings."

Heart-Freedom: Close Your "Ex Files" and Make Room for "The One"

Carrie couldn't believe her eyes. Big was standing just a few feet away with his new girlfriend. She hid behind the wooden chest that her boyfriend, Aiden, made at his display in the furniture expo. Her heart raced, she became giddy and clumsy, and when Big saw her, her cheeks went red with embarrassment as she stumbled into view. "Act cool!" she thought as she sheepishly greeted him.

Most of us know the story of Carrie Bradshaw (fictional character from the hit HBO series, *Sex and The City*) and her dysfunctional dating life all too well. Whenever she would fantasize about Mr. Big with her way-too-patient friends over cosmopolitans, we would groan (if you didn't, we must talk). *Why couldn't she just move on from this elusive, cigar-smoking, narcissistic, model-chasing, commitment-phobic man?* We went on to watch how she sabotaged her love life, over and over, ultimately settling for the very man who let her down even after they ultimately got married.

Do you have an inkling that there's still unfinished business lingering from your past?

Whether you're single or in a relationship, unhealed relationships from the past can compromise your future. In my assessment,[2] nearly 66% of women still think of their ex, and their emotions range from annoyance, anger and hurt to endlessly wondering what they did wrong. Common wisdom says, "Time heals all things" but as a relationship coach and a woman who's lived through my share of heartbreaks, I've realized it simply isn't the case –through our relationship "disasters," we accumulate baggage and subconscious beliefs about our unworthiness, and we become self-doubting and mistrustful. We lose a bit of our soul and end up "performing" in the dating game to find a partner. Scars are formed on every level—physical, emotional, spiritual and mental. Our hearts become blocked and guarded, risking us to shut down from love altogether.

One of the things that we don't do so well in our society is learning how to properly get over a past relationship or another painful event from our life. There's a whole grieving, forgiveness and wisdom process that we forgo. The questions haunt us: What were we supposed to learn? Why did it happen in the first place? What should our relationship be with those who have hurt us? What could we do differently to attract healthy, lasting relationships?

2 - "Love Magnet Quiz: What's your goddess archetype and what types of men are you attracting?"
https://sarikajain.com/love-attraction-assessment/

One of my biggest fears after my last devastating breakup was, "Can I trust again?" I noticed that my heart was closing up, and I felt tired and exhausted with life. I began to wear big sunglasses and dark clothing, donning the "jaded" look. Even though I thought I was ready to start dating, deep down, I had a fear of being hurt again. If the pain wasn't bad enough the first time round, it would be worse in the next one, right? These were possibly signals to the universe that I was not ready to be with Mr. Right.

Some women know that they are still hooked onto an ex. Comments I've heard from women on how they could be sabotaging their love life include:

"There is definitely a lack of trust in guys because of past situations that always seem to repeat themselves. Maybe it's a self-fulfilling prophecy!"

"I still have pain from my past heartache. I met someone new recently and I feel unsure … perhaps I compare the new guy with my past love."

"I'm still hoping my ex will realize he wants me back."

"I am having trouble meeting quality people and still cannot get over the heartache of my last relationship (over a year ago). I can't seem to get over him, even with therapy and trying to move on."

"I had a breakup six months ago and am only now processing the pain and loneliness attached to that."

"I am still somewhat overcoming past heartache, healing myself to be in love with myself and seeing my own worth."

Do any of these resonate for you? If so, you've been through some real heartache in your life. I get it. It seems like there is no easy path to finding and attracting love without pain. On average, a person goes through three major romantic heartbreaks in their lives, and the pain from each one is real and lasting.

Here's the good news for you, Love Goddess. Your past relationship is your proverbial philosopher's stone, through which you become an alchemist, turning your gunk into gold. It's an opportunity to learn about your patterns and the root causes, dealing with unprocessed hurt and pain, and honestly exploring where you were inauthentic, gave up on your power or hid your truth. It's also a unique chance to take responsibility for your role in the relationships and clear them. You might have been too controlling or emotional or had a wobbly foundation upon which your relationship became a house of cards. It's better to face it and find the root cause, embrace healthy solutions and move on.

It's Time to Close Your "Ex Files"

I want to support you in taking that pain which I call the "Ex Files" and transforming it into something beautiful and powerful. Even if you are over your ex, you may still have a block in your heart, a belief around unworthiness or an energetic cord that needs to be cut.

If you're divorced, you may still be recovering from the emotionally wrenching experience of the divorce itself, or have some physical connection with your former spouse, such as sharing custody of your children or disputes over property, for instance.

Many women, after each breakup, shove the painful memories under the rug and are almost instantly ready to get back up and fight for love as true warriors. In my experience, if you haven't cleared your past on every level – emotional, mental, and spiritual – you simply can't pave the way for a different type of love that's healthy and lasting.

Whether your last relationship was a marriage which lasted ten years or a two-month rendezvous with someone you thought was "the one," you may still have some unresolved issues; **but, most impor-**

tantly, you can use that relationship to heal your love blocks and attract the right relationship. I believe that your last relationship has all the information you need to take the right actions for attracting a healthy, loving relationship.

EXERCISE: BEACH MEDITATION

Get into a comfortable seated position, relax your body, and take a couple of deep, slow breaths. Now, imagine that you're sitting on a beach by yourself. You feel calm and content. Out of the blue, a man comes up to you, and begins chatting away. You talk about everything under the sun. As evening draws closer, he invites you to dinner. You find a cozy, romantic restaurant overlooking the ocean, and time flies. You both share your dreams, desires and fears, sometimes even eating in silence. You look at your watch and see it's midnight! You tell him you have to go home and pack, because you have a flight to catch the next morning. He asks if he can walk you back to your hotel, and you say ok. As you're saying goodbye, you hug, and he leans in for a kiss. Pause. *Now begin to come back to the present moment.*

(Note: I've included a recording of the Beach Meditation exercise which you can download here: https://sarikajain.com/Soulmate-Plan-Resources/)

Journal what came up for you during and after this meditation. What thoughts, feelings and sensations arose? Be specific and comprehensive as you're writing this down. What did you learn about your "Ex Files"? Don't worry if nothing comes up.

> Journal: What can I learn from my past
> relationships and "Ex Files"?

A breakup rarely happens overnight. Usually, it's the final straw on the camel's back; a part of a larger process where at first, a couple might experience an emotional breakdown or disconnection, followed by mental, and then finally, the physical manifestation. Can you think back to your past relationships, and track where the breakdown started happening? This is why I emphasize emotional connection and healing as first and foremost in creating a lasting relationship, and the unique role that we women can play in emotional leadership. And of course, *it's important to recognize why it can never work out with an emotionally unavailable man; the connection cannot be sustained.*

The ending of a relationship is, of course, terribly painful. When you experience disillusionment or a breakup, there are usually five stages of recovering from the trauma, called catharsis. As I shared earlier, we rarely go through all stages, and find ourselves getting emotionally stuck. Take a look at the below and think about where you might have ended things in a past relationship.

Five stages of catharsis:

1. Shock and Denial

Initially, you wonder if what you're experiencing is even real. You go about your daily life, clinging on to hope that things will change, and find different ways of disassociating with the pain through activities like television binging, having long complaining sessions with friends, drinking or throwing yourself into work. Your body might have an actual reaction of feeling numbness and a sense of disconnection. Your ego feels like your life has literally ended before your eyes.

2. Pain and Guilt

When you begin to actually come to terms with the chaos and devastation, you begin to feel a sense of pain – which is sometimes even physical due to increased cortisol levels. The pain within the heart is real. Meanwhile, you may feel a sense of shame and guilt about the situation. If you were in a relationship that ended, you recognize that you played a part in it ending, consciously or not. You feel like kicking yourself for doing and saying the things that led to the ending. Also, you might face social rejection or blame due to your situation, which could exacerbate the hurt. When you experience disillusionment, you may feel that it's unfair, or that something is wrong with you, which is why you brought it to yourself.

3. Anger and Bargaining

Once you begin to come to terms with the situation, you begin to feel enraged. You were robbed of your dignity, freedom, your happiness and sense of safety, and you feel stuck – and suddenly you want to revolt. The anger may bring up other things that have hurt you, and like an avalanche, the anger and resentment keeps growing. Your judgement becomes drastically altered, and you see no way out except to retaliate – and this is when people hurt others and violence occurs. Sometimes you can sidestep the anger by "getting even" with the person. You begin fighting to win back the love and connection that you lost, and sometimes even maintaining your sense of sanity. You bargain with the people who hurt you. On a very deep level, you are angry with yourself: "How could I have put myself in this situation?" You wonder how you could have been so foolish, didn't see the signs, weren't proactive enough or somehow created it.

4. Depression, Reflection and Loneliness

Once you're done fighting and see that you're not getting anywhere, you become depressed. There's a sense that everything that was worth fighting for is now lost, and you have to accept your situation as it is. There is no way out, and sadness, heartbreak and confusion are here to stay, *so it seems*. It is dark and lonely and you feel depressed and stuck. You find it hard to find people who understand your situation. You reflect on your past, feel sad about your mistakes and your situation.

5. Acceptance, Meaning and Upturn

After going through the above stages, there comes a natural turning point when you begin to see a light at the end of the tunnel and new possibilities begin to emerge in your life. You begin seeking meaning, and experience something heart-opening or even magical. Perhaps you are a recipient of an act of kindness, or you come across a book on meditation that resonates. You become grateful for the things you already do have in your life, and you're able to see and understand your role in the past. You're able to appreciate the experience that you did have and gain a greater sense of clarity about what you desire going forward. You channel your pain into creativity, service or sheer presence. You recognize that there's something greater at play, and that life is inherently kind and loving. When one door shuts, another opens. You've heard these phrases, and yet...you begin to see it actually happen in your life, and you feel a sense of hope and even happiness. You've been through the full emotional ringer...and you've made it to the other side like a heroine!

> Journal: When you think back to your past major relationship, how did it end? What emotions or thoughts are you still clinging on to, and where in the catharsis process are you?

Usually, most people never make it through the different stages of catharsis, as it's not something taught in our society – we're used to shoving things under a rug, hoping that our life will turn around on its own. No matter where you are with your past relationships, you can use this time to heal and release what no longer serves you, which I'll be sharing in the Close Your "Ex Files" process below.

Here's some great news – after doing all of this, if your ex is right for you, it will work out *naturally*. **In the same token, if you're done with the relationship, you can simply let go and open your heart to new possibilities!**

EXERCISES: CLOSING YOUR "EX FILES"

EXERCISE 1: WRITE A LETTER TO YOUR EX

(Don't worry, you don't have to share it with him. This exercise is for you.)

1. Bring a significant relationship with an ex to your mind, one that has deeply impacted you most recently.

2. Make a list of different moments in your relationship that you appreciated or that hurt you. Create a table (such as the below)

with ten rows. **List 6 negative experiences, and 4 positive experiences.** Take your time.

Incident	Feelings	Needs met/ unmet	Your role in the incident

3. For each of the incidents, journal on the feelings that came up. What needs were or weren't being met at those times? Be as thoughtful as possible. Feel into your feelings – allow yourself to embody them. It's ok to feel angry, happy, sad or withdrawn as you're writing this. Also, acknowledge your own role, taking responsibility for actions or things that you wish you had or hadn't done.

4. Now, turn this list into a powerful, fully expressed letter to your ex. Incorporate all the incidents in the list. Handwrite the letter if possible. Tell him exactly what you want him to know, using the feelings and needs, sharing both happy and painful moments. Let him know everything. *Be as compassionate as possible, trying not get into the blame game – rather owning your own experience and sharing your feelings and needs.* Accept responsibility for some of the things that you may have done for making the situation painful for him or you. Take as much time as you need. The longer and more heartfelt the letter, the better. Get it all out!

5. Put it under your mattress for a few days. By doing so, you're allowing a detox to occur on a subconscious level while you're sleeping – words have vibration. During this period, go through the catharsis process, using the emotional well-being tools I shared earlier for being with your emotions. Sometimes I even use play-acting, where I stand in front of a mirror and act all the scenes out in a highly dramatic fashion, while *feeling* all the emotions. Set an intention to release your ex from your life. When you think of him, practicing Ho'oponopono, thinking, "I'm sorry, thank you, I love you."

Go through your house and remove anything from your ex – letters, photos, gifts. One of my clients still slept on a bed that she shared with her ex-husband, and she wondered why her back hurt so much! No matter how hard it is, try your best to clear your home of memories, and of course your ex's energy in different forms. I'll be sharing more on decluttering in the Prepare for Love chapter.

EXERCISE 2: CUTTING CORDS WITH YOUR EX

Follow the cord cutting exercise as shared above in the Father Wound, burning the letter in the end. This is your time to release your partner, once and for all! If you would like, during the ceremony yet after cutting cords with your ex, you can also call in other partners and practice cord cutting with them.

Allow whatever time you need to, to do this completely.

Clear the house and your body with sage afterwards.

End with this prayer:

Dear God,

Please disconnect my body and soul from this past relationship that does not serve.

May the cords that bind my heart, or any other part of me, be cut.

May we no longer have any cords together.

I release this person into your hands.

Please help me disconnect any psychic hooks I have on him.

Restore back my power and love.

May we forgive, love and accept each other for things in the past.

May we learn what we needed to, heal, and transform any past pain into wisdom and growth.

May this person be happy, have peace and be free from suffering.

May I be happy, have peace, and be free from suffering.

Free us from each other.

Please lead me into your light, into your love. Show me how to love unconditionally, with wisdom.

May I begin anew in the spirit of love.

I surrender this relationship to you totally and completely, dear God.

May I learn to love with faith and trust, and be open to true, healthy love going forward.

Amen.

Let's say you desire to meet with your ex to get closure or reconnect. First, recognize that reconciliation is a journey. It's a gentle, slow and deeply humbling process. You have to remove your focus on a "perfect" or expected outcome and trust in the process. Your intention should simply be about increasing understanding and forgiveness. During the process, both of you can grow as people in your ability to have empathy for the other, and truly understand how you may have caused suffering for the other.

It may take months or years before a reconciliation can truly happen. It first starts from the inside, and ultimately may lead to you actually meeting the person and having a heart-to-heart conversation. You can make a few more attempts to meet or speak with your ex – and if they aren't ready, that's fine. You've done your best, and you just have to be ready to move on. Just know that whatever is meant to happen, will; and be prepared to be surprised as well!

Beginning Anew

Once you have completed these exercises, congratulations! You have finished all the steps in "Heal Your Heart and Close Your 'Ex Files.'" This is a marvelous, courageous undertaking – and this is a time for you to celebrate and love yourself like no other. Have trust that everything you have done is supporting you in releasing your past and setting you up for a future that's aligned, overflowing with love, and filled with miracles. Be there for your heart, loving and appreciating her for her resilience and wisdom. **Acknowledge that you have gone where most people haven't dared to go – to face your past wounds and inner demons – which is what makes you a true spiritual warrior.**

You might still feel tender and uncertain. *Imagine how a caterpillar feels while going through its chrysalis phase?*

There is an expansion waiting to emerge in your love life because you have made a commitment to tend to your Love Garden and release weeds that no longer serve.

EXERCISE: ROSE PETAL BATH

- Do a forty-five-minute bath, using rose petals strewn in luke-warm water. Surround yourself with candles and peaceful music. Use a white cloth to bathe yourself. You can also add some Epsom salt or frankincense pieces in the bath water to collect negative charge.

- Then, for fifteen minutes, meditate about your past.

- For the next fifteen minutes, meditate about your present.

- Lastly, spend time meditating and envisioning your future. Partnership, romance, life, family, career, secret dreams ... let your fantasies go wild!

- When you're done, put the cloth in Ziplock bag, then place it under your mattress for a week.

- After a week, you can throw out the cloth. This is a sacred ritual to capture any remnant energetic charge and release it and infuse yourself with the high vibrational energy of roses.

- Note: If you still feel a sense of resentment, anger or bitterness in your body, especially after completing the Heal Your Heart exercises, use lemon peels instead of rose petals, as the peels have the ability to absorb your bitterness. Then proceed the following week with a rose petal bath. Baths are powerful for healing. At different junctures, you can consider doing baths with frankincense, Epsom salt, minerals or a combination of milk and honey, as Queen Cleopatra used to do. How luxurious!

STEP 3: DISCOVER YOUR "WOW! FACTOR"

Align with Your Unique, Feminine, Sexual Self

When I was young, I was mystified by my mother. She was my archetype of a woman, and I wanted to experience the world through her eyes and body. I marveled at her gemstone-colored silk blouses, pearl necklaces and her high-heeled shoes. I used to rummage through her makeup and hair accessories, and by the age of twelve, I was adept at using a curling iron and hairspray for my hair. I observed her every move and was fascinated with her interactions with my dad. I so wanted to grow up and be a woman! I loved girly things like short skirts and flirty dresses, dreamt about dating and awaited my breasts to come in. I wanted to be in a romantic relationship with a handsome, princely man, and I read countless romance novels. However, I felt largely insecure and clumsy because I was dark-skinned, hairy and skeletal in my build – I was not one of the cool girls by any means.

By my teens, I could see the messaging in our society about being a young woman: "Don't get pregnant. Don't distract men. Don't invite too much attention. Sex before marriage is bad. Dark women end up alone; fair women are beautiful. You're too fat (or skinny)." The list went on, and I felt confused and even sometimes ashamed of my body. I tried not being too loud or boisterous, as to do so was considered unladylike. I wanted to look and behave a certain way to feel feminine, beautiful and sexy, yet those were the very things that got me into trouble. The media didn't help – there were images of sensual women galore in ads and television, and women's magazines were filled with messaging around pleasuring men and looking fashionable. I was smart and did well in school, which I'm incredibly thankful for; but the conflict between pursuing something masculine – I ended up studying Computer Science & Engineering as an undergraduate, and an MBA – while being in my feminine was confounding to navigate.

In my twenties, being a woman was both fascinating and hard. I had no problem dating men, yet had trouble keeping a relationship. I read books about succeeding in the game of work and love as a modern woman. When it came to my career, I was told to not be so nurturing and too sexy or emotional, and when it came to dating and winning a man's heart, I was advised to turn up my sexuality, kindness and femininity. I dressed professionally for the office and got many power suits tailored, and for my personal life, I dressed in gypsy, feminine and flowing wear. On dates, I was sculpted, wearing something elegant with a slightly sexy edge. When I went to India to visit my family, I would rock my Indian outfits, while rebelling against customs that I thought were too patriarchal or oppressive. I always felt "too much" or "too little." My loved ones kept asking why I wasn't married yet, and I felt constantly embarrassed or even wondering if I were cursed because I was single.

I had a love-hate relationship with my sexuality, feeling grateful for the prospect of giving birth one day and experiencing the joy of sex and intimacy, but also finding my menstrual cycle to be debilitating and a pain. My sexuality felt confusing, especially when it came to dating or making a relationship last. It's sad to admit, but I felt disempowered, like I was just basically trying to scrape by through sheer hard work and intelligence and playing games to win affection and love.

I had interests in metaphysics, growth, art, relationships and service, but I had no idea how that fit in with my explorations in creating a life of success and freedom. I thought that I could pursue those later, maybe even after I got married or, better yet, retired. In fact, I was constantly trying to figure out what I was passionate about, outside of work. There were so many seeds within me, so many yearnings… yet they all felt caged in, and at some point, I became disconnected with my desires, which I considered selfish or impractical.

However, after I began to love myself and heal my heart, I started feeling lighter, and saw a glimmer of new possibilities opening up to me. I began to question things in my life: What am I here to really do and what's my purpose? Do I really want to get married and have kids? What kind of lifestyle would support me in realizing my spiritual potential? How could I share my talents with the world in a joyful, authentic way? What other gifts do I have that I didn't know about?

The answers to all of these questions started appearing when I began to embrace my feminine, intuitive, sexual side – at least however much I had the courage to. I was sick of playing by someone else's rules in terms of how to live and be happy and wanted to claim my own path.

I was having the best time of my life connecting with my heart's desires. I was falling in love with myself and my life, seeing the world with a sense of wonder, and dancing to the rhythms of my heart.

It was in this journey of inquiry and taking courageous risks in exploring my purpose that I met Krishan. He was inspired by my vision and values and wanted to support me. I too could see the gentleness and generosity in his heart, his fierce commitment to truth and integrity, and his passion ... which turned me on! I was living in my divine feminine and there was real chemistry between us – nothing fake, manipulative or based on instinctive, instant attraction, like I was used to.

I knew that my life is way more precious than what I had thought it was – and life is too short to be playing small. If I wanted to live into my true power as a modern woman, and create a life of meaning, love and fulfillment, then I needed to embrace all sides of me, including the parts that lay hidden, and even what I considered ugly, shameful or dark.

You, my divine Love Goddess, are unique, beautiful and frikkin' gifted. There is a perfection and exquisiteness in you that exists in no one else. When you are in your power, there is nothing that can stop you – you are a Queen on a mission, ready to slay self-doubt and rule over your kingdom with confidence and grace. You have the capacity to be a love magnet wherever you go, performing alchemy in your environment through your presence.

Now that you are (mostly) baggage-free, you can begin envisioning and creating this new life that your soul is itching to create. But how do you get there, and what is it exactly?

You have an inner compass and a secret weapon – it's your unique soul blueprint, and the temple of the body you were born in. When you align with your "Wow! Factor" - your true essence and unique vision for your life – and restore your feminine and masculine balance, you will become "turned on" by yourself and your life … this is when others are turned on by you!

This step not only involves connecting with your soul and its purpose, but also sexual healing, and restoring your feminine sensuality and desire for love, relationships, life and creativity. You discover the many facets of being a woman, mastering different talents and skills, along with your unique spiritual power that courses through your body, once it is unleashed.

First, though, you have to discover that your first true soulmate is … you! When you become your own lover, your own greatest champion, and recognize your own allure and spiritual strength as a woman, you can begin to emanate a sense of confidence and electrical radiance. You're turned on by *you*, and lead a turned-on life, as you step into your "Wow! Factor". You become a force to reckon with, a magnet for love. *Your partner will fall in love with you for who you are deep inside – your uninhibited, unapologetic, unleashed self.*

"When the feminine wakes up, it wakes up to self-love, creation, giving birth and to pleasure. It wakes up to heaven." – Giovanni Cavalieri

Being a woman is way more magical and powerful than our patriarchal system has made it out to be.

Is it any coincidence that young girls and teens are so drawn to love and romance? How women support others empathetically and are drawn towards creating a healthy family and society? Or how a woman's beauty, grace and sensuality can inspire art and even stop wars? These are not weaknesses. There are studies that show men with older sisters and men who marry live longer because they have a woman to open up to and will always feel cared for. I always marvel at how women multi-task to the nth degree, feeding and nourishing everyone around them.

Through your love, pleasure and an open heart, you have the power to bring the world to your feet and instill a sense of ecstasy and sacredness in the others around you.

In their heart of hearts, men want to be with women because women have what men don't – our connection to bliss and creation. Women have a *joie de vivre* and deep understanding and reverence of life that men can never compete with – and it's what actually drives them to want to be with us.

As a woman, you too have latent powers that you don't know about – but as you begin to sweetly nurture these aspects of yourself, you will begin to create a life and world that is driven by your deepest desires and your God-given gifts. In this chapter, you will be discovering your "Wow! Factor", which is through embracing your full unique, feminine and sexual self. This involves healing any shame or sexual blocks from your past and stepping into your feminine power. You will discover facets of your soul's unique path and what gives you a sense of purpose.

This step covers a lot – and may initiate years of discovery. I encourage you to simply do the exercises provided and move on to the rest of the book in order to complete your 90-day transformation. Use this chapter as a guidepost for deep self-discovery and claiming your true, loving, sexy essence.

Awakening Your Sexuality

Rose, a soft-spoken, soulful and beautiful thirty-something woman, was on a path of heart openness and happiness. However, she still carried a whole host of regrets, shame and guilt. As a child, she was sexually molested, over and over, by her tuition teacher who began visiting their home when she was four. She felt defenseless and too ashamed to tell her mom, feeling somehow responsible for inviting the abuse and being in the situation. She struggled to excel in school, and constantly compared herself with her sister, who was a star student and adored by the family.

As an adult, Rose had long forgiven everyone, except for one person – herself. She felt unable to trust in herself, let alone others, and felt mistrustful of men in her life. She found herself in relationships with emotionally unavailable men who wouldn't commit and felt that she needed to use her sexuality to create connection and keep a relationship, which ended up falling apart anyways. Given the general taboo over casual dating and sex, especially for women, she wondered if she were somehow tainted. Rose had numerous health issues, including an auto-immune disorder, and sometimes felt too exhausted to get out of bed.

As she began to release her past and heal her sexuality, Rose began to feel a sense of empowerment and freedom. She felt comfortable stepping into her feminine and started feeling a sense of connection and pleasure in her body, which allowed her to access her intuition. She began to find the right medical treatments to help heal her body and witnessed a surge of energy and newfound passion! Rose felt sexy and comfortable in her body. She felt a sense of renewal and possibility and began to approach dating from a place of joy and discovery, with loads of self-confidence to boot.

As a woman, you have the power to create, and sustain life, through your body. Wow.

Why do I start here?

Self-love starts with radical self-acceptance and understanding and honoring yourself and your body. Knowing, implicitly, that as a woman, the sacredness of your body is key. Whether or not you can or decide to have children is not important – it is the very essence of your femininity and sexuality that gives you the greatest power given to mankind: to create almost *anything* out of nothing through the power of your desire. Your body has access to universal, creative intelligence that specifically flows through the feminine body.

As a woman, you also have the ability to experience great pleasure in your body, process the ultimate depths of emotions, access deep intuition and wisdom, and heal through the divinity of your presence. Whether as a lover, wife, mother, CEO, community organizer, gardener, or any other role you find yourself in, you have a vital essence that, when harnessed, captivates hearts and minds and can move mountains.

In essence, your body is a temple, which requires great honor. When you respect your body, mind and soul, others will invariably do the same. When you're deeply connected to your body and sexuality, you are in your truest, greatest essence and power.

Men are ultimately vulnerable to women, which is why they have to work so hard to stay strong and in control of their emotions, especially around sexy women. Sexuality is power, my friends. Why else would patriarchy have created a complicated, multi-generational, multi-layered system to control and oppress the feminine?

The challenge for women, for over millennia, has been the sexual shaming and institutionalization which has kept women in submission in different ways – whether it's the pressure to be a "good girl," to look and dress a certain way, be a doormat in the bedroom, keep a handle on her emotions or to not have too many sexual desires. Most religions have made the woman's body to be sinful and lust-creating, and natural processes like menstruation and childbearing to be considered unholy. Moreover, hundreds of millions of girls and women are sexually abused and violated around the world. In many cultures, women are forced to get married young and to men they don't know. When a girl gets her period, she is sometimes considered a liability because of her ability to get pregnant. Pregnancy out of wedlock is considered taboo, and when a girl is molested or raped, she is made to feel it was her fault. Sadly, girls and women aren't protected in our society, by and large, which leads to much trauma.

Perhaps one of the greatest ironies has been that women are some of the greatest gatekeepers in this patriarchal system, pushing old institutional ideas around sexuality, body image and marriage, curtailing each other's freedoms. They do this by condemning and judging each other, requiring their daughters to behave in certain ways, or through jealousy and contempt, which our system actively promotes. Even modern-day norms push women into traps of having to "do it all" or "have it all" in terms of career, marriage and having children, which I've personally found taxing on my love life and body.

While women have gained many freedoms and have fought for equality, it's vital not to forget the basics of masculine and feminine essences in our human bodies and spirits, and find a natural, healthy complementary relationship between the two.

The sexual violence and gender war is rampant, and it hurts one's love life. It is a social breakdown, and the sense of heartbreak and grief is devastatingly immense. The crisis continues into the bedroom, where nearly 60% of women are not able to experience sexual climax during intercourse, while many experience pain during sex. Most women don't know what they want in a bedroom, and some are even afraid of sex. Poor, unfulfilling sex, and sometimes coercion or having sex out of obligation has become the norm, which further affects women's libido. All of the shame, fear, anxiety and rage that women carry in their bodies can end up affecting their reproductive systems and hormonal health, leading to health issues.

How can you love when you have such deep pain within your body – where it even *hurts* to love? How can you love a man, when, deep down, there is such distrust? When your body rejects such vulnerability because it is frightened or powerless? Or when you deeply feel disgusted by how your body looks and feels?

The good news is you don't have to carry the weight of your personal and generational trauma any longer! You can begin to lighten your own load and create a whole new relationship with your body and sexuality through the power of self-love. When you feel connected with your body and have a general appreciation, you will begin to step into your sexuality in an openhearted way, one which honors both your vulnerability and resilience while living a life of pleasure and authenticity.

EXERCISE: IS MY SEXUALITY BLOCKED? SELF-ASSESSMENT:

Answer True/False for the below statements. There is no right answer – we are all in the process of discovering and healing our sexual blocks.

1. I have healthy, non-co-dependent relationships. _____
2. I tap into my creativity regularly. _____

3. I have a healthy sex life (even if I'm single, I know how to provide myself sexual pleasure and touch myself in a sensual, loving way). _____

4. I know what I want and how I'm going to get it. _____

5. I handle my emotions well and anything life throws at me. _____

6. I enjoy sensual pleasures in my life guilt-free. _____

7. My hormones, sexual organs, urinary tract and lower back feel fine and healthy. _____

8. I embrace my body, sexuality and sensuality. _____

9. I don't have any major sexual trauma. _____

10. I am generally free of addictive behaviors, like smoking, alcoholism, being on my phone, causing myself physical pain, etc. _____

Count how many Fs you have. The more you have, the more it indicates that your sexuality may be blocked and that you may need to release baggage to thrive in a healthy relationship.

Allow yourself to fully feel all the emotions and concerns, accept them, and let them go. Find the tools from "Be a Love Magnet," such as self-empathy, to be with these emotions and accept where you are in your sexual healing journey. Have faith that shining light on any potential blockages or beliefs is the first and most important step to healing your sexuality!

EXERCISE: BRINGING AWARENESS TO YOUR SEXUALITY

Journal: This is a space of stream of consciousness journaling. Try to simply write, without judgment or analysis or getting caught in stories. Simply observe the thoughts and sensations that arise.

1. How do you currently feel about your body?

Do you take pleasure in your body? Do you love your body or have disgust? Do you feel ashamed, or simply feel like ignoring it? Do you deny your sensuality? Or do you struggle with pleasure through pain, addiction or repression patterns in your life?

2. How do you currently feel about yourself sexually?

Do you enjoy your sexuality and feel confident in its expression as a sacred gift? Or do you repress, control, deny or overuse your sexuality in any way that causes you, or others, pain? Do you feel ashamed about your sexual experiences from your past?

3. When was the first time your sexuality was considered taboo or bad?

Many sex experts point to girls getting cut off from their sexuality when they become young teens. Basically, when you go from innocently enjoying your body's pleasures to feeling ashamed of it; and usually a specific moment is the turning point.

4. What was it like to get your period? What are your memories around it?

Reclaiming Your Relationship with Your Body and Sexuality

Navigating your sexuality can seem overwhelming at first, especially if you've never paid attention to it. Yet now you have an opportunity to gently focus on your body and sexuality with no external pressure.

Your body is such a magnificent, intelligent creature of its own.

Your breasts are an entire system that's magically set up to nurture a child – a miracle that only nature can intend for! Breasts are incredibly complex and beautiful – doesn't it almost look like a flower on the inside? The amazing thing is that breasts come in all shapes, sizes and color; every woman has a unique pair, and they are perfect as they are, no matter what the situation is – if a woman has small breasts, had her breasts removed, had breast enlargement, shrunken or sagging breasts, breasts are still beautiful. Breasts, and especially the nipple areas, are also incredibly sensual and delicious to touch and are a gateway for feeling pleasure in your body.

Your reproductive organs in the lower part of your body, which include your womb, ovaries, uterus, fallopian tubes, etc., are active during your menstrual years and play a special role even later in life. Not only does it perform the sacred function of supporting conception and giving birth to life, but it also communicates with the rest of your body, in terms of hormones, general well-being and more.

I am enthralled by the mystical power of the womb. The womb has so many divine functions, including energetically manifesting your vision, calling in your soulmate and other healthy relationships, holding and processing your emotions, and is the chief supply of source energy and vitality, called *prana* or *chi*. Whether or not one is menstruating, these organs are the source of feminine intelligence and power for a woman.

Your *pussy* consists of your vaginal area, labia, clitoris, and more. In fact, the woman's pussy is deeply intricate, and performs some of the most important functions for your body. Apart from being a part of your anatomy for giving birth, it is also a pathway to enjoy sex, pleasure and intimacy and is your personal guide to leading a turned on life. When you develop a genuinely curious and appreciative relationship with your pussy and learn what gets her excited and aroused, you begin to lean into what truly resonates with you, at a body and soul level, because you're being led by authentic desire. The clitoris has over eight thousand nerve endings (whoa!) and, as such, is highly sensitive and is the pathway to heightened pleasure. Unfortunately, many women have negative perceptions, pain and trauma associated with their pussies. Whether it's due to the annoyance of having periods, the smell, the looks, how she feels, the bad memories of pain or shame, you may have negative associations to heal.

I could go on about how powerful and incredibly awe-inspiring your body is (which I've come to truly appreciate after having a baby, and now, learning from my elders about the powerful, cleansing, rite of passage known as menopause). I leave it for you to discover and learn about the incredible nature of your body on your own. There are many resources available which I'll share at the end of the book in the reference section.

What are some ways to begin healing your sexuality? Below I share some exercises:

1. Honor your body

Begin looking at yourself naked in the mirror, from head to toe. Make funny faces, be curious and have a fun adventure with it! As you examine different parts of your body, think to yourself, "My sacred eyes, my sacred nose, my sacred breasts, my sacred thighs ..." You might notice different thoughts coming up about your imperfections, but don't allow them to arise. Continue to honor the sacredness of your body this way, dancing, noticing your body's contours, edges and textures. You can also do different affirmations in the mirror, such as, "I'm magnificent. I'm enough. I am worthy!" When you get your period, be grateful to your menstrual flow, respecting your body and its needs during those days.

2. Create your heart-womb connection

Here's a simple practice to start with in the morning or before falling asleep. Lie in a comfortable position. Place one hand on your womb, and the other on your heart, and begin to breathe deeply, and slowly. Watch the breath follow through your throat, heart and womb ... and release your breath. Say to yourself, "I love you, I accept you, and I forgive you," or "I am safe. All is well," or any other affirmation that feels good to you. Your heart and womb will feel loved and reassured, and you'll deeply connect with your body.

3. Conscious Body Touch

Conscious body touch is an exploration of the body, where you consciously give attention to each body part, offering your love and gratitude. You use the healing power of your hands to send energy to each part. In doing this practice, you heal old abandonment wounds and rejuvenate your body, helping her feel desired, alive and deliciously fulfilled.

Set aside forty minutes to an hour.

Lie on your bed. Now, place both hands on top of your head, close your eyes, and send love to your head, thanking it for all the ways it supports you, it's miraculousness. How your brain helps you think, how your skull protects your head, the preciousness of your hair follicles and hair. This is truly an intimate process! Continue down your body, touching your eyes, ears, neck, shoulders, breasts, all the way down to your toes. Spend a few minutes per body part. Imagine sending healing energy through your hands as you're doing this.

Now, go to your breasts, and using some coconut oil, massage them in a slow, gentle way. Get to know your breasts, lovingly caressing each part. Move down to your pelvis and do the same. End with getting to know your pussy, moving from the outer labia, the clitoris, the lips, to the inner parts. Be curious, kind and loving. You can end with self-pleasure.

Your body has probably never received this kind of physical attention before – so if you notice certain emotions come up, like resistance, grief or anger, or simply pleasure and joy, just be with them. There is no right and wrong, and that in itself is the healing process.

4. Playful Self Pleasure

Spend an evening pleasuring yourself. Take a warm bath with rose petals, wear sexy lingere, dance in front of a mirror, and end up in your bed or floor. Then, spend time pleasuring yourself. What turns you on and what arouses you? What hurts, or what kind of resistance do you feel when you're doing this? What thoughts come up? Do you. Be present for all of this, yet continue to get sexually intimate with yourself, and see if you can get horny. You can reach orgasm if it naturally occurs, and keep going, or you can stop when you feel you've had enough sensation.

Your pussy is ready to reemerge and play, and guide you in a gentle, feminine way of reconnecting with your sexuality and pleasure.

Try to pleasure yourself every day. Get to know your sexuality and desires, and fill up your body with sensual delight that's inherently yours!

5. Release cords with people tied to your sexual *chakra*

The sexual chakra, or energy center, is located below your naval, and supports your sexuality, emotional health, and on a physical level, provides vitality to your sexual organs. As a woman encounters various relationships, even ones in which she was sexually intimidated in some way, she collects cords and memories in the chakra which creates energetic blocks.

Take time in cutting the cords, using the cord-cutting tools I provided earlier.

You can declare, "I am sovereign. I am free to choose how I share my sexuality with others. I release any wounds, suffering or limiting beliefs about my sexuality. I am claiming my love, respect and integrity, and vow to take care of my sexual health, from here on forward."

6. Face Your Madonna/Whore Complex:

Unfortunately, we've grown up in a society where both women and sex have been reviled, commoditized, sensationalized and more. We're facing the aftermath of it. Within you, where do you have a conflict between being a good girl or bad girl? What are you ashamed/proud of? When do you consider other women too slutty or prudish? Do you put yourself or others down for how one dresses, looks, talks, feels, etc.? Do you feel ashamed to follow your sexuality or ask for what you desire with your partner?

Contemplate these things, as you begin to create a whole new relationship with how you desire to dress or show up in your relationships with both men and women.

7. Practice Sacred Self Care and Honor Your Inner Sexy

Explore ways to honor your body and listen to what she needs. You can research personal feminine products, supplements, diet, yoga and exercise regiments that support your body's sexual needs. I have personally let go of using tampons, and instead use a menstrual cup (which saves money, feels sacred and is safe and eco-friendly). If you don't feel comfortable taking birth control pills, ask your partner to use a condom. If you don't feel like having sex with someone or are uncomfortable with them ejaculating inside of you (which, I recommend, unless this person is your life partner, as their energy stays in your body), then set those boundaries. It's more than OK – it's your sacred duty to your body! Practice communication skills to express your feelings, needs, requests, and setting healthy boundaries, which we will cover in the next chapter. Avoid activities that drain you, and practice regular self-pleasure and other pleasure-filled practices like dancing, flirting, pole dancing, or whatever else gets your mojo going! Be your naughty, irresistible, unreasonable self, wear sexy clothes and have fun! When you create emotional safety and trust within yourself, in terms of your sexuality, you'll be happier and find all of your relationships improving.

Bonus: Advanced Sexual Practices to Manifest a Magical Life

Once you begin to develop a new relationship with your body and erotic nature, then you can begin to actually leverage your sexual energy for even more powerful healing and manifestation practices, such as calling your soulmate and dream life. Below, I'll be outlining two that you can play with either now or later.

1. Rewiring negative beliefs through orgasmic energy

Your orgasm has immense healing power and vitality, and you can actually rewire your pain and beliefs using this energy. When you are self-pleasuring and reach heightened ecstasy, bliss or orgasm, then you can use this opportunity to say positive affirmations out loud, like, "I am magnificent! I am worthy! I deserve healthy love with a soulmate! I am a baller, kick-ass, sexy woman!" or anything else that you believe is hindering you.

2. Manifesting through Sex Magic

While self-pleasuring or having sex, breathe your orgasmic energy throughout your body, from head to toe. Then, imagine what you would like to have or create in your life. What is that divine vision that you hold sacred in your heart and body? Bring to mind your desired partnership, your home, a bank account with lots of money, a peaceful world... whatever it is that gets you excited and filled with euphoria! As I mentioned earlier, your womb is a magical, intelligent being of its own, and through its manifestation power, along with the power of your intention and being in a state of orgasmic pleasure, you can begin to conjure your world consciously.

As a woman, you hold the powerful key to love and intimacy, both within yourself and your partner. We women can heal the world through our ability to love and teach others to love. Our bodies were designed for pleasure, giving birth, emotional alchemy and love. This desire and pathway to love is both sacred and divine, and men yearn for this special connection to God through love with a female partner. This is not just about sex –it's about connection on every level.

Here's a secret: Most men *want* to pleasure and please women. This is what they desire most! What most women don't realize is that the biggest turn off for a man is when she doesn't know what she wants or desires. This is your chance to get to claim your relationship with your sexuality, Love Goddess.

Activating the Divine Feminine Within

What is being a woman to you? What are her traits, what does she look like, and what's her role in society? Our idea of the woman is largely shaped by the media and major icons in religion and society, or from the women we've known in our life. The woman is somehow supposed to be beautiful and accomplished, married and a wonderful mother, living a supremely manicured, perfect life.

Yet the reality is very different. The average woman is overworked, shuttling between different obligations, caring for her family or the people around her, and finds pleasure in the simple things like resting, talking to her girlfriends, yoga, working out, spa time and travel. She lives in a boxed world, with an identity shaped by society around her. Does she feel feminine in this role? Due to the constant shame, guilt and overwhelm of balancing so many taxing obligations, many women are having health issues and nervous breakdowns in their forties, if not earlier!

As a modern woman, you get to define what it means to be feminine – to you. When you're connected to your true source of womanhood, you access a deeply forgotten spiritual, regenerative power that is meant to flow through the woman's body, *and also specifically your body,* **that has been shut off.**

In Hinduism, there is the concept of the god and goddess, Shiva and Shakti. While Shiva lives in the crown of the head, and embodies the realm of thought and consciousness, Shakti is pure primal, creative, manifestation energy that lies in the bottom of the body. Without enlightenment, Shiva and Shakti are separated, and they each live in their own wounded realms. Think about how disembodied we are as humans as we live in our heads, trying to navigate life from external sources of information? How we need others' advice and approval to propel us forward, without tapping into a life force within ourselves?

In the journey of awakening, when the blocks in the energetic centers in the body (known as *chakras*) are cleared, the Shakti energy can rise up the spine, finally reaching up to Shiva in divine union. There is bliss in this state, and even an ambrosia-like nectar that can emanate, and awaken the pineal gland, creating absolute ecstasy in the body. The masculine and feminine engage in an eternal dance, creating joy and vitality. *This kind of union is possible between a man and woman, but first, each must find this sacred bond within themselves.*

Many of us have been living in a wounded feminine state for so long that we've forgotten how to *truly* feel and be feminine. Our energies remain stuck in the lower realms within our body, caught up in low self-esteem, shame and impoverished perceptions of being a woman. When we're in our divine feminine, we can create chemistry within ourselves and others, and become irresistible to strong, grounded, masculine men. We feel whole, energetic and unbelievably sexy! (In the next chapter, I'll be talking more about *sexual polarity,* and how to create that magical, dynamic tension and pull between the masculine and feminine, which is the secret to creating chemistry.)

Through the work in this book, you've already been clearing your inner blocks, and your feminine energy has been rising. **But the true power lays in you claiming what femininity and womanhood looks and feels like for you, unapologetically.**

Five Feminine Archetypes

One of my favorite ways of understanding the woman is through the study of different archetypes. Psychologist Carl Jung used them for understanding human behavior and what drives our ego and soul. In order to understand the different aspects of woman, and her different strengths and shadows, I'm going to share a framework.

In this framework, which is adapted from Sheila Foster's work on the sacred feminine, I'm sharing six archetypes – the Mother, the Warrior, the Wise Woman, the Lover and finally the Queen. *There are countless other archetypes, but I'll be focusing on these for the purposes of this book.*

Through breaking down each of these types, we can explore their essence as well as the light and shadow aspects. It gives us a chance to explore and understand each of these, owning them with a sense of curiosity and discovery and releasing any shame or sabotage patterns related to each.

1. The Mother is perhaps the most well-known archetype and is revered in many religions and pagan cultures as the ultimate creator of life. She bestows her children and those around her with love and nurturing. Her role lends her to a certain vulnerability as she focuses on taking care of her family's well-being. In some cultures, she's seen as the leader of her family, the matriarch. Sometimes, this archetype is seen as virginal and holy, and at other times, she's seen as the ultimate divine protector driven by her fierce love for her children.

In the light, the Mother is kind, intelligent, devoted and compassionate. She receives with grace and bestows her goodwill and unconditional love on others. She's responsible, caring and nurturing, and open to different perspectives. The Mother's always in service, helping others live in their potential. She seeks to alleviate peoples' problems through her prayers, compassion, understanding and wisdom. She's brimming with patience, tolerance and forgiveness.

In the shadow aspect, the Mother is a martyr, is prone to conditional ways of loving which hurt her children, struggles with low self-esteem and even self-contempt. She's constantly taking care of others to the point of denying her own needs – abandoning and betraying herself. She's critical of her children and her husband. She is beset with overwhelm, guilty and contempt. She mothers the men in her life and can become overbearing and expectant in her love.

In this book, we cover the Mother Wound, and the idea of mothering ourselves. In what ways do you see this archetype in yourself, in both the light and shadow aspects?

2. The Lover is intoxicated with life and an explorer of all things – relationships, men, nature, art, culture and life itself. She's connected with her sexual nature and has a joyful innocence about her. She fills herself and others with her abundant life force and knows the art of connection. The lover is a sexual priestess, healing through intimacy and the body.

Unfortunately, the Lover's been given a bad rep. In ancient times, she was a courtesan and sometimes chosen to be the consort of Kings and noblemen. Women who were married often felt jealous of her stealing their husband's hearts and enjoying freedoms that they didn't have.

In her light, she brings joy, discovery and pleasure into her life and isn't afraid to be sexually expressed. She's sensual, wild and has plenty of *joie de vivre* to boot. She's the master of relationships and connection and awakens the fire of desire for those around her. She's confident, bold and beautiful. She honors and respects herself and sees her body as a temple. She's the ultimate teacher in self-love and how to love others in a healthy way. She has different names in various cultures as a Goddess – Isis in Egypt, Aphrodite in Greece.

In her shadow aspect, the Lover is prone to co-dependency and losing herself in relationships, to the point of submission. She's a master manipulator and can use the power of sex and seduction to get what she needs. She's jealous of others' success and beauty and feels powerless and insecure in her relationships. She is placed on the opposite of the Mother, as the two are seen as in conflict, such as the Madonna/Whore complex.

In the previous section, you've been exploring your sexuality. What role has this archetype played in your life, and what ways does it feel hidden or alive in you?

3. The Wise Woman is a prophet, grandmother, who has seen and experienced life. She is deeply connected to the underworld and the heavens. She's spiritual, mystical and intuitive, and is always seeking truth. She is a medicine woman, a shaman, bringing healing to her community, and she's talented in esoteric and ancient arts. She is a teacher and way-shower and draws on ancient customs. She's the wisdom keeper of her community and people turn to her in times of distress for guidance and council.

In our culture, she's sometimes seen as an old hag or crone, which is seen as denigrating. The Salem Witch Trials heavily persecuted women, on the basis of their intuitiveness and psychic abilities.

In her light, the Wise Woman is intuitive, grounded, spiritual and wise. She brings enlightenment and awareness to the world around her. She's supremely humble. Each of her words and actions are sacred and thoughtful. She's always learning and seeking for deeper truths.

In the shadow aspect, she's prone to wrong perceptions, fundamentalism, and hiding behind her ego. She has the power of casting spells, and curses either consciously or unconsciously through her negative thinking and jealousy. She can be self-righteous. On the flipside, she may be in denial of her Wise Woman side and shunning it in order to seek safety and approval from society, bringing other women down.

Is the Wise Woman alive in you? In what ways have you supported her shining, or hidden this side of yourself? What qualities do you resonate with?

4. The Warrior is a strategic fighter; she's a goal-driven, mission-oriented woman who gets what she sets out for. She is an architect, builder and is known for her strength and aptitude for creating structures. She is the opposite of the Wise Woman, as they are both dichotomous energies – the Wise Woman is still and introspective, while the Warrior is out in the world, in pursuit of worldly endeavors.

Most of us are in touch with this archetype as we're in a go-getter culture, especially when it comes to our education and careers. In a sense, we are taught to train and hunt for opportunities, money and even men.

In the light, the Warrior is strong, courageous, committed to contributing to her society at large. She is driven by her fierce love to bring justice and order and has a strong sense of self. She knows that she is of value and that her work is needed in the world. She fights only when needed and knows the value of surrender and grace. She's the peaceful, spiritual warrior that knows the ultimate battle is a spiritual one.

In her shadow, the Warrior is always in battle and is in high defense. She ploughs through difficult terrains with relentlessness, exhausting herself and the people around her. She's angry, defensive and on a mission, and her ego's in charge.

In what ways do you relate to the Warrior? What strengths and short-comings do you see in yourself when you're playing this role? How has this affected your love life?

5. The Queen is the integration of all of the above archetypes, in the highest form. She has the wisdom and compassion of a mother, the open heart and sensuality of a lover, the spiritual and intuitive ability of a wise woman and the courage and determination of the Warrior.

The Queen is venerated and exalted by both men and women for her ability to bring divinity in the human form. She is a complete woman who has gone through various life experiences and continues to integrate her past and shadow aspects so that she can be the best version of herself. She's adored and respected by her family and community. Through her own example, she inspires others to rise in their own love and consciousness. The Queen has balanced feminine and masculine energies and knows how to play in each of these polarities, depending on the circumstances. She's magnanimous, generous and lives an abundant life, on her own terms. She's sovereign and is a creator of her destiny.

In her light, she is humble and responsible in how she conducts herself and is concerned for the greater good. She has all the positive traits from all four archetypes.

In her shadow, she can be vain, proud and selfish. She's aware of her power and uses it for her personal gain. In addition, she has all the shadow traits from the Lover, Warrior, Mother and Wise Woman.

Do you recognize this archetype in your life, and at what times does she show up? Who are some people whom you think resemble the Queen archetype for you? What are your aspirations?

The journey of love awakening has allowed me to integrate each of the archetypes in me. I've spent a lot of time exploring each one, and it's been a delicious, exciting journey to discover and water the seeds for each. I'm now really proud and thankful for my life's experiences and who I was in each of them, which gave me plenty of opportunities to learn and heal, so I can become the woman that I am today. I've loved relishing each of my stories, even the heartbreaks, failures and drama, celebrating my insights and how far I've come as a woman. Although I started off feeling like a princess that needed to be saved by her prince, I now feel confident as a Queen to my King, to my children and my community, and adore my different sides.

This path of feminine awakening is a lifelong one, and each moment of time, you get to visit your archetypes in their light and shadow, which may sometimes bring you down to your knees or elevate you. This is the heroine's journey, which ultimately leads to the princess within you that needs to be "saved" and united with – *by you.*

Your partner will be excited to be a with a woman who engages in this inquiry honestly and vulnerably. You'll likely attract a man who's doing the same!

EXERCISE

Journal about each of the archetypes. What specific experiences can you remember that helped you embody each archetype? What insights did you gather? What tendencies are you ready to release, and which traits do you want to grow? What are you proud of?

Take one day per archetype, so you can relive it, play with it, even consider role playing!

Just know that by going through this book, you are healing and integrating all these archetypes. *How cool is that, right?* That is the power of the journey of love – it is all encompassing; the perfect heroine's journey.

Honoring the Different Seasons of Womanhood

Sometimes, you might just need to focus on one archetype for a time in your life, letting go of others. For instance, you might find your Warrior archetype getting in the way of your love life or motherhood. It's ok to let it go into the backburner, as you channel a single one predominantly, maybe for a couple of days, months or even years. At the end of the day, all of these are different aspects of the Queen, who goes through different seasons in her life. For me, I've found that I was predominantly a Warrior in my twenties, a Wise Woman and Lover in my thirties, a Mother in my forties, and am finally feeling like I'm stepping into my Queen. Of course, I'm always watering the seeds of my other archetypes especially as I'm playing different roles. I also revert into the shadows of the different archetypes and have additional healing to do.

The journey of womanhood is like a spiral. For each woman, her path is unique and magnificent, no matter what archetype she is called to embody in that moment.

Healing the Sister Wound

Do you struggle with comparing yourself or feeling triggered or jealous by certain women? Have you been hurt badly by your mother, sister, or a girlfriend in the past? Given that so many women struggle with different wounds, it's natural that we hurt each other in unconscious ways, because of our superiority and inferiority complexes with each other, and painful mothering patterns.

Sure, there are always going to be people that trigger you, but when you heal your Sister Wound – your wounds with other women – you begin to feel more secure, accepting and confident within yourself.

Every other girl or woman is a manifestation of you – and whatever they're struggling with, on an unconscious level, you may be too.

Take time to nurture your relationships with other women and join a women's circle or two. Be as loving, affirming and supportive of others, and of course practice healthy boundary setting and letting people go who don't serve. If you have women who are close to you that have hurt you, you can practice forgiveness or even have a compassionate, honest conversation.

A note on jealousy and envy: When you notice jealousy arise, breathe, love yourself, and bless the person who has what you yearn for. **Jealousy is a natural indicator for what you deeply desire.** When you notice it, rather than feeling ashamed, which is our normal tendency, just breathe and acknowledge the envy – and smile! As women, we've been conditioned to believe that there is a lack of good men (and general abundance), and that somehow, we're not worthy. There is a plethora of love and abundance waiting for you to be had. Blessing and appreciating what others have aligns you energetically with experiencing what they have.

Aligning with Your Purpose & Igniting Your Passion

One of the sexiest qualities of a woman is when she's self-expressed in her genius and flowing with a sense of purpose in her world. A woman with purpose is like honey, attracting bees all around her. She imbues a creative energy, a sense of "I don't care what anyone thinks" and, trust me, she's having fun with life!

When you're driven by a sense of purpose and service and deep self-knowing of both your gifts and sabotage patterns, you'll feel aligned with your higher self and your soul. We're most authentic and abundant when we're contributing our gifts to a greater cause. The sexual *chakra* comes alive when your creative energy is being channeled, which is sexy and alluring to men.

Imagine how you would feel to be so good at something or contributing to the world in some meaningful way, or spending time in learning and discovery about skills that you never knew you had?

Unfortunately, so many women are disconnected from their inner beauty and creative gifts. This is a natural byproduct of living in a world that is materialistic and has been pushing women into narratives that are palatable to the average mind. This leads to so many emotional blocks for women and can even show up as addiction or disease. Brené Brown says, *"Unused creativity is not benign. It metastasizes into grief, rage, judgement, sorrow and shame."*

The truth is that you have many hidden gifts that were born with but can only begin to be revealed once you've released your inhibitions and old, wounded conditioning, and you start aligning with your authentic life path. This is because you've been taught to think and behave in a way that society tells you is safe and where you'll feel like you belong.

Purpose isn't about doing something special or exceptional – it's about living a life that's service-oriented, pleasure-filled and meaningful to *you*. Everything that you do is contributing to your state of being awake, present and deliciously alive.

Often times, our gifts come in the simplest of ways. Regularly serving at a soup kitchen at a local shelter, offering to care for your sister's children or spending your free time doodling funny caricatures or gardening are all ways in which you can tap into your gifts. While beginning to flow into your sense of creativity and passion, you can also go deeper and discover what really turns you on, and what your soul's unique life path and gifts are. For instance, maybe you're meant to be a teacher or healer, or a yoga teacher. Or something off the beaten path like a tree-whisperer or an amazing dessert chef, or your thing is that you are amazing at connecting people. In this complex fabric of life, we're each a unique thread and bring our own exciting color and texture into this phenomenal creation.

Amy, a corporate marketing executive, discovered that her "thing" is her own recovery from alcohol abuse and her calling to help others in recovery and leading empowered lives. It took her a long time to finally accept that healing alcoholism was an important value for her, especially on her dates with men where she would simply avoid drinking. Yet when Amy started sharing her dreams and values and aligning her life accordingly, a man she was dating fell in love with her and became her greatest champion.

The question is, how do you align with your soul's unique path, and how do you begin to start leading a life that sets your heart free, lifting yourself and everyone around you through your untamed spirit and quest for authenticity? Below, I'll share a couple of pointers and exercises that will get you on your path. This is an exciting, intriguing journey, so don't worry about getting it right – be like a kid, having fun exploring!

[Reminder: It's easy for women to get stuck on this part of the process, as finding one's gifts and 'turn on' is intriguing and exciting – and could potentially take years. For now, simply do the exercises, identify a single inspiring action continue to explore during your dating journey, and move on with the rest of the book.]

Discovering Your Life Path

As I shared above, each of us has a unique personality, purpose and frequency, and a life purpose and path that we're on. We also have specific personal struggles, sabotage patterns that we're here to learn and heal, and our very own gifts and talents.

There are many books dedicated to life purpose, several of which I've shared in the Resources section. Astrology is a very powerful way of understanding your energetic blueprint, your personality traits and your various life stages, beginning from the moment you were born. Getting a reading with a western or eastern astrologer is highly illuminating, and while you're at it, you can also consider Tarot reading, a numerology assessment, a psychic reading or an Akashic Records reading that will help reveal your gifts and purpose. Lastly, transformational coaching and personal development programs are wonderful at helping you break through your sabotage patterns and begin to live a more authentic, powerful life.

There are, of course, many resources out there; the key is to tune into your heart and ask the universe to guide you in finding your life path and purpose.

EXERCISES TO HELP DISCOVER YOUR PURPOSE

1. EXERCISE: FIND YOUR DOMINANT ENERGY CENTER(S)

We are born with natural gifts and qualities, and these are aligned with specific energy centers or *chakras* (see chart below). When you begin to utilize your gifts, especially those with your **dominant energy center(s)**, you feel more energized and alive – more *turned on!* Most people have one dominant energy center, and some have two (and possibly three).

In the table below, identify one or two energy centers that you most resonate with. Your purpose may be linked. (Hint: it may not be something that you've picked up through work, etc., as those may be compensating/learned behaviors rather than truly connected with your innate gift).

Chakra/Energy Center	Qualities	Sample activities
1. Root chakra	Connection to earth, rootedness, earthiness, related to stability and safety	Gardening, nurturing, cooking and baking, caregiving, etc.
2. Sacral chakra	Emotional expression, sexuality, creativity	Inventing, art, writing, and anything else that's creative, entrepreneurship
3. Solar Plexus	Will power, strength, determination, control	Leadership, organization, business, athletics
4. Heart chakra	Unconditional love, connection, empathy	Relationship, healing, caregiving, counseling, mentoring
5. Throat chakra	Communication, expression	Music, speaking, teaching, self-expression, activism
6. Third eye	Psychic, visionary, Intuitive	Advisor, leader, visionary, psychic
7. Crown chakra	Spiritual, connected to higher realms	Spiritual teacher, seeker, guru

2. EXERCISE: JOURNALING ON YOUR HIDDEN PASSIONS

What hidden desires/passions have you been suppressing, and what is a small way you can start exploring it in your life starting today? Here are some seed questions for reflection:

- *Who do you feel jealous of?*

- *Connect with your inner child. What were you good at as a child? What would your eight-year-old version of you say to you now, and what did she enjoy doing?*

- *If you had a million dollars in your bank account and unlimited time, how would you be spending your time?*

- *Ask your mom (or someone who knew you as a child): What were you good at as a child? What were your favorite activities?*

- *Ask your friends for the top three skills or talents that they think come effortlessly for you (be prepared for a completely different response than what you've thought of for yourself). Sometimes the things that come effortlessly for you are the very things you take for granted for yourself – and yet, when you're doing these things, you're living in your essence.*

3. SERVICE: A POWERFUL PATHWAY TO LIVING WITH PURPOSE

"The best way to find yourself is to lose yourself
in the service of others." ~ Mahatma Gandhi

Service of any kind allows you to heal your heart and transcend your life's hurdles and limitations. Service also has the added benefit of boosting your self-esteem and making you feel connected to others and something greater. You end up meeting people who are at a similar wavelength – and who knows, you might even encounter a wonderful man! I've personally had almost all my opportunities (including meeting my husband) arise through my spiritual and service communities.

Whether you are extremely busy in your career, or have lots of spare time, it's the perfect moment to start taking steps in leading a more purposeful, intentional life. This can be in conjunction with your love life, wherein you begin taking baby steps in the direction you want to go. This is a lifelong journey, and it begins by a small act, starting today – even if it is to do a random act of kindness, joining a faith-based volunteer activity or taking a painting class.

STEP 4: PREPARE FOR LASTING LOVE

As a professor in a university in New York City, Maria had just met a wonderful man online which she had successfully done after stepping into her magnetic feminine power. He was kind, reliable and emotionally available – different from her ex.

After a few months of the honeymoon period of dating, she noticed there was something about the relationship that made her feel disconnected, shut down and afraid of commitment. She was reaching an impasse in her relationship and her doubts began to weigh in on her whether he was "the one." Every small thing he did was starting to irritate her, and she became busy and distant, which began to frustrate him. She began testing him by making him jump through hoops to prove his love for her.

Noticing this pattern, Maria asked for a break and began to delve deeper into herself. She intuitively felt that her relationship foundation was weak and that she needed to first build it before potentially sabotaging her relationship even further.

During our coaching work together, Maria began to understand the source of her problems. She discovered that because her parents' marriage was so tumultuous and her mother was largely disempowered, she struggled with faith that a marriage could really work. She lacked trust in herself, didn't know what she truly wanted for her life and regularly sought approval from others about major life decisions. She also felt unable to communicate her true feelings, and during disagreements, she would either shut down, boil up with resentment or become submissive.

Maria was in all worlds an independent woman, and she knew she would be fine being single; yet she wanted more! Maria desired a companionship in which there was deep respect, love and intimacy between the two. She realized that she needed to prepare for the kind of love that she wanted in her life, much like how she had paved her path for getting tenured as a professor – with exceptional diligence and care.

Maria began to clear her schedule for love. She got rid of memorabilia and gifts from exes and anything else that didn't resonate and made her home into a beautiful love nest. She released any vows that were keeping her single and focused on learning healthy communication and relationship skills. She strove to understand her own psychology and that of men and creating healthy sexual tension. Maria began to rewire her lack of trust in men into one of curiosity, openness and respect.

As Maria became more intentional about creating her Love Garden and stepping into her "Wow! Factor", she began to feel confident that her sabotage patterns wouldn't block her anymore. She felt ready to invite this partnership into her life from a place of resilience and love, rather than fear and self-doubt. She created a manifestation prayer for what she wanted in her life and stepped into creating a life that turned her on – a life of vision, purpose and fulfilling partnership. She knew now that she was "in it to win it" in her relationship, and so was he. Now they are married, living near a beach in California, working on passion projects – their latest being a baby girl!

EXERCISE

Do this meditation: *Imagine yourself five years from now. Who are you with, what are you doing? How does your day look? What is your partner saying to you, how is he looking at you? What are you two doing together? Where do you live? Do you have children? If so, how would you describe them? How would your friends describe you? How would your partner describe you? What do your children love about you? What is your relationship like with yourself? What kind of home do you have?*

The way to manifest a great, fulfilling relationship is by **Cultivating the Conditions for Love to Manifest in your life.**

You are at a ripe, potent juncture in your life. You've let go of much of your conditioning and heaviness. Like a painter, you are free to draw broad, bold brushstrokes on a blank canvas, creating an illustration that moves your soul.

You're about to call in your ideal match and manifest the life of your dreams through the power of your intention. Maybe you have even discovered that being single isn't as terrible as it's made out to be! In fact, it's given you the opportunity to love and heal yourself and discover what truly makes you tick. Moreover, you get to define the kind of relationship you want, without compromise.

You have already done the most important work of creating a strong foundation within you – by learning to love and reparent yourself, release your old wounds and limiting beliefs that are no longer serving you, and stepping into being a Love Goddess, a Queen.

Now, you're ready to set the stage for the next phase – of **consciously calling in healthy, juicy love with your King.** You're doing it in the feminine way of creating your nest and calling in your mate, so you can nestle in together, make ecstatic love and face life's exciting adventures and challenges together from a place of resilience and strength.

> "There is a candle in your heart, ready to be kindled.
> There is a void in your heart, ready to be filled.
> You feel it, don't you?
> You feel the separation from the Beloved.
> Invite him to fill you up, embrace the fire.
> Remind you that tell you otherwise that
> Love comes to you of its own accord,
> And the yearning for it cannot be learned in any school".
> ~ Rumi

If you are longing for a partnership, you're in the right place! Honoring yourself for this yearning is important – there is nothing wrong with you for having a desire for partnership and intimacy. Rather, this is an enlightened, self-aware desire coming from a place of self-love – and it means that your heart is open to exploring intimacy and partnership.

Yearning is a holy feeling, filled with love, and is deeply feminine. When you yearn, you are consciously opening up, asking, and receiving, without any attachment to the outcome. **There's no shame in longing for deeper connection with men and for being with your soulmate – honor it and know that it's one of your superpowers!**

If you're like how I was after my Love Recovery, in that I was happy being single and felt reluctant to get back to dating and even questioning why be in a relationship in the first place, then you're also in the right place. If this is so, I would urge you to continue this path. Sometimes the greatest things in life are the very things we're afraid of or skeptical of! These are just your defense mechanisms acting up.

Relationships are meant for healing. An intimate relationship with your soulmate holds the most potentiality for profound alchemy and experiencing unconditional love. There is a reason why love is considered the holy grail in one's life. It's not just for safety and security that we seek our soulmates – it's for experiencing transcendence. Your partnership will elevate your state of consciousness and magnify the love in your heart, a million-fold. He will break down your barriers in your heart till he merges with you, and you will hold him in love and safety, allowing him to be his full, unabashed self. You will learn to conceive your reality together, through an eternal dance of Shiva and Shakti. In this process, you will evolve into a loving, beautiful creature that you couldn't have even imagined, and new powers and desires will be unlocked in you. Through the power of the union of healthy masculine and feminine, you get to experience heaven on earth together.

In this chapter, you will begin to consciously invite love into your life. You will learn Feng Shui principles for setting up your life to *energetically draw in love*, naturally, while clearing out any remaining obstacles. You will become crystal clear about your values and what you stand for, and what type of meaningful life you envision and want to create. Moreover, you'll find yourself upgrading your love consciousness so that you really know how to manifest a rock-solid relationship with a sexy, masculine man, and keep your relationship alive through sexual tension.

Feng Shui Principles for Calling in Love

> A friend told me a story. He had a client who was looking to meet a wonderful man to settle down with. Yet, when he went to her home, he noticed that her closets and drawers were full, her bathroom was filled with products and personal items, and her home felt cluttered. Her bedroom was busy with electronics, books and a TV. She had a two-car garage, yet both the spots were taken. Quite literally, there was no space in her home for a man, nor was it inviting. He gave her this feedback, and she realized her folly. She got rid of everything that no longer served her, made her home a haven and miraculously, soon enough, a man entered her life!

Do you wonder whether your home and lifestyle are **attracting** or **repelling** lasting love? Maybe you haven't even considered it.

For many people, being busy with work, having a full social calendar and living in a cluttered home is normal.

Yet, if you want new opportunities and relationship possibilities, and in general, love, beauty and abundance to flow into your life ... then you've got to make space for it. I call it the Feng Shui principles of love. Everything in our life is energy, and if you want to generate directional flow, then you have to create an opening for that energy to flow to. This occurs on many levels, including the mental, physical, emotional and spiritual.

As you can see, you've done much clearing work till now, simply through your intentions and the exercises. You can be assured that you've taken all the right steps in clearing space for the right kind of love.

Now, it's about inviting this kind of love into your life through your vibration and intentionality. This is how synchronicity and abundance work.

So, how can you start attracting love through your home (and lifestyle)?

1. Declutter your home and turn it into a haven.

The truth is everything in your home – including every book – has vibrational quality. The colors, the words, even the intention behind each item, determines the vibration of your home. This lower vibration could not only be draining you, but also be sending mixed signals to the universe about who you are, and what you are manifesting.

It's time to get rid of the old! I use a rule "If I haven't used it in 6 months – out it goes" (of course, make exceptions for seasonal items). If you have items from exes, books you've already read, papers, old decorations that don't give you joy, lifeless kitchen items… donate them. It's better to have less than more. Marie Kondo (author of The *Life-Changing Magic of Tidying Up*) has a relatively simple principle. If the item no longer gives you joy, throw it out. Go room by room. Dedicate a few months to this process if it feels overwhelming. Get rid of furniture items you don't use – even items you somewhat like but feel guilty about throwing out.

Decluttering can be an emotionally intense process. There are many items that are sentimental or give you a sense of identity or security. Sometimes looking at old items may bring up memories or emotions, so if you need support in this process, seek it out.

Your home is the physical manifestation of your mind. The process of letting go of a lot of your old items will quite literally open up space in your mind and heart.

Air your place out:

Open your windows and simply enjoy the open space. There's something magical about nothingness. You can chant some prayers or mantras and light some sage. Bring a healer or shaman home to clear the space.

Host a "goddess circle" to ritualize this phase of your life and sanctify your space. You are beginning anew!

Decorate to your heart's content:

Start finding items that resonate with your soul and decorate or refurnish. Make your home your *love haven* – your pride and joy. A place you want to spend time in, which energizes and rejuvenates you.

To bring in the vibration of love, place rose quartz crystals and pictures of love, couples, nature or anything else that inspires that feeling. Establish a meditation corner or a place for your love rituals and an altar. Play music in the house that's angelic, spiritual, beautiful and romantic.

Make your home delightful to the five senses. Sensuality is key. Buy artwork that inspires you. Decorate with warm or bright colors, candles, books, carpets, plants, a comfortable bed and a kitchen that you enjoy using with beautiful dishware. Make sure *you're* turned on by your home. Be outlandish and wild – you can always redecorate!

Turn your bedroom into one of love, romance and rest. Take out any electronics or excessive books, and instead make it sensual – a perfect place for making love. Get a new duvet and beautiful pillow covers, clear off your dressing table and bedside tables. Put flowers and a candle near your bed. Get a diffuser so you can have healing essential oils like lavender and eucalyptus infusing your lungs at night. Create a little pleasure chest for yourself, with lingerie, self-pleasuring toys, romantic books. **If you work from home, then set up a separate desk** outside of your bedroom and try to set a healthy boundary between work and romance, which is important for your psyche.

Invite friends over for dinner:

As modern women, we become accustomed to meeting friends for drinks/dinner or entertainment. Make your home a place of community, sharing and love. Well-wishing friends bring positive energy into your home – and cooking for others creates a virtuous cycle of sharing, gifting and fulfillment.

2. Wear clothes that bring out your "Wow! Factor":

Donate clothes that are no longer "you." We have this idea that we need to look grown up and serious, and sometimes even masculine. Wear clothes that turn you on, that make you feel feminine, free and powerful. Colors have certain vibrations; for instance, red and pink connect one with love and sexiness, while yellow and gold with joy, and purple resonates with royalty, transformation and sensuality.

Notice where you have blocks around your clothing due to your body image or not wanting to be visible. Those are important to address and heal gently. In fact, I would encourage you to get clothes that accentuate or reveal your breasts, hips, shoulders, legs or any other body part of yours that you are proud of and bring out your sexy siren! There's nothing to be ashamed of, and you being in your feminine is a tremendous boon to the world.

3. Create space in your life for love:

If you have a busy schedule between work and your social life, or are entangled with family obligations, then you need to begin to place strong boundaries, and carve out space for love.

Love doesn't just happen on weeknights or weekends ... rather, love is an intention, and requires plenty of air and space. Luckily, while doing this book, you've been carving that space out.

If you are busy, that's understandable, yet you need to prioritize the space for love and say no to extra work obligations or dinners that no longer resonate. You may even have to put other things on hold, like starting a business or seeking a promotion.

You must create a large, open space in your life, heart and mind for love. During your spare time, instead of filling it, focus on relaxation, taking time for pleasure and cultivating your love practices.

When you're out and about, smile and talk to people. Don't wear earphones, and instead be present to what's going on around you. Smile at the cute guy at the coffee shop. Be approachable and inviting to love, in all its wondrous shapes and forms!

Establish Your Queendom

"If you build it, he will come" ~ From the movie Field of Dreams

Sometime around now, you may be wondering, "Wow, what comes next? What do I want? Who do I want to be with, and where do I want to live?" Whether or not you have these questions, now is the perfect time to take a step back, recalibrate, and begin to consciously articulate your vision.

Your thoughts, words and creative feminine energy can begin to conjure this life for you. *It sounds like magic, right?* When you're clear about what you desire, you attract a partnership and opportunities that align with your authentic self. Plus, men are wildly attracted to women who are connected to their deep knowing, are grounded in their vision for life and feel turned on!

In this section, you will begin to articulate your dreams and desires, and declare them to the universe, once and for all.

Your Values – The Sexiest Thing About You

Ellie was falling in love with Dan and wondering if he was "the one." She had never felt this way before about any man, because all her past relationships had been painful. Due to her mistrust, she began testing him. Realizing that this could be a sabotage pattern and that the relationship was potentially going off a cliff, she decided to take a step back and reflect on what her values were. She identified growth, integrity, and kindness as her top three. She then asked herself, "Do I embody these when I'm around him? Does he support me in living these values? Does Dan have these qualities too?" To her surprise, she found the answer to be "Yes!" for all three, and deeply contemplated each, realizing how much she truly loved Dan and their relationship. Reflecting on her past relationships, she always had trouble maintaining these values, and she noticed that she would feel tested rather than supported in these values. She decided that she would move past her resistance, give this relationship an honest chance and take a true leap of faith.

In mountaineering, when you're in a precarious situation like falling down a cliff, you place your climbing stick into the ground, and courageously lean into it and surrender.

Values are the same – they are your inner compass, your guiding light through life's ups and downs, and it's how you consciously create a life that's meaningful and fulfilling to you. When you're clear on your values, you begin to live more authentically and make courageous decisions in alignment with them.

For instance, if you value discovery over security, then you may choose not to have a typical 9-5, steady-income job, and instead align with a career that allows you to do research or spiritual inquiry. Likewise, if you value family and community, then you make choices to fuel that intention which may require letting go of certain things like a promotion. If you value compassion and communication, then you may choose to have difficult, vulnerable conversations with your loved ones even if it feels uncomfortable.

This is not about not having it all. Rather, it's about becoming truly self-aware about what's important to you and what you're willing to give up or let go of. It's also about who you truly are when times get tough. It's the most helpful tool to have when making important life decisions, and it supports you in living in integrity and honesty. When you're aligned with your values, you feel happy.

When you're unconscious about your values, you fall into people pleasing, approval seeking and following herd mentality, even when it comes to dating and finding a relationship. You follow a path that's been laid out by your parents and the culture you're in. This path is not heart-centered or soul-inspired… and it can feel mechanical – and may lead to depression later on.

As you're entering this new stage of intentionally creating your life, I invite you to find out your top three values. *Note: Values can change over time as you enter different life stages, so feel free to revisit them whenever you're feeling unbalanced or needing clarity.*

EXERCISE: DEFINING MY VALUES

1. Journal on the following. Use the Needs Inventory from the Center for Nonviolent Communication for reference.

- *Name an incident in your life that you're most proud of, preferably in your personal life. What makes you proud about it? Identify needs that were met.*

- *Identify a time when you were most fulfilled and satisfied. How did this experience give you meaning? What needs or desires were fulfilled?*

- *Think about a time in your life you were angry. What needs or desires weren't being fulfilled? How does it show what you truly believe in – what you may even be willing to die for?*

2. Determine your top values, based on the journaling above. Use the Needs Inventory to identify your top ten values. Then, begin to whittle them down to three if you can! Use a dictionary to understand the meanings behind the words, as sometimes it's hard to find the exact word that resonates. Also, a value can encompass many other values. For instance, maybe one of your values is love, and underlying it are other values like empathy, compassion and communication that help you to adhere to the value of love.

My Top 3 Values
1.
2.
3.

How does it feel to know what your values are? Where do you think it may be useful?

EXERCISE: DEFINING MY DESIRED NEEDS IN A RELATIONSHIP

Sometimes when we think of being in a relationship, it makes us feel all warm and fuzzy. Yet, there are some really tangible needs that are likely important for you, especially given your own needs and childhood experiences, or your recent discoveries of your values and what you cherish.

Take a look at the NVC Needs Inventory and identify top five needs that are important to you in a relationship. Is it adventure, security, safety, intimacy, communication, compassion or growth? Of course, a relationship may fulfill more than these five, but knowing what is important to you will help you build your relationship accordingly.

My Top 5 needs in a relationship

1.

2.

3.

4.

5.

Declare Your Intentions to the Universe

One of the most powerful things you can do is to write down what you want to manifest in your life. Your life is a creative endeavor, and through the power of your word you can begin to write the story of your life, envisioning what you desire. Your subconscious mind, when moved by this vision, begins to draw in this reality to you and filters in those affirming experiences.

EXERCISE: CREATING YOUR MANIFESTATION PRAYER

The way to do this is by writing your Manifestation Prayer, a story about what you desire to create in your life. To make your manifestation prayer as juicy and magic-infused as possible, here are a couple of pointers:

- Write it as though it is already flowing into your life. Don't write it from a place of lack or "I want." Rather, *know* that it is already yours, as you write it.

- Take out anything that's egoic, like specific jobs, type of man, locations, amount of money. Rather, write about what needs of yours are being fulfilled, and how you *feel*. Feelings are an important part of this. Also include traits that are important, and activities you imagine doing.

- Remember to include the values that are important to you.

- When you're done, put one copy under your mattress.

- Have another copy on hand. You can recite your prayer every morning, followed by spending a few minutes visualizing it.

Know that your prayer is already happening and embody a feeling of gratitude and humility while receiving the grace that is flowing to you. If you feel a sense of yearning or longing, that's perfect and divine – honor that! Recognize that everything occurs in divine timing, and that the universe wants to support you in your happiness and your soul's evolution. Your vision may occur in a way that's different than how you thought it would, so it's important to let go of your attachments to outcomes. "Let go and let God," so they say. Declare your intentions to the universe, and simply surrender.

Bonus: If you're feeling courageous, share this vision (out loud) to up to five people. The more you share it, the more intensity is added to the manifestation power of your word.

Here's an example of a manifestation prayer. Make it your own! Take plenty of time, light a candle and play sensual or calming music while writing it out. You can even do an erotic dance before writing to infuse feminine energy. There's no way you can get this wrong, and you can always change or rewrite your prayer.

My life partner

I am manifesting into my life a partner with whom I can practice mindfulness and continue to evolve my consciousness and awareness. I feel cherished, safe and loved in his presence. He is authentic, can express his emotions openly, is mature, and has balanced male and female energies. He is handsome, attractive, romantic and glowing, and I feel joyful and content around him. Someone who's presence I can feel from far away. He is caring, generous, makes me laugh, is witty, strong, selfless, and is concerned about my well-being. We cook and clean together, take care of each other in beautiful ways. We practice equanimity, joy, peace, loving-kindness and compassion with each other. He is filled with love for himself and all other beings; and has trust in the universe.

My partner is patient and kind and shows me that it is possible to love truly, simply, and deeply with deep mutual trust and respect. We give each other confidence to grow and explore and to face challenges, whether big or small. We help each other stick to our values of compassion and joy and we help each other grow deeper and more confident in them. Our relationship is simple, playful, and deep. There is a contentment and simplicity to being together. Our sex life is strong and healthy, we bring each other pleasure that brings us closer and I feel exhilarated and curious. He helps me understand and feel why people say sex is a beautiful thing.

Likewise, you can add to the prayer by writing out the different aspects of your life, such as your career, your community, a project you're working on, your relationship with your family, etc.

EXERCISE: CREATING YOUR VISION BOARD

A vision board is a tool used to help clarify, concentrate and maintain focus on what you desire to create. Literally, a vision board is a board in which you display images that represent whatever you want to be, do or have in your life. The colors, visuals and the feelings that are evoked work well for the subconscious mind.

Make a vision board around what you want to create in your life. This is a great activity to do with your girlfriends. Get magazines, scissors, glue and a sturdy white poster board and find images and words of things you want to manifest in your life, including your romantic partnership, family, hobbies, career or wild dreams. Place pictures of where you want to travel and what kinds of experiences you want to have. Have fun, be sexy and creative! Remember, there is no wrong way to do this. Explain your vision to others when you're finished.

When you're done, you can place this board on your altar or near your desk. Looking at the board daily will program your subconscious mind to filter in and attract what you desire.

Invite the Masculine into Your Life

Ah men, how much we love them… and love to hate them! For all their shenanigans, they somehow find a special place in our hearts and we *yearn* to be with them. Our heart knows what's true – with men, we get to experience heart-fluttering romance, make ecstatic love, flirt, build a beautiful home, experience fabulous adventures, do business, have a family, and on a bigger picture, create a peaceful, thriving world together. Whether it's our father, brother, lover, work-spouse, the electrician or even the local bodega owner, the men in our lives make our life better and more fulfilling in their own ways. It's also fun and juicy being around men – they are strong, determined, intellectual, sexy, funny, loyal, protective, supportive … the list goes on. *In fact, I've found that most of my growth has happened through my relationships with men.*

Yet, what I've found is that so much of our lives as women is putting up defenses around men. For good reason – whether at home or at work, we've faced our fair share of challenges with them. We've experienced betrayal, hurt and intimidation from the very people we seek approval and acceptance from. Mansplaining, misogyny and double standards seem to be part of the norm in our society. We've also watched women in our own lives struggle with men, whether it's seeking independence at home, equality in the workplace or safety from some sort of abuse.

For this very reason, women have created roadblocks when it comes to inviting healthy love with men. We send energies of being independent and not needing a man and not trusting them. We easily go to fight or flight mode when we feel attacked, and feel defensive against being taken advantage of in some way.

Here's the irony of it all: *we're so afraid of being needy and insecure, that we end up being needy and insecure around men!*

Len Hew, the psychiatrist who brought the practice of Ho'opono-pono to the world, shared that the most prevalent "program" that he works on healing is the one of women's distrust of men. It's like a wild weed that keeps growing in our consciousness, that he spends all his free time clearing. The problem with this program is that it keeps men and women in a gridlock – women being untrusting of men, and men feeling mistrusted and ashamed, furthering the program through their unconscious dynamic.

Unfortunately, our fear and natural defensiveness gives rise to a whole host of unwholesome behavior that have become commonplace for women: emasculating men through criticism and judgment, being controlling or withholding love and appreciation. I'll be getting into ways women push men away in the next section, but just know that it takes two to tango … and that as women, we've played an equally painful role in our gender dynamics.

You might be on your best, most self-aware behavior when you're dating or starting a fabulous relationship, but trust me, the minute you get triggered or insecure, you will begin this unconscious downward spiral into darkness if you're not careful.

I say this with tremendous humility, because I see myself playing out emasculation patterns in my marriage *nearly every day* and I now know how many men I have put through hell. In fact, I see this as one of my primary areas of spiritual growth – releasing the barriers around my heart around my husband and other men in my life, and learning how to grow my love, respect and sense of interdependence with them.

While you may have needed this defensive shield in the past, it's time to lay down your arms, dear Love Goddess.

From this day forward, you can begin to truly believe in the inherent goodness of men (especially the higher vibrating ones you are attracting in your life!) and create positive dynamics that only increase your sense of fulfillment and well-being. You can be your most powerful, loving and authentic version of yourself, confidently attracting men into your life that love and respect you for who you are.

In this section, you are going to begin to learn to lay down your guard, release old "wounded feminine" barriers and consciously invite the masculine in your life.

EXERCISE

Close your eyes, drop your awareness into your body, and say, "I desire to open my heart to men, trust them, need them, but something is blocking me." Notice the sensations in your body. How does it feel? What physical sensations arise – a chest tightening, a rumble in your belly, or maybe just warmth and relaxation? Where do you feel denseness, resistance or blockages? What feelings, thoughts or stories arise? None of this is good or bad – it's just an understanding of where you may have blocks.

Journal on what you discovered.

Love Goddess, I desire for you to go into the dating world with an open mind and the belief system that most men are good, caring, loyal, and kind. Especially the ones that you will be attracting now!

So, what are some steps you could be taking begin to consciously bring down your barriers, and invite the masculine into your life? Below are some tools and exercises to support you.

EXERCISES: INVITE THE MASCULINE INTO YOUR LIFE

1. Journal: What do you love about men? What positive things have male relationships in the past (including that with your father, brother, exes, colleagues, etc.) provided you? Soak in, with a deep sense of gratitude, all these qualities that you have experienced with the men in your life.

2. Write a letter to your soulmate. In it, share how excited you are to meet him, what you will be doing together, how you will cherish your time together with him. Tell him about your prayers and dreams for the future. Begin to imagine and feel him in your life.

I once met a man who met his wife by beginning to speak with her and write her letters, even before she arrived in his life!

Remember, your partner is out there, and even if you aren't together physically, the first place of manifestation begins when you two connect in the spiritual realm. *It is through the ether that the mysterious process of manifestation begins, which then brings in the spiritual body, energetic body, emotional body, mental body and finally the physical body ... in that order.*

3. When you see men around you or passing by, begin to think, "I love you. I need you. I trust you." This is a perfectly safe practice which not only helps you face and heal your triggers, but also sends healing energy to men. This is a heart opening, spiritual practice. You can even practice Ho'oponopono with men, which is "I'm sorry, thank you, I love you, please forgive me," every time you feel triggered.

4. Begin to hang out with men, including your married friends, with whom you resonate with, in a friendly, openhearted way. Observe how you feel around these men. Let go of exes and other men that don't resonate anymore and may be energetically blocking you from inviting healthy masculine in your life.

5. Begin to have playful interactions with men around you – at work, the coffee shop, even your brother that you're normally serious with. Humor and play are transformative and are a big part of the manifestation process.

Secrets to Creating Sizzling Chemistry with Men

In Discover Your "Wow! Factor", you explored your own brand of sexuality and how to lead a turned on life. Now, how do you take that confident sensuality you hold and turn it into juicy chemistry with men?

In normal dating guidebooks, women are regularly taught how to flirt and get a guy's attention, how to pleasure a man in bed to keep, make men feel special and how to use the right verbal "script" in order to build connection. All of these are very helpful to know. However, through my experience, you cannot sustain a long-term relationship simply based on this.

Over the years, I've found two principles to be super helpful for creating chemistry with men, on top of simply being your magnificent, authentic, free-spirited self: Sexual Polarity and being a Communication Expert. These principles are based on the dynamic between masculine and feminine energies and what creates sexual tension, trust and intimacy between men and women.

Secret #1: Sexual Polarity

"The positive and negative poles of a battery create
electrical flow. The masculine and feminine poles between people
create a flow of sexual energy in motion." ~ David Deida

As you're stepping into your true feminine power, you now have access to a sacred principle that creates long-lasting attraction and chemistry between women and men – it's understanding the fundamentals of how sexual energies flow through us and generate a magnetic pull between partners.

Sadly, in our world the idea of being feminine and masculine is getting more and more diluted. Many women are taught to be in their masculine at work and school and fight hard to keep their feminine side alive while in their relationships or mothering. Men are taught to hide their emotions and pride themselves in their intellect, success and physical strength, elevating an alpha male archetype, while dimming down their own feminine side; yet regularly feel emasculated in their personal relationships. *I recognize these are broad generalizations and what's occurring is much more nuanced.*

Men and women are confused about their gender roles, while unconsciously playing out both wounded masculine and feminine sides. This leads to watered down sexuality and attraction, and couples get into a dissatisfied loop of being too busy for love, sexual displeasure, addictions and seeking for something outside their relationship to fulfill their unreachable itch. *Yet, a relationship has everything in it – an entire world – if a man and woman were to truly mine the richness of their essences.*

In order to understand what some of the traits for the masculine and feminine are, take a look at the below.

Core Masculine Traits	Core Feminine Traits
Sense of mission leading to freedom	The search for love and intimacy
Competitive	Compassionate
Living on the edge	Deep, radiant beauty
Analytical	Emotional
Growth from challenge	Growth from support and praise
Definitive and decisive	Ambiguous and unpredictable
Goal-driven	Intention-driven
Seeking of knowledge through information	Seeking of wisdom through higher connection

In which circumstances do you embody the masculine traits and feminine traits? Can you see that all these characteristics are complementary and necessary, yet can feel conflicting or combative if both are embodying the same traits at the same time in a relationship?

Sexual polarity exists when one takes on a more feminine essence, and the other, a more masculine one, especially when it comes to their relationship. Polarity is important, because it has the electromagnetic pull that creates dynamic tension between the two – an electromagnetic field of pure potency, creation, sexuality, propulsion towards something greater than the two.

In a traditional sense, a man is strong, stoic, provides protection and strategic direction, and is the trusty warrior. He penetrates his woman's heart and body with his love. The woman is vulnerable and sensual and a receiver of this love. She empowers his masculinity, and he is able to relinquish control and surrender, being anchored by the strength of her feminine love. **When both partners are both masculine or feminine in the relationship, the polarity is lost, and chemistry fades.**

Of course, as evolving spiritual beings, we desire to nurture both our masculine and feminine sides, and as we grow, we get to experience having a divine union between the two. We also have the ability to tap into our masculine and feminine sides as needed in a situation, and sometimes in a relationship, the polarities are reversed – there is no hard and fast rule that the woman must always be in her feminine, similarly for men.

However, if you want your man to feel strong, grounded, sexy and masculine – then, lady, you gotta own your feminine side!

When you follow the principle of being in your divine feminine and refusing to emasculate men, men will quickly start to transform before your eyes.

Whereas before you might have found them confusing, frustrating and intimidating, you can now admire, appreciate and understand men in a way you never thought possible.

What Do Men Really Want Anyway?

Now, before we get started with solving how to improve your dating life and relationship with men, it's important to clarify what the opposite sex is looking for. As shared above, women and men are 180 degrees apart – we couldn't be any more different! There's beauty and also deep frustration that goes with that.

On a more affirming note, on a human level both men and women thrive on the same exact needs such as safety, connection, communication, belonging and love. It's just as important to know that on a biological and spiritual level, masculine and feminine energies have different, yet complementary roles to play, and your main job is to allow the magical dance to happen between the two.

The good news is that in this book, you've had a chance to explore what being in your feminine power is all about.

As you're stepping into the Love Goddess, you have an opportunity to reinvent your relationships with men into ones that are healthy, fulfilling and fun. Normally, we as women flounder about, trying to figure men out. However, through years of beta testing (hehe), as I'm finding out it's relatively simple.

I'm going to dispel the confusion for you, with these three principles about what men (the real, grounded, masculine type) want from you:

1. **Men want to pleasure, protect and serve you.**
2. **They want to feel free to be themselves around you.**
3. **They want to know you trust, respect and need them.**

You need to know this, deep in your heart, Love Goddess. Write these down and keep them with you. When you're in your masculine then you're competing with these very same energies with men, thereby impeding sexual chemistry.

For more clarity on each, let me break it down for you.

1. Men want to pleasure, protect and serve you.

It's hard to for women to imagine this because we've been conditioned to do the opposite for our entire lives – to pleasure and serve men, and even protect their feelings. Yikes! Think about all your past relationships with men. Were you the one doing most of the work, trying to figure out what his favorite dish is, how to get him to call you back, or when there was something bothering you, not bringing it up, so as to not push him away? Did you constantly feel stressed and anxious around these men, especially after the honeymoon phase? Do you do the same with the men in your career or your family?

What if the reverse were actually required from you? To be receptive, grateful and simply allowing men to serve you in the best way they can?

Let's understand what motivates men, shall we?

Men are wired to be warriors and soldiers. Think about men in the army. They are loyal, moved to serve, even risking their lives for their cause. They are driven by their goal to protect their country, to kill the enemy and bring about safety for their land. They follow orders from their commander and will always follow through without resistance because they value integrity, honor and respect. They bond through a common purpose – service to their cause. They are also typically stronger, taller and more muscular than women.

Men are also hunters. They can work in solitude, and through their single-minded, tunnel vision, they hunt down their prey and kill it.

250

They are determined and won't come home till they have food for the family.

I share this because this is a special type of human being – it's the man! Our industrialized world may have taken men out of these more traditional roles, yet it's helpful to look at these as archetypal forms existing in men's psyches.

Now, let's say that *you* were the prize, the very thing that your man loves and wants to protect and serve? From an early age, **men are wired to be driven by their attraction and love for women. Whether it's their sexual drive (which is actually sacred – their "Ero" or primal, instinctive erotic energy) or their innate desire to be in sacred union with the feminine, the man will always work towards attracting, serving and delighting his woman.**

Why do men seek out status, fancy cars, high incomes or having a six pack? They don't do it for other men – they want to be as appealing to women as possible!

Of course, the real grounded man, the King, won't be necessarily driven by all this on the outside; he seeks out his Queen, you, and wants to fulfill you in leading a joyful, pleasureful, ease-filled life, and be of service to you and your family. He wants to pleasure you, sexually, and wants to turn your life upside down (for the better) and show you the world as Aladdin did with his love, Princess Jasmine.

Women regularly get in the way of men's natural instincts by competing with them, showing them that they're independent and don't need any help. They show a man that no matter what he does, she's not happy or content, and can do most things herself, or make a man feel incompetent. Or, on the flipside, women behave like damsels in distress, drawing on these precious energies from men like energy vampires.

It's our role as women to find contentment within ourselves, be in gratitude, articulate our desires and honor the men in our lives for these natural, beautiful tendencies – whether it's at home or work. <u>We have</u> <u>to get out of men's way and cheer them on as they serve and protect us</u> <u>and fuel our pleasures in their own unique ways.</u>

When you're around a man, ask for help in something and receive with grace. When he offers you something, or wants to serve or protect you, accept it with kindness. Thank a man and appreciate him for his efforts, no matter what. You can always let him know about your preferences down the line in a kind, gentle way.

2. Men want to feel free to be themselves around you.

"You must love in such a way that the person you love feels free." ~ Thích Nhat Hanh

What do men do when they're away from women? Eat, sleep, watch TV, play video games, burp, work, talk crap and compete with other men, masturbate, lift some weights at the gym, nerd out on something inane (to us) like car engines, wear sweatpants, eat take out, spend time zoning out, goof around … the list is endless. When men are upset or ashamed, they retreat into their cave; and when they are mad, they feel like roaring and beating their chests. Yet, when a man is around us, he is measured, refined, well-groomed, caring, inquisitive, romantic. What gives!

Women bring out the best in men, otherwise they would be floundering away purposelessly. But at some point, men begin to get tired playing a charade around women, and their natural tendencies begin to shine through. As they fall in love and feel more comfortable around their sweetie, they can finally begin to let their guard down.

Can you begin to have empathy for men, as they work so incredibly hard to curb their natural biological tendencies, in order to be better, *for us*? It fills my heart with so much appreciation and love as I write this, and I'm incredibly humbled by their genuine desire to curb these instinctive qualities and be their best around us.

As a woman, your greatest service to men around you is to help them feel understood, seen and cherished for *who they are*. Without judgment, complaint and criticism, period. This isn't to say you can't have issues with them. However, to have your man on a constant "Performance Improvement Plan", to think of him as being less capable than you or to view him as a project is simply not fair and thwarts his natural life force energy.

"People will forget what you said, people will forget what you did, but people will never forget how you made them feel." ~ Maya Angelou

When a man feels great around you, his oxytocin level rises, and this powerful bonding chemical creates a sense of attachment and the feeling of being in love.

The magic you bring is to give men a great experience around you.

This doesn't mean you have to please men, simply submit to their desires or avoid confrontation and speaking up when things don't resonate. You are your own beautiful, free spirit with your own will and unique needs. **Yet, you can set the intention to do what it takes so that men can feel safe, loved and understood around you.** There is no seduction, manipulation or faking it necessary.

There are some common things that women do that thwart a man's beingness and intentions. Here are some ideas of how you can shift into being in your sexy feminine:

- If your man is feeling horny, don't embarrass him. Instead, honor his erotic energy, and if you're not feeling like having sex, just playfully tell him, "Ooh, how sexy! Darling, would really love to, how about a little later?"

253

- If he's talking about work, don't go into the analytical with him, simply hold emotional space for him, affirming his ambition or dreams.

- If he gets you a gift, or takes you for an adventure that you're not really that excited about, simply say, "Thank you sweetie, how kind!"

- Don't analyze every single thing a guy does, as it just amplifies your anxiety and creates stress for a man.

- Don't complain to him, roll your eyes at him when he does something wrong or blow off his ideas.

- When he gets emotional and cries, or gets sick, hold space for him in a kind way, without thinking of him as weak.

- On dates, avoid talking about work or politics, or anything else highly analytical, instead stick to topics that are emotionally honest, meaningful and values-driven.

- Try hard not to burden your man with unprocessed stories and emotions – men love solving problems and finding solutions, and this can feel overwhelming and confusing for them. Instead, share them with your trusted friend, coach or therapist.

- When he does work to solve a problem for you, thank him, give him a hug and look at him with wonder and appreciation.

- Work to curb your tendencies of seeming competitive or argumentative around a man, because in that setting, men become competitive and begin to treat you like a man; this is simply how they are designed biologically.

Your power lies in you being your nurturing, supportive feminine self, that's emotionally expressed and full of grace, heart and possibility.

"First you have to focus on the practice of being. Being fresh. Being peaceful. Being attentive. Being generous. Being compassionate. This is the basic practice.

It's as if the other person is sitting at the foot of a tree. The tree does not do anything, but the tree is fresh and alive. When you are like that tree, sending out waves of freshness, you help to calm down the suffering in the other person." ~ Thich Nhat Hanh

Imagine the impact you can have on men when you embody these qualities. If you are in the powerful state of compassion grounded with self-love, you can create a safe space for a man to share his fears, desires and dreams with you, and feel great afterwards. In those micro moments of seemingly mundane conversations over dinner or a walk, you've created connection and safety.

When you add in playfulness, flirting, humor and following your pleasures, you've created a haven for men. You can be affectionate with men like caressing their hair, staring into their eyes with genuine awe and hugging them, letting them know you cherish them. You can practice the 5 As of Love with him. You don't have to fake any of this – you can activate the Love Goddess side of you that truly honors the beauty and sacredness of connecting with each man you meet in a joyful way.

3. Men want to know you trust, respect and need them.

In our world, love is elevated to the highest level, and we watch romantic movies of couples falling in love and setting off into the horizon on their white horse. We assume that things will work out for the unassuming, rose-tinted glass wearing well-intentioned couple!

Yet, what I've found to be the nitty gritty of making a relationship last is to have a foundation of trust and respect and making sure the other feels needed and valued.

If you are having trust issues with your man, then break up with him. It's plain and simple. If you keep wondering if he's trustworthy and find yourself snooping on him or becoming controlling, then sooner or later, your mistrust will corrode his own faith in himself and he will begin to make mistakes and leave. Trust is the foundation of any relationship and is even more important than love.

Trust is built over time, through careful, discerning speech, consistently showing up for the other even when it's uncomfortable and following through on what you said you would. You are relatively equanimous in your emotions; of course, you are allowed to have your ups and downs, but always coming from a place of compassion. When you do these things, you let the person know you have their back no matter what, and they can rely on you, emotionally and physically. Over time, trust gets built like a wall, brick by brick. Interestingly, when you break trust even once, an entire portion of the wall can come crumbling down! Trust is sacred, which is why you've worked so hard, Love Goddess, to build strong trust within yourself first. As I shared earlier, women have a tough time trusting men, and this is a much-needed area for healing.

Respect is a quality that has also been steadily declining in our world. We are regularly taught to condemn or make fun of people who don't act or think like us or have a different way of solving a problem. In our modern world, we view people through the lens of productivity or worthiness. This is not the natural law of love – in fact, each and every being on this planet, whether it's an ant or a child, has their own gift, significance and contribution.

Men, due to their values of honor and integrity, and their constant desire to serve a cause, thrive in an environment of respect. When you treat your man with unequivocal respect, even if you don't agree with him, you are supporting him in being his best self. How do you do this? You listen to him with an open mind, affirm his way of looking at things, and thank him for all of his contributions.

Finally, men want to feel needed, which is why I began the book with recommending that you ask men to help you when you need it and receive with grace. Many women talk a big game about being independent, and that they could do everything themselves if they had the time and money. Of course, sometimes they are coming from a place of being hurt by men. However, where does that leave men? This is a real problem in our society, and so many men are isolated, single and hurt because of this.

From Me to We

"In the progress of personality, first comes a declaration of independence, then a recognition of interdependence."
~ Henry Van Dyke

As a relationship coach, I can definitively say that **women are seeking to break out of the mold of simply being a strong, independent woman, and moving into being an openhearted, tender,** *interdependent* **woman who** *does* **need a man, from a place of inner security and stability.** A woman ultimately needs a man to feel sexually whole and complete, and she longs to experience true, romantic, sexual rapture in a man's arms, having his body enveloping her, his love penetrating deep inside of her. She feels safe, loved and cherished in a man's unwavering gaze and devotion. She is driven by her erotic nature to seek this kind of union, and she can't deny this need for too long. Let a man know when you find him sexy, and cuddle, kiss and adore him often. There's no need to hide your appreciation or withhold love – men thrive in affection.

Sometimes though, it requires a bit of reprogramming how we think about interdependence in a modern-day partnership. Currently in our household with two young ones, I'm taking care of the day-to-day household activities that include cooking, cleaning and care of our children, while carving out time to write and coach. My husband is hacking away at his computer, taking care of business and making sure our house is in fine working order, while spending his free time chasing the kids. Meanwhile, he works tirelessly quietly in the background, taking out the garbage, moving our compost, fixing the lights when they go out, scheduling the handyman. He's on the rescue whenever we need him. Without Krishan, I know our home would fall apart, and I wouldn't have the freedom to spend unlimited time with my kids as well as my creative pursuits, which is such a blessing! I love my life and am committed to turning our home into an oasis, a true Love Garden.

As a Type A woman coming from the corporate world who used to work around the clock, this lifestyle is a huge shift. I used to believe that a man and woman should be financial equals and have similar roles and contributions in the house. Now, I'm simply seeing our roles as complementary and equally important, and I have deep respect for what I and my husband and even our kids each contribute.

There are numerous times when I feel like rolling my eyes when my partner forgets to do something I ask him, or does something in what I would consider an inefficient or ineffective way. Or punishing him by withdrawing, staying silent, being defensive or condescending using passive-aggressive speech. These are tendencies I work hard to curb. I have come to realize that being respectful and trusting of him is my greatest gift to our marriage, being appreciative of all of his efforts, while opening up to needing him without guilt, shame or obligation.

I recognize that in playing our playing more traditional gender roles while honoring our inner masculine and feminine sides, helps to generate the polarity needed for the sexual tension and chemistry between us. I'm the wise, loving Queen of our home, and he is the loyal, righteous, sexy King.

Every couple has to work to find the right balance, depending on their desired lifestyle and their shifting roles, so that sexual polarity can exist in all its glory. I know of men who take care of their kids while their wives are working, or situations where both work full time. In all the scenarios, couples can find sexual polarity if they make their relationship as their #1 priority. **Getting professional help, like couples' coaching or counseling, is a key component to the relationship's support structure.**

Secret #2: Keep a Man Hooked Through Sexy Communication Skills

I couldn't seem to muster up the words to express my frustration with my fiancé (now ex). During our honeymoon phase, things were easy. We would joke about things, gossip, share about our days, dreams and desires. Yet when things bothered me, like his work schedule, or his not showing up to an event that mattered to me, I would bottle it up. I didn't know how to share my feelings, without breaking down. I wanted to be a good girl, be compromising and not shake the boat. In that way, what I was with him was manicured, put together woman who was mature and relationship ready. Yet, I would hide my resentment, insecurity and contempt, which would boil up as snarky and hurtful comments here and there. I would bargain and negotiate for my needs being met.

During my love awakening, I got to understand more about how to actually make relationships work, and how to communicate effectively. I became an earnest student of nurturing a healthy relationship through my words and intentions. Looking back, I could see how I had no idea how to communicate nor maintain a healthy relationship and would regularly go between being a doormat and a bitch.

When I started my relationship with Krishan, I made a determination to not hurt him or anyone else through my words. I wanted to create a sanctuary around me, where people felt seen and heard, where we could have real honest conversations and share things from our heart, even if it meant being vulnerable to rejection. I wanted a relationship of authenticity and deep connection, which felt juicy and exciting!

Intimacy is the ultimate experience a person wants to have in life – it is the nectar of love, the ambrosia.

Intimacy can be broken down into In-To-Me-See.

Nothing parallels such a connection where two people feel a divine union, breaking down all their barriers and bare their hearts to each other. When they look at each other, they see an ocean of understanding and love. They can express anything around the other person, even something potentially painful, but are generous and kind in intention. They can argue and have breakdowns, yet they have the ability to get through it together while growing in understanding. They play and laugh together, free in each other's arms, safe from the outside world. They are a team in every sense and can see each other's potential and support each other in rising up out of their own pity or darkness. There is a healing quality to the relationship. They are both in it to win it. Sounds yummy, right?

What creates intimacy? How do we get there in a relationship? The key lies in communication, which, Love Goddess, you are destined to be an expert in.

You are a divine sorceress through your words and presence. Everything that you utter has vibration and power. Your words have the power to heal and connect or hurt and disconnect you from others. Most people I meet struggle with one thing in their relationships at home and work – communicating effectively.

While communication skills are a whole art and science, I will share two skills with you that will rock a man's world and create chemistry: Deep Listening and Compassionate Communication. These two skills are the beginning point to giving you what you need to attract a great man and keep him hooked!

1. Deep listening:

One of the greatest gifts you can offer a man is to simply listen. Honestly, there's nothing sexier! As women, we're used to gabbing away, talking about exes, our work, things that bother us, people we're mad at. When someone's talking, we can hijack the conversation by bringing in our own thoughts and experiences or turn it into an advisory session.

Yet, as a Love Goddess, you know that a man wants to be seen, heard and understood. Don't worry about getting your needs met of being listened to – it will. Men have very few avenues for sharing their feelings and ruminations, and if they have a non-judgmental ear who will listen, especially from a beautiful woman, they feel safe to surrender their heart and open up to vulnerability.

While listening, try to remove all filters and judgement, and place your full attention on the person. Put away your phone and other distractions and turn and face him. If appropriate, smile, ask questions, and maybe even reflect back what you're hearing. You can use statements like, "So, what I'm hearing you say is…", "What else?" and "Tell me more," looking into their eyes with wonder, nodding where it makes sense. When a person's done sharing, simply say, "Thank you for sharing," without adding your own two cents (this is probably the hardest part for us women). You can do this for five or ten minutes straight, or in some cases where someone is struggling with something, even an hour! If you're coming from a place of genuine curiosity and compassion, this kind of listening won't feel fake, and instead, over time it will feel more and more natural.

Even if it's not someone you plan to spend the rest of your life with, this person deserves your full attention and presence in that moment – and remember you are getting great practice in listening and holding space for others, and you are in service to the universe as a Love Goddess.

Listening is a superpower, and the better you are at it, the more you'll be a master in your relationships. There's a healing quality about being listened to, and silence in a conversation is sometimes is so cathartic. Whenever you're in doubt, simply listen, even if it's to yourself. As the saying goes, there's a reason why God gave us two ears and one mouth.

I once heard a miraculous story about a boy who was ill in a mental institution, who had been quiet for years. No one could get him to speak, nor his parents, doctors, or the priest. He sat there, mute and despondent. An uncle, who was a meditation practitioner and compassionate communicator, asked to go see him. He went and sat with him, simply being in his presence, and listened. At first, nothing came out of the boy's mouth for days. He would ask a question and simply listen. Then, the words started coming out, slowly. A week later, he was talking about everything under the sun! All his thoughts, hurts, hidden truths. Through the miracle of listening, he felt so much better, and recovered! He could finally leave the facility, and his illness went away.

EXERCISE

Find someone to practice deep listening with. Schedule time with them, set a container for twenty minutes or an hour, whatever feels good to you. Remember to practice self-empathy and grounding before and after meeting with them. If you're able to do this once a week, you'll watch your personal life blossom!

2. Compassionate communication:

There's nothing so sexy as a woman who's raw and emotionally honest; it's so incredibly refreshing. A woman who speaks her truth in a compassionate way is rare. Just imagine if every sentence you said created even more connection in a relationship?

Men are terrified of silence, and would rather hear real honesty, than fake words. Whether you walk on eggshells around a man or start your sentences with "I need you to ..." in a firm, masculine way, a man will start to withdraw from you. Changing how you communicate in a feminine way will be a game-changer in every single relationship of your life.

The good news is you've started making some headway into healthy communication by practicing self-empathy, mindfulness and meditation and dealing with your emotions through emotional self-care. In the "Love Alchemy" chapter, you learned how to deal with triggers, about not taking things personally and about the power of discernment in what you say. *In fact, at this point, I would recommend that you go back and read that chapter as it is all vital in building healthy relationships.*

As women, we struggle with everyday communication conundrums. How do you relay your joy and frustrations, deal with disagreements and have a man fulfill your needs? What do you say when a man doesn't show up on time, sends you a suggestive picture of himself after a first date or doesn't call you for over a week? If you're in a relationship, how do you avoid future blowouts, and use difficult situations to grow in your understanding and connection with each other?

I have found the teachings of the Center for Nonviolent Communication to be invaluable. Borrowed from their concepts, below are some quick guidelines in communication to get you started in your stellar communication skills as a Love Goddess:

How to share how you're feeling:

Whenever you need to complain or share a frustration with a man, it's helpful to own your own experience, and explain your feelings and needs. For instance, you can say, "When you didn't show up on time for dinner, I felt concerned and irritated. I really value integrity and communication." As you can see, I used the feelings and needs from the NVC inventory, which I invite you to reference regularly in your communications. In this case, you state an observation without blaming the other person (i.e., not showing up for dinner on time), and you share what you felt and needed. It's that simple! You don't have to make the other person feel bad or ashamed. After you say it, you are welcome to add, "I'd be curious what's coming up for you?" while genuinely holding space for him to share without judgement. Likewise, if a man sends you a text that irks you, you can text back, "When you sent that text, I felt embarrassed and irked, and my need for respect wasn't being met." Of course, paraphrase in such a way that feels appropriate to you, recognizing that some of this language is new to you.

Moments like this can seem scary, yet if you approach communication in an emotionally honest, yet values-oriented way, and end with asking the other a question, you can actually create powerful moments of even deeper connection.

Remember, you can also share positive things too. "Thank you for inviting me to the concert for this band I love. I feel so incredibly delighted and touched. I really value celebration and beauty, so this fits the bill!"

How to make a request:

After sharing your feelings and needs, you can follow with a request. Remember to make it specific, bite-sized and realistic, and be open to the other saying no.

As an example, from above: "When you didn't show up on time for dinner, I felt concerned and irritated. I really value integrity and communication. Next time we have dinner together and you might be late, would you mind calling or texting me?" Sometimes the other person might not be able to fulfill on your request, in which case, you can work out alternatives with him. This is what collaboration and teamwork is all about.

How to practice empathy:

As much as you've learned to hold emotional space for yourself, it's just as powerful to hold that for a man. While you're practicing deep listening, you can ask him questions about his feelings and needs, while of course being mindful of not interrupting him, or making it sound like a psycho-analytical interrogation! As an example, if he's sharing about a tough conversation with his dad, you can listen and after a while ask him, "Do you feel annoyed, angry or drained?" He might not be able to name his feelings at first, but your questions will stimulate him to con-template. He might say no, so ask more question, "Do you feel irritated or maybe even heartbroken?" No matter what, he will feel touched by these questions, and will likely share more about his feelings. You can follow it up with, "Are you needing clarity, respect, or communica-tion?" See if you can get into his shoes and guess his feelings and needs.

You can end it with, "Thank you for sharing," with a sweet smile. Practicing empathy is a true Love Goddess practice. You're not trying to give a guy advice or fix his problems in any way. You're simply holding emotional space for him. That is your genius!

Expressing regret:

Sometimes you will make mistakes or inadvertently say something to trigger your man. Feel your sense of regret, and then let him know, "I'm sorry if what I said hurt you. I can see it was coming from a place of insecurity and fear, and I didn't mean it, and next time I'll be more careful." Apologizing and taking ownership of one's own actions can heal so many old wounds, and it's tender and heart opening for both people.

As you're employing your communication skills, it's important to stay grounded and self-aware through mindfulness. Your self-love practice is an important part of being able to communicate with men without losing your balance or coming from a place of insecurity or a need to control.

Love Goddess, you're on the path to inviting a King into your life, and you can bet your horses that he will incredibly turned on by you and your sexy, wise relationship skills!

STEP 5: LOVE AND DATE
WITH CONFIDENCE

Myra, 41, was ready to get out there and start dating. Yet, she was scared. She had very little dating experience because she had married her high school sweetheart. A tall, slender and beautiful dancer with a fiery personality, she was concerned that she came off as too intimidating. She struggled with how to balance her gregarious, extroverted, ambitious side with her tender, nurturing and feminine side. Prior to coaching, she had dated online but felt like she had failed miserably and was wary of trying again. She was afraid of rejection and of the possibility that there was no one out there for her. Yet, she also deeply wanted to experience the adventure of dating and meeting her beloved whom she ached to be with.

Now... could Myra trust the process of dating... and let go? Could she just be the most open, vulnerable, courageous version of herself and get out there – and actually enjoy the dating process? Or would it feel like a draining task, filled with heart-break and rejection?

After we created Myra's profile and worked on her dating strat-egy, she felt ready, yet before putting up her profile, she got cold feet. She had to face her fear head on, holding it with com-passion. Yet, like a true love warrior, she made the commitment to get out there, whether it was online or to singles' events. We created a strategy that felt easy for her to dip her feet into dating, while ramping it up to a sustainable level that allowed her to continue her daily activities that made her life joyful and fulfilling.

The first few guys who wrote to Myra online, she felt turned off; yet she kept up her momentum, focusing on her attitude and simply showing up to her love life, even if it felt uncom-fortable or frustrating. Through the process, she learned a lot about herself and grew as a person. She went on many dates which was a mixed bag of interesting, fun or annoying experi-ences. She maintained a positive attitude!

She met a man that she fell in love with – a kind, down-to-earth yet charming man who was thoroughly smitten with her. They hit it off like a house on fire. However, after several months of dating and thinking he was "the one," they hit a rough patch. During it, she learned that he had a drinking problem and that he emotionally shut down, and no matter how hard she tried to keep up with communication and possibly seek external sup-port, he continued to withdraw. She contemplated her best course of action, and through coaching support, she decided to end the relationship. Even though it felt scary, she was deter-mined to make her breakup a conscious one, practicing deep understanding and honest, heart-felt communication, and releasing spiritual cords. The breakup was heartbreaking, and she allowed herself the time to grieve.

When Myra felt ready, she got back up and started dating again, mindfully caring for her tender heart. Surprisingly, through that relationship, she learned so much about herself which helped her become a more confident, self-aware and even more loving woman.

Through continuing to keep her heart open and dating, she eventually met Mr. Right, a man who ended up being so similar to her on many levels. He too was divorced, and because of that they both felt mature and ready for a real relationship. They celebrated a spiritual yet romantic and intimate wedding at a picturesque Buddhist monastery, which was her dream. He even built her a house with her own yoga studio inside!

Love Goddess, congratulations for making it to this final step! If you have completed the previous ones, then you are a true love warrior – someone who knows what she wants and is disciplined and determined to get it. You've been cultivating your Love Garden, learning the art of love and have a strong inner foundation. You already are the partner who your man has been waiting for – someone who's loving, sexy and self-aware.

If you jumped ahead to this chapter, no worries at all too. Make sure that you have completed "Step 2: Heal Your Heart and Close Your 'Ex Files'" first, as this is vital to making sure you've released your past for good. You can continue to do Steps 3 and 4 while following through with dating, however, I highly recommend that you make the commitment to finish those at a steady pace. In fact, you will see that as you keep doing the inner work and stepping into your whole, loving, heart open self, that you will keep attracting better, high-quality men.

In this chapter, you will learn a new, feminine, powerful way of dating. You'll be guided in creating a magnetic mindset, discover keys to conscious and joyful dating and begin to embody your feminine grace and wisdom as you date. You'll feel sexy and empowered as you meet new men, while having tools on hand for dealing with your pesky fears and sabotage patterns. You'll discover red flags to look out for in a man, and how to know if someone's "the one".

Whether you've dated before or are beginning for the first time, it's important for you to have a beginner's mind – a fresh, open perspective. In fact, pretend like you've never dated before. The reason is that you can feel jaded and all your old thoughts and fears will come back. *"Dating sucks! There are no good guys online anyways. I know because I've already done it,"* might be some of the thoughts you're having. If so, practice self-compassion and self-empathy, know that it's just your fearful ego talking, and let it go. You're way more brave and capable than that.

"Whenever we strive to become better than we are, everything around us becomes better, too." ~ Paulo Coelho, The Alchemist

Remember, **you are a whole new person now, vibrating at a new frequency.** If you're doubting that, and struggle with really believing that things aren't going to be different, I would still urge you to look at this as a whole new experience. Because it is!

Note: If you're already in a relationship, you'll find the principles in this chapter to be invaluable in creating a fun, grounding basis for a satisfying relationship. The principles of dating in a relationship never go away. Remember, couples who consciously date each other throughout their lives rarely lose their romance or connection, and in fact find their love growing and evolving.

This would be a great time to go back and brush up on the concepts in "Cultivating Your Love Garden" and "Love Alchemy Tools," as they will support you in continuously honing your love skills. Also, use the skills in self-love, as you will need to keep building your inner foundation, especially during the ups and downs of dating.

A New You, a New Kind of Love

There's a new paradigm of love that's emerging. It is the H-shaped relationship, in which both partners are connected through the heart, versus the A-shaped relationship, where each one is leaning on the other, economically, physically or otherwise. There's a dependency in the latter, while the former is about joyful *interdependence*.

The H-shaped partnership is one in which there is connection on every level, physical, mental, emotional, spiritual; a relationship in which both partners feel free to be themselves around each other and have mutual respect and love. They're individuals brought together through a common vision, a soul-level resonance along with a desire to heal and grow together. Their lovemaking feels exploratory, connected and natural. This soulmate couple creates a ripple of joy and romance around them, making the world stand still. This kind of love fills the air with beauty and the sweetness of true, unconditional love, and people in their company feel blessed and held.

One of my favorite poems is by Kahlil Gibran, a forward thinker of his time, in which he spoke prophetically of what this sacred relationship (as a marriage) looks like:

On Marriage (The Prophet)

Then Almitra spoke again and said, and what of Marriage, master?
And he answered saying:
You were born together, and together you shall be forevermore.

You shall be together when the white wings of death scatter your
days.
Ay, you shall be together even in the silent memory of God.
But let there be spaces in your togetherness,
And let the winds of the heavens dance between you.
Love one another, but make not a bond of love:
Let it rather be a moving sea between the shores of your souls.
Fill each other's cup but drink not from one cup.
Give one another of your bread but eat not from the same loaf.
Sing and dance together and be joyous, but let each one of you be
alone,
Even as the strings of a lute are alone though they quiver with the
same music.
Give your hearts, but not into each other's keeping.
For only the hand of Life can contain your hearts.
And stand together yet not too near together:
For the pillars of the temple stand apart,
And the oak tree and the cypress grow not in each other's shadow.

How simply majestic is this vision of love! Having a healthy relationship with yourself, and ultimately with your soulmate, and creating this Love Garden or temple together with your man is one of the greatest ways to feel fulfilled, along with being such a contribution to society.

As you're stepping into your feminine power, releasing the barriers around your heart and learning the art of love, there is no doubt that you are opening up to this kind of (r)evolutionary love.

You Will Meet Your Soulmate, Guaranteed

Through my years of working with clients, I have seen that women who continuously focus on their love life, even if it's thirty minutes a day of practicing self-love or planning a date, eventually meet the man of their dreams. How does this happen?

As I shared with you, everything is frequency and vibration. When you do the work of staying loving and openhearted and take active steps in your love life, you begin to naturally align with healthy love. **Through cultivating the conditions for love and grace in your life, you begin to attract your perfect match through the principles of synchronicity, magnetism and resonance. It's simply the inevitable outcome.** I once read a study that nearly 95% of people ended up meeting their mates in their lifetime. When you're vibrating at the frequency of love, the odds are 100%!

Love is the natural life force and field that we're all operating in, and when we're alignment with the intention of being loving, we're supported by benevolent, intelligent energies that flow through us, on a natural, loving path. *The ultimate desire of God and the universe is for you to be happy and joyful. God desires for couples to unite, create families, experience romantic, healthy love and lead a life of pleasure and spiritual fulfillment.* Love is the most healing, potent, natural energy there is. When you align with love, you are in alignment with life itself. The magnetic attraction of love is what pulls particles together, the material formations around us and creates our reality – it's literally the stuff we're made of.

Your soulmate is seeking you, just as much as you're seeking him. My husband once said in one of my workshops, "If I had known I was going to be with Sarika, I would have enjoyed my dating life way more." The women in the room chuckled and so did I. It's true – the time that you are single and dating is fleeting, and filled with abundant and juicy possibilities of being a *courtesan extraordinaire*, meeting sexy men, self-discovery and having fun or at least interesting dates.

Knowing that you will inevitably meet the man of your dreams, how would you approach dating differently?

Before we get started, I want to burst a few myths that have been floating around that make women miserable:

a) My biological clock is ticking, so I gotta hurry up!

I remember counting backwards from the time I thought I would want to have kids. This would put so much pressure on me to perform my seductive magic and stronghold a man into my life. I would get anxiety attacks just thinking about my biological clock and I was sending desperation vibes to men I met.

When this happens to you ... stop, breathe, and smile.

First, ask yourself – is having children a necessary condition for your happiness? I would argue that you can be happy, right now, exactly as you are. Also, wouldn't you want to first have a great relationship, and let children be a natural byproduct because your relationship is strong and can support this beautiful expansion? Being a mother now has made me realize that motherhood is indeed magical and lovely – yet to be honest, I'm more grateful to my partnership and our dedication to self-love and building a strong relationship foundation first.

Taking the pressure off yourself allows you to become more Goddess-minded – open, expansive, free-spirited – and when the timing's right, you will meet the right guy, and having kids (even if adopted, or otherwise) will always be an option.

If you know deep in your heart that motherhood is important to you, then **I encourage you to consider freezing your eggs as early as you can.** This will take the pressure off dating and your future relationship.

Also, if you know having a child is a deep soul-calling, something you must do now - then give yourself the permission to go ahead and have a child! When you follow your bliss, even if it feels scary or irrational, you begin to become magnetic to all your desires. I have met many couples who met after one individually decided to have children – because true love truly has no filters.

b) All the good ones are taken or aren't interested.

Living in New York City, I developed a narrative that all the single men were either players, unavailable, taken or gay. I went on dozens of dates with seemingly decent men and fretted. Some men seemed to only want one thing. Why wasn't I attracted to these guys? Where are the smart Renaissance men, the ones who travel, are spiritual and have many interests outside of work? The one who will adore me, and keep a relationship as their number one priority?

The truth is that most men want what you want – a happy, healthy, fulfilling relationship. They struggle with the same issues as women do. As I shared before, the world is your mirror, so whom you may have attracted before is certainly not a reflection of where you will be going.

In fact, the best is yet to come!

The right man *will* appear when your life feels in alignment and you feel happy and balanced from within. You may meet him through online dating, work, community service, or your friends. Trust me, he will appear when you're truly ready to receive him. *Will you recognize him when he does?*

c) There must be something wrong with me, which is why I'm single.

You probably have a lot of friends who met "the one" randomly at college, on their first date off of a dating app or through an acquaintance. Yes, there are plenty of cases of people who seemingly do nothing, and yet, they get to meet their soulmates magically! The world can seem unfair in this way.

It is true that some of us struggle more than others in certain areas, or don't have the same luck. Yet I believe that the best things in life are those which are intentional and consciously created.

You are perfect just the way you are. We all have life lessons to learn. Relationships are the best way to learn about yourself, to grow and evolve, and to heal in many ways. **You being single now is not an accident and actually it's a gift. It's a great place to be because from now on, you can begin to consciously draw in the extraordinary, soul-shaking kind of loving relationship that you desire and deserve.**

Just to be clear, there is nothing wrong or broken about you. Thoughts of "I am too old, young, short, [fill in the blanks] to find love" are all myths. You can begin to let go of your limiting beliefs around what makes you lovable or worthy. *I know of a ninety-seven-year-old woman who met her soulmate (after being married to her late husband) in a retirement home!* The reality is there is no right age, looks, education or any other physical requirement that's necessary for finding love. When you achieve personal harmony and genuine love for your amazing and imperfect self, you'll be at the right point in your life to build a strong foundation with the man you are meant to meet.

Enlightened Dating

Layla, a dainty, soft-spoken, beautiful South Asian woman, and nurse practitioner. When we began working together, she wanted to meet a man of the same background and dreamed that they would live in the suburbs together near her parents. She was excited to experience dating as a part of her healing and discovery process, especially since she was coming out of a long-term relationship with an emotionally unavailable man.

Layla went on dates with different men, going through ups and downs while learning about her preferences and practicing her relationship and dating skills.

She saw a profile of a handsome Chinese-American man online and decided to reach out to him. When she met him for coffee, she was amazed with how comfortable she felt with him, what a great listener he was, and how kind and accepting he was of her. As it turns out, that was the biggest turn on for her – that's what she had been seeking all along! He was immediately besotted by her radiance and gentle confidence. The only challenge was that he was a diplomat who would soon be stationed in Morocco within a year.

Layla kept dating him, even though she knew that he would leave for his assignment. During the first few months, everything was light, carefree and romantic. She threw caution to the wind and began falling in love. That's when her "commitment wall" began to come up, and she suddenly felt defensive and afraid – was he was "the one"? Was she was going to have to give up her lifestyle and career in order to be with him, including submitting to his aspirations while discarding her own? She was scared of creating the same pattern all over as she had with her ex.

However, we worked through her fears, and from accessing her inner knowing, Layla realized that she could navigate this relationship differently. She realized that her desire to be with him was greater than anything. He would do anything to be with her, including give up his own career. He was different than her ex, and she could trust in the process of building the foundation of their relationship together, with common values they both cherished.

They decided to co-create their future together, and she opened up to the adventure of living abroad with her new beau – leaving behind her home, job, everything. She soon got a job in a clinic and has started her own life coaching practice, pushing her beyond her frontiers. She gets to live a passionate, loving, discovery-filled life with her dream man, her best friend, her life partner in a foreign land. How romantic!

Like Layla, many women start off with their own idea of what her life could and should look like. Yet, by owning your feminine power and using dating as a discovery process, you can begin to define and design life on your terms, claiming your deepest values.

By the time you attract your man, you'll be a much more loving, sexy, confident woman who has weathered the storm of dating successfully, a mature, resilient Goddess whom a man greatly admires and knows without a doubt that you are the woman of his dreams.

Keys to Enlightened Dating

1. Use dating as a platform for growth and self-discovery

"We cannot change our past... we cannot change the fact that people will act in a certain way. We cannot change the inevitable. The only thing we can do is play on the one string we have, and that is our attitude. I am convinced that life is 10% what happens to me and 90% of how I react to it." ~ Charles R. Swindoll

Remember, your Attitude Is Everything.

When you recognize that dating is a spiritual journey, then you will see the learning and value in everything, and it will support you in staying optimistic and grounded. This isn't naïve – rather, this is a key fact of life. Life isn't a set linear path of success – rather, it's a series of ups and downs, and our attitude is everything in how we react to different situations.

The criteria of success in love is simple: show up every day with a loving mindset, take small steps and detach from the results.

You can view dating from the lens of a powerful path in becoming a better person – learning to be more heart open, vulnerable, noticing your beliefs, blind spots and learning about your relationship patterns. Through staying the course of dating, you are making a powerful commitment – to taking bold steps in creating a love life of your dreams. Each person who writes you or you go on a date with is someone you can learn from about yourself and improve your love life.

When you begin dating, you can observe your own patterns and perhaps even have the perspective that the man you're dating is a mirror to you in some way. This may seem complex, so it's helpful to share a few scenarios with a man you're seeing:

- *In what way do you judge or criticize yourself, that you're projecting onto him? Do you feel secretly unworthy or undesirable?* Maybe you need to love and accept yourself more.

- *Does he come across as arrogant, intimidating or insecure?* Likely there's a part of you that still struggles with it or you still haven't let go of that pattern in your life.

- *Are you afraid of communicating your truth, making him angry or distant?* Perhaps you need to grow your inner confidence and improve your communication skills.

- *Do you need his or others' approval for your choices in life?* Maybe your soul yearns for more of approval and love from you.

- *Are you repeating a pattern, like falling into relationships too fast, or getting jealous and controlling as soon as you start getting serious?* If so, it's time to be honest with yourself, resolve to do what would be of greatest service to your relationship and seek support if needed.

You can also begin to fine-tune your relationship skills and contemplate your dynamics with men. For instance: *How do you deal with insecurity and uncertainty, and what do you hold on to for comfort? Are you competitive and struggle with power issues? Are you unable to maintain healthy boundaries? Can you let go of your expectations, while still honoring your desires and longing? How much faith and trust do you have in yourself, the universe, God? Do you feel feminine and relaxed, or masculine and controlling on your dates?* Noticing these patterns will not only serve your love life, but they can also serve as a healing blueprint for all your relationships to come.

Moreover, through dating different men, you can learn about what you truly care about and what resonates. For instance, maybe initially you wanted to date a spiritually-minded man – but over time, the conversations you have with him feel disconnected. You begin to wonder about your own preferences and realize that you don't want to wake up doing yoga every morning at five a.m. with your partner (something he does) – it's simply not you! So, you actually recalibrate your own preferences, sharing it with him, but recognizing that you both may not click. You examine reevaluate the role of spirituality in your own life. Like this, there are many, many aspects of one's life that we might not consciously think about, until we meet and have an open, honest conversation with someone – especially a possible love interest.

That's the power of romance – it has the power to help us transcend our own egos and open up to new dimensions of ourselves.

This doesn't mean that you aren't open to others' views on life and preferences, however, it's a great time to begin discovering what really makes you tick, and the kind of life you want to lead. Maybe, in the beginning of dating, you are keen on a life of marriage and kids, living in the suburbs in white-picket-fenced home. And yet, as you keep dating, your mind and heart are opened to new possibilities that you never would have considered.

2. Be the partner you want to attract

One of my friends told me her story of meeting her man. She was sick of her dating patterns and was about to give up on dating. She had already done a lot of inner work, and she realized she could be happy on her own. She decreed to the universe, "God, I'm done with dating men who aren't right for me. Send me a man who is kind and generous and is my divine match – otherwise I'm fine being single." She also had an epiphany – if she wanted to meet a man who was all of those qualities, then she needed to *be* that.

She started living her life more consciously, cultivating her Love Garden. She practiced respect and kindness to every person she talked to or saw, ranging from the cashier at her grocery store to her mom on the phone and to the men she met. She smiled at people and put away her phone while out in public so she could be more mindful and present. She honored and respected herself, and was honest, yet discerning in what she shared with people she hung out with or her colleagues. While on dates, she was unguarded, compassionate and forgiving. Soon enough, while at an event and glowing like a Love Goddess, a friend of hers said, "Oh my gosh, I need to put you in touch with one of my friends. I think you guys will get along." She ended up meeting this dreamy, funny, handsome guy – and they hit it off immediately! They are now married with a beautiful baby.

Whatever qualities you value, there's no time like now to begin living it, being it, breathing it. As in the book *Five Love Languages* by Gary Chapman, you can discover what ways you like to be loved, and subsequently offer it to people you meet. You'll see that who you are is who you will attract.

3. Channel your inner courtesan

Remember how I shared about the women in ancient times who were the apple of men's eyes, the beautiful, intellectual, sexy women who were the king's consorts – the courtesans? These women loved men, amongst other things – they loved other women, science, art, nature, exploration, sex, dressing up in regalia and sexy clothing, anything in life that was beautiful and exhilarating. These women were great at flirting, communicating and the art of love. They also held men's secrets and were their greatest confidantes – no doubt they were compassionate and wise healers, too.

This is your chance to be her, in whatever way feels good to you. In fact, make a commitment to never let this side of you die! I have found her to be very powerful in keeping a relationship alive, no matter what stage you're in.

Three courtesan-like, divine feminine qualities that I've found helpful in love include Presence, Play and Pleasure. When you bring these into any date, or while you're communicating with men or women, you become a joy to be around – and you get to have fun, too! You can transform even the most uncomfortable situation into one of healing and connection.

Presence: By far, the greatest gift we can give to ourselves and our loved ones – and the greatest turn on for men – is our presence. Presence is the ability to bring full awareness to our thoughts, feelings and sensations in our body, along with our surrounding environment. It has the inherent quality of being in the present moment (and not lost in the past or future), a timelessness and awareness. Presence is super sexy because not only are we in complete control of our reactions to things that trigger us, but also it allows us to immerse ourselves and enjoy the moment – *and experience the glory of rapture and falling in love.*

When you're present, you can genuinely feel joy and compassion despite having uncertainty about the future. It helps you not get lost in all the drama of dating (*"Why didn't he call?? What does his text mean? What if he's seeing anyone else? Why did he reject me?? Is he a player?"* – you know the drill).

While dating, practice breathing and staying present – not getting lost in the past or future. Sometimes it's easy to become over-analytical or feel paralyzed when you're meeting someone on a date, wondering whether he's is "the one" or if you'll get hurt. Rather, use the time to get to know him, bringing your full presence to each date, and practicing mindfulness and self-awareness. Put away your phone when you're with him and request him to do the same.

Being present helps you access your deepest intuition during dating, which gets hidden when you're lost in heady analysis, fear and anxiety. **Intuition and wisdom are divine feminine qualities that help us women navigate which man is right for us, when to go on a second date (or end a date early) and when to leave a relationship or job.**

Perhaps most importantly, being present and mindful is a very important quality in undoing your deepest painful conditioning and patterns around love. You become present to the ways in which you're sabotaging yourself and are able to make healthier choices. It also allows you to have more acceptance, appreciation and compassion for yourself.

Play: Play is a feminine quality and is often seen as child-like or naive in our society. Yet, I find it one of the most important ingredients in relationships! Play is about having fun and not taking things too seriously. It involves the use of imagination, humor, pleasure, flirtation, exploration, enchantment or any other quality that creates joy and connectedness.

Playfulness while dating takes the pressure off and brings ease and fun into a situation. For instance, say a guy asks you a question that puts you off, like "So how come you're *still* on this dating site?" which could cause you to roll your eyes. You could respond playfully, "Well, I've been waiting to meet a man like you, sweetie," or "I just can't get enough of going on fun dates with tons of interesting men," making light of their comment or even saying something edgy and sexy.

Curiosity and wonder are components of play. On your dates, ask a lot of questions, including provocative or deep ones, like "What's a story in your life about you that you're most proud of?" or "What aisle of the bookstore do you find yourself drawn to?" When you're genuinely curious, then you can look at dating as a way of getting to know the man or gaining different perspectives on life, in a non-judgmental way.

Also, don't forget to bring your flirting game. On your dates, laugh and giggle, poke fun (lightly, of course), touch the man's arm, give a warm hug, and gaze into a man's eyes when he's talking. Try to stay away from serious topics until the third or fourth date (for instance, about past relationships, politics, etc.), and stay in the present moment. This doesn't mean that deeper topics aren't important; rather, find topics to talk about that are universal, about values and even simply being present and joyful with another.

For date options, be open to a man's ideas, but also suggest things that you enjoy doing, whether it's a yoga class, a walk in the park, an outdoor concert. If a man's really into you, trust me, he'll join!

Pleasure: Perhaps one of the greatest sights to behold is when a woman's in her pleasure. When she's turned on by herself, her life, and connected to her natural, feminine, wild side. Whether she's creating poetry or playing with a dog, eats a decadent scoop of gelato for lunch everyday while on vacation or she decides to wear sexy lingerie for the heck of it, she's following her pleasures from an authentic place, which she knows is good for her body and spirit.

When you're turned on and in your pleasure, men find you to be utterly sexy, and they feel defenseless and even vulnerable around you. The radiance you're emanating even shines through in your dating profile.

When you're dating from a place of pleasure and being sexually empowered as a woman, you aren't afraid to say no when something doesn't feel right. You trust in your innate intelligence to guide you in choosing healthy dating experiences, while walking away from men that are toxic. You feel bold enough to ask for certain needs and desires to be met in a playful way.

Sprinkle pleasure into your life every single day. It could be slow, joyful self-pleasure, having dance breaks, swimming, eating chocolate cake, creating some art. Before your dates, do a fun or sexy dance break to shake off nervousness and expectation. Wear sensual, beautiful clothing and perfume. Dating is inherently vulnerable and sometimes scary, so having a playful, pleasureful attitude can support you in actually enjoying it without all the drama.

Getting Started with Dating

Love Goddess, now you're ready to start getting your beautiful journey of meeting men started, if you haven't already.

Your mindset is of vital importance. If you're feeling uncertain, afraid or insecure, now is a good time to get some support. No matter what, just know in your heart that you are worthy of love, and that the only way to begin your soulmate journey is to get out there with a tender yet resilient heart that knows great adventures await her.

The goal of dating, especially in the beginning, is to practice flirting, communicating, and understanding men. Ideally, you would be getting to know two or three men at a time. Dating just one man at a time or getting committed early is old-fashioned and takes all the fun out of dating!

Where to Meet Quality Men

Now the question is, where do you meet exquisite, sexy, emotionally available men? Here are some recommendations:

1. Online Dating

If you're feeling wary about online dating and feel like you've been there and done that, I hear you sister. Yet, I would strongly urge you to reconsider and open your mind to viewing online dating with a fresh perspective.

Through my coaching and personal experience, I've found that online dating apps are an excellent way to meet men. Most of my clients have met their partners online, *even though they started off strongly resistant to it.* It's a great way to extend your network, go beyond your radius and meet stand up guys. Studies show that nearly 40% of people are meeting their partners online now.

Think about your brothers and your guy friends – aren't they online as well? Didn't many of your friends meet their partners online?

So, my friend, online dating *does* work, and you can meet "the one." The way I look at it, online apps are a way that technology enables us to live better lives. It doesn't replace meeting people in social settings – it's just another channel for calling in your soulmate. Sometimes it's hard to be grateful for something that potentially has caused you a lot of pain – but remember that our mothers and grandmothers didn't have a chance to meet and date men outside of their limited social settings. We do! And here's the plus side: you have the opportunity to date and choose a man who's right for you, someone that you would have only been able to find given these technological advances. *So, try to approach online dating with a mindset of abundance and gratitude.*

Some tips to master online dating:

Use gorgeous, striking pictures of yourself: This is the most important tip. Men are visual creatures (and so are we, by the way). I've seen men swipe through apps really quickly and stop at a picture of a beautiful woman. I recommend getting professional photos done, where you are wearing sexy, colorful, elegant dresses and outfits. Have fun in the photo shoot – and even get your hair and makeup done. The best part is, once you get these photos done, they can be used for a variety of purposes, like your social media and professional website (and believe me, you will always treasure them).

Make your profile humorous, yet authentic and values-oriented. We all love a little chuckle. Especially in dating! Take the opportunity to use your online profile to bring out your less serious, more fun side. Create a unique username, even if it's kind of silly, like Puppy-Whisperer or YogaBear. Make it related to something you're passionate about. Add a tagline that's witty and related (if taglines are supported in the app), like "Smarter than the average bear!" for the YogaBear example. *(In this case, YogaBear is a play on Yogi Bear, and relates to this woman's interest in yoga.)*

In your profile, share your interests and background in a casual yet interesting way. Talk about what you value in life and use anecdotes and language that draws in the five senses. You can even be vulnerable and share some of your quirks. Most importantly, try to be light-hearted and flirty, yet sincere. If you do mention your job, make it just one aspect of your profile – remember you are way more than your career.

Try not to mention things that you don't want (e.g. "Not looking for a one-night stand") – these can look like red alerts or signal that you still have issues you are working through.

Your profile is a chance for you to stand out from the crowd and share your unique essence. What makes you *you*, magnificent goddess! Also, it doesn't matter if it's long (as long as the app allows it) – the longer, the better. I've seen men read every single word if they are piqued by a woman. The more you share, the more a man will be able to see if there is resonance with you – and also find a hook to connect with you.

Note: I recommend you get professional support in creating your dating profile. Also, plan on being on a maximum of two dating sites at a time in order to not feel overwhelmed, and when you feel that you've exhausted all your options on one, switch to another. There is no perfect app. I've seen women meet men on almost all dating sites.

2. At a bar, party or restaurant

Single men can be found in abundance in social settings where they can be out with their friends. Remember, men who are single want to meet great women like you – and a bar is as good a place as any. You can practice flirting by going up to a man and saying something funny or cheeky, and when a man approaches you, be open to chatting casually. The great thing at a bar is if you're bored (or you don't want to linger for too long), you can always end politely and make an exit to the bathroom, or find your girlfriend. Go with friends who are also single and are just as open as you to meet men and start conversations.

3. Meetup or interest group

Meetup.com is a forum for people to form groups based on shared interests. Depending on where you live, the options may be quite vast or rather limited. For instance, there may be groups that meet for hiking, tennis, culinary experiences, spirituality, books – you name it. Go through the list and see if any appeal to you, even remotely. If a particular interest doesn't show up and you're inspired to form a group – why not?

4. Service or community organization

If you're interested in meeting kind, generous men, then look no further! Joining a soup kitchen, a faith-based group, a mindfulness group, or local community events supporting a cause are great ways to meet other people (and men) who are into giving. Plus, they are healthy environments to get to know someone in a way that's fun and authentic, with a lot of heart.

5. Personal growth or educational seminars

Many men and women who are single are introspective and looking for ways to grow and transform their lives. Look around at community forums and billboards for activities, or courses, where you can have fun learning. There are always opportunities to meet men in these places.

6. Singles events

What's the best place to know whether a man's single? You got it! From speed dating to after-work mixers or trips for singles, you can meet a myriad of interesting men. Nearly every city has them in multitude. If you go to an event and are disappointed, don't worry. Just keep attending different ones. You never know. Plus, working on your flirting and dating skills at this stage is important and such events are helpful.

7. Through friends

Let your friends know that you are looking to date. Be grateful and kind when they set you up with men, even if you think the guy isn't the right fit for you. Remember, your friends are doing their best and have your interest at heart. They want you to be happy in a relationship.

As a coach, I always encourage women to try to get to at least one event or activity per week. Dating is a marathon, not a sprint. A good dose of humor, play and openness will go a long way in making the experience enjoyable. If you ever feel disheartened, remember that this is a vulnerable experience for both you and the men you meet, and requires immense courage and compassion. Celebrate and practice self-love every time you go to an event. You're already ahead of the curve by getting out there and being proactive in your dating life.

Goddess dating tips

1. Communicate with guys online as you would in person

One common issue that so many people face is that the conversation online feels forced and artificial. What if you were to meet a guy in person? How would you speak and communicate? Try to bring that same casual, curious tone when communicating with someone online. Ask questions about something he said in his profile, and answer his questions in short, fun ways. Feel free to use emoticons and be flirty – it'll keep him on his toes! Give chances to men whose profile you think are not so great. Sometimes a man's profile might not represent him well, and you may be surprised when you actually meet him in person.

2. Create healthy, sustainable dating habits

Take small, daily steps to move your love life forward. I generally recommend earmarking thirty minutes a day to communicate with men online – no more, no less. In this way, dating becomes an integral part of your life, and you aren't consumed by it. During those thirty minutes, send fun, interesting messages, get on the phone, find a singles event or plan a date. Focus on the quality of your interactions, rather than quantity. For instance, if you're only able to write to one or two men, but your messages are kind, funny and mindful, then that's a great use of your time. Take a moment to meditate or practice deep, calm breathing before you go online or on a date, do the same after. Lastly, have an open, fresh mind each time you use your dating app or meet a man – each day is a new day. Another healthy metric is carving out three evenings a week for dating and if you're not on a date, then use the evening to read a book on love, or date yourself.

3. Remove artificial filters and criteria, and genuinely be open

I have clients who have dated men who are younger, much older, shorter, less educated, living in different parts of the country, of different ethnicities and religions, interested in different things ... the list goes on! And these men are perfect for them. The reality is that your soulmate is someone who might come in a different package than what your ego thinks it needs. So be open to possibilities.

4. Invite men into your life

I have found that we women can play a special, powerful role for men – that of inviting them into our lives and letting them know we find them intriguing, sexy or handsome.

In the new, empowered, heart-centered paradigm, women and men get to choose to be with each other, and both partners work at keeping sexual chemistry alive. As such, you can approach a man and let him know that the door is open, metaphorically. When you're online, don't just wait for men to reach out to you – you can be the first one to send a thoughtful, funny message letting them know that you're interested in getting to know them. Likewise, at a party, you can look over at a guy and smile, or go up to him and make a funny joke about something. The goal is to get your flirty, sassy game on – and be bold! Sometimes men are clueless or confused how to approach a woman they find attractive (especially men who are shy) and do require women to be obvious with them. I have had so many clients meet and marry men that they reached out to first.

In my own story, I was the first to call Krishan up and invite him on a date, and looking back, I'm so glad I did. I didn't overthink it – I was genuinely just interested in hanging out with him, no strings attached!

5. Play it safe

For a woman, dating can feel vulnerable and can even sometimes trigger fears around safety. There are many safeguards you can put in place to maintain healthy boundaries and yet enjoy dating.

- To maintain your privacy, I recommend creating a separate e-mail account for communicating with men, and even using this e-mail for your dating apps.

- Never give out your phone number unless you've communicated via the app or e-mail a few times and you feel comfortable with the person.

- Refrain from connecting with a person on social media unless you want to be friends with him or you're getting into a committed relationship with him.

- If a guy says something sexual and inappropriate and you don't like it, let him know it made you feel uncomfortable, and end the conversation, wishing him luck.

- Offer to meet up with a guy on a date only after you've spoken with him once or twice over phone or video. You can make the request seem sexy, like, "Ooh I would love to connect with you over the phone, are you free this evening? ☺" Nowadays, dating can feel like eating fast food – but you can approach it mindfully and slow down the communication and meeting up if that feels better for you.

- When you meet, arrive and leave in your own mode of transportation, and meet in a public place. Only show your place to someone once you've gotten to know them well.

- It may sound obvious, but it's worth mentioning that you should never feel like you have to sleep with a man just because you feel obligated or he wants it – maintain your standards and determine when, and with whom, you want to have sex and at what pace, making sure it's coming from a healthy place of desire. **Healthy boundary setting will allow you to maintain both a sense of safety and also create a sense of mystery for a guy.**

6. Date more than one man

This sounds counterintuitive, but even if you've met a guy you think is "the one," continue to date other men. There are many reasons for this, but a main one is it takes you out of your head, otherwise you will analyze the relationship endlessly because you are putting all your eggs in one basket. It will allow you to chill and just enjoy getting to know men, keeping your options open without focusing on the outcome. When you have many options, you become a prize to be sought after, and men find it super sexy!

In fact, I generally recommend that you get to know a man for over six months before committing, or preferably after having gone through a crisis or two together to see how you weathered the storm and grew, and seeing whether you both resonate with each other.

This is contrary to what women are taught – to date one man at a time, know early on whether he's marriage material or not and get him to commit. This is unfair and is a recipe for disaster, as it makes it harder to create a long-term relationship based on mindfulness, trust and growth in connection through friendship. Women who date with this mindset reek of desperation, and they become susceptible to men either running away or manipulating them.

Trust me, after dating several men, when you finally meet and commit to Mr. Right, you will feel even more confident with your choice!

7. Enjoy the dates and don't take things personally

Generate a positive mindset around dating, and don't take the process too seriously. Remember, rejection is just part of the game, and everyone is looking for the right partnership that will last a lifetime. If you aren't interested in dating a man, let him know honestly and firmly yet with compassion and love.

If a man ghosts you, leads you on and then disappears, says something disrespectful or rude, or shows red flags like anger or addiction issues, then take this as a good piece of information that you can use to identify that he's not a good match for you. You can thank the universe for helping you see the signs and simply let the man go. No more projects or guessing games, thank you very much! Practice Ho'opono-pono and wish this man love, healing and grace on his path.

8. Date based on resonance and values, rather than chemistry

Try not to write off a man based on superficial reasons. Give a man at least three or four chances, especially if he's kind, generous and shows up for you. Over time, you can see whether you feel energized or drained while you're with a man – this is a good test for resonance.

While dating, see if you resonate on deeper things, like your values, vision and lifestyle preferences.

When you're on a date, you can ask questions that let you get an insider's view into your man's world. With curiosity, observe things about his life. Is he close to his family? What are his friends like? How does he treat waiters or people he meets? Does he show up for you every time, or is he flaky? What does he envision in his life? Does he love children, and how, through his daily actions, does he show self-awareness, generosity and kindness? You don't need to interrogate a man; simply be present and have a sense of wonder and forgiveness. The truth about a man, and whether you two make a great couple, will slowly and surely begin to reveal itself over time.

I find using chemistry as the basis to attraction is an overrated concept because it focuses on our biological wiring, sexual instinct, and wounding from one's past. Instead, I invite you to listen to your intuition and what resonates with your soul. You might discover that a man you didn't find attractive in the beginning ends up being the true knight in shining armor, a man who will steal your heart through his integrity, personality and a true soul connection with you.

9. Be a partner in the dating process

The model of dating where a man chases and serenades a woman, wines and dines her is archaic. Don't get me wrong, I love being wined and dined like any woman does. But I recognize that I have a more partnership-oriented view of love.

You can take turns paying for dates and inviting each other for different experiences – for instance, in the first one, allow him to pay for dinner, and after dinner, you can treat both of you to ice cream. The following date, you can organize a hike or go to an outdoor movie. These don't have to be expensive, yet it could be fun and meaningful. I find that doing things that don't require money to be some of the best dates!

Men have gotten burned by spending tons of money on women who feel entitled to be treated like princesses – you don't need that, because you are a Queen, and you don't need to be seduced through money or grand gestures. When you show up as a kind, confident and respectful woman, you will turn a man's world upside down.

Trust me, when a man wants to be your King, he will do everything in his power to pleasure you, woo you. When he falls in love, he will make you a beautiful palace to live in (even if it's a cozy little home ☺) and will make sure you are taken care of.

10. Maintain your Love Goddess rituals

When you vibrate with love and live from a place of intention and grace, you naturally align with your divine plan. Remember to keep doing your morning rituals, affirmations, visualization and meditation along with activities that bring your body and soul pleasure.

You can do a daily prayer or affirmations to call in your beloved, such as:

- "My perfect partner is already selected. He is arriving in the right way in divine timing. I am so delighted and grateful to receive him."

- "Dear God, dear all beings, teachers, mentors, parents, guides, lovers, colleagues, family, friends, who have shown me unconditional love and support on my path, thank you, thank you, thank you. May I align with my higher self, my highest intention for the greater good of all. May I access deepest wisdom from source. May I release my barriers to love. May I align with the energies of love, healing, grace, ecstasy and surrender. May I be guided on a path of miracles, a path of love and abundance. May I open my heart to the life partner and life you have in store for me, dear God. I know that if my beloved

296

came here, I would adore, honor and cherish him and serve our relationship. Please give me the opportunity to expand my heart into the life that you would have me lead – one of love, integrity and true intimacy, which fulfills the divine purpose You have for me. Thank you, God. Amen."

• There is also a powerful Sanskrit mantra which you can chant 108 times daily: *Sat Patim Dehi Parameshwara*. It means "Please bestow upon me a man of Truth who embodies the highest and most pure masculine attributes."

After every date, I recommend that you practice a little meditation and self-empathy, tuning into your feelings and needs. With my clients, I ask them to send me their feelings/needs after an evening out with a man – rather than an analysis of how things went.

Whenever you feel a sense of doubt or insecurity, you can pray to God to hold you, ask for guidance and simply surrender and receive grace. Remember, you are a daughter of God and are infinitely loved and supported.

11. Establish your support system and strive to maintain a Goddess mindset.

Let's face it. Dating is inherently vulnerable and can bring up old fears and wounds. For many women who have had to be strong and independent, being vulnerable and feeling powerless is tough and it's a muscle that needs to be exercised. Vulnerability comes in many forms – reaching out to a guy online even though you're afraid of rejection, having sex or being intimate, sharing a personal story, making requests, talking about how you feel, kissing someone or opening up your heart to a man while being uncertain of his feelings for you. *Your vulnerability is your strength. This is the very quality that makes you alluring and attractive and invites men to instinctively want to hold and protect you.*

We're all creatures of habit and are afraid of rejection and getting hurt. **Yet dating is the most vital thing you could be doing to releasing your barriers to love and inviting in partnership.**

It's important to have a team of supporters on board who cheer you on – a caring girlfriend, therapist and maybe a family member – who understand you and who you can rely on when you're needing a mindset boost, help you reflect on your dating patterns and keep you focused on your mission of finding your soulmate. It's also important to do that within yourself. Keep loving yourself, giving yourself the compassion and attention your body needs.

I highly recommend working with a Dating and Relationship Coach or mentor who can support you in staying positive, creating healthy dating habits and getting out of your own way, which is perhaps the biggest challenge. A coach will help you overcome your fears, hold you accountable, identify your patterns and support you in making the right choices in your love life. They are your partner and confidante in a journey that can often feel lonely and confusing.

Dear Love Goddess,

If you've reached the end of the book, hooray! I am here celebrating with you at the finish line of this courageous journey that few women (and men) venture to take. Surely now, you must feel relieved, but also a bit nervous. Where do you go from here? What's next? What if all of the work you did was in vain? Before you let your analytical, fear-based thinking get in the way, go out and celebrate your accomplishment of this major milestone! You deserve to fill yourself up with love and approval, be your greatest champion and know that you're worthy of love no matter what, every single day. Prepare a bath, grab some champagne and relax to some seductive, uplifting music. Or go out and dance!

Rewiring for healthy love is no easy feat, and yet, you did it. Whether it's apparent right now or not, the fruits of your labor will begin to grow and ripen when they're ready. Maybe you feel a little softer and more tender around people and you've experienced a couple of miracles. You've noticed that you're less judgmental, more forgiving and appreciative of yourself, and more open to receiving love. Your heart feels a little lighter and your vision of what you want to create in your life is clearer. You've gained a new perspective on relationships outside the mental model you grew up with. These may seem like small wins, yet they're big, and they show that you're on the right path of experiencing love that is ecstatic and profound, that transcends all your old painful patterns – a Higher Love that you've been yearning for.

This is a self-love journey, in which not only do you step into being your own beloved, but you will attract a beloved relationship with a man. Ultimately, your soulmate is your best friend, to share your path with you while seeking connection with you on every level – mentally, emotionally, physically, spiritually. When you're spiraling down emotionally or you find yourself going down the wrong path, he will lift you up, and likewise, you will do the same for him. You're each other's accountability buddies, champions and you have each other's back. Your man is your King, ready to serve and protect you, and you're his Queen, nurturing him and exalting him even higher as a man. You're a team, and you're growing and evolving together, overcoming different challenges. There's bliss in experiencing this kind of love, harmony and growth.

The foundation for this kind of relationship begins when you're single, yet some people wait until marriage to develop this kind of understanding (which, by the way, isn't necessarily too late either, yet requires focus and commitment). The great news is, you've begun this process which will pay off in your love life long-term.

So, chica, get ready for a wild adventure of meeting exciting men, facing your fears and stepping into higher and higher levels of bliss! Dating and being in relationship is for valiant women who know what they want – to lead a life of fulfillment and heart openness – and no doubt you are this woman! I wish you the very best on your journey, and I personally hope that our paths cross in different ways.

LOVE MANTRAS

In closing, as you're beginning your love journey, I leave you with a few nuggets of wisdom to guide you as you forge a path of true, blissful love. No doubt, your man is on his way, and even if he's here, these mantras will support you in turning your relationship into one of fun and deep connection.

- Love is the path of miracles.

- Breathing in: "Today is a new day." Breathing out: "It's a beautiful day. I vow to approach today with mindfulness, joy and openness."

- Love flows in the path of least resistance.

- Separation is an illusion. In reality, we're all interconnected.

- Choose love, kindness and generosity. Love trumps everything else.

- Fear is False Evidence Appearing Real.

- A little bit of humor goes a long way.

- Always speak with kindness.

- Ask and you shall receive.

- When in doubt, tune into your heart and body. The heart will always guide you through uncertainty.

- Fear, uncertainty and discomfort are your compasses towards growth.

- Forgiveness is your greatest power.

- You are worthy of love, abundance and fulfillment.

- Change happens through acceptance. Find acceptance first and life will unfold, naturally.

- God loves you and is always there for you. You are protected. When in doubt, pray for love, healing, guidance and grace.

- Be vulnerable and strong enough to seek help and support. It's a courageous act of self-love.

- The more you respect, love and honor yourself, the more others will do the same.

- Choose to allow your heart to be broken open, for that is where the light enters into you.

- Your vulnerability is sexy.

- Lay down your armor and defenses. Your heart will start shining through.

- Your authenticity and free-spiritedness are a turn on for men.

- Your femininity is healing and empowering.

- Let go of your addiction to work, career, and success. True fulfillment comes from your relationships – with nature, yourself and others.

- If you're single, it's because the best match is on his way, and you are preparing for his arrival.

- Let go of your need to be right.

- Trust is a muscle. Keep exercising it. You'll ultimately reach a place of deep inner knowing.

- Faith it till you make it. Faith is your greatest virtue and strength.

- Focus on emotional safety and connection. Everything else will follow.

- Insecurity breeds neediness; confidence breeds vulnerability and honesty.

- When you release emasculating men, you unleash kings.

- Your heart and love have the ability to surrender the ego.

- Your man is seeking you, just as much you're seeking him.

- Each bad encounter, date or rejection is a step closer to meeting "the one."

- Every man you meet is a mirror to you. What are you projecting? What needs to be healed? What do you truly value? What can you learn, accept and let go of?

- Girls just gotta have fun! Pleasure, play and presence are your secret powers.

- You never need to commit to someone until your heart, mind and soul feel ready, and you both feel a sense of resonance with each other. In this state, partnership will arise easily and naturally.

- If he shows up for you, he's interested.

- No relationship is wrong or a mistake. Each man takes you on a journey from A to M, N to P, Q till so on.

- Keep showing up for your love life, every single day. Love is a marathon, not a sprint.

- The best is yet to come.

- Smile and breathe.

ABOUT THE AUTHOR

Sarika Jain is a leader in love strategy and transformational coaching. Her unique approach encompasses everything from uncovering relationship patterns and closing one's 'Ex Files' to practicing self-love and mindfulness in relationships, all with the goal of inspiring women to live the lives they've dreamed about – experiencing profound love, success and fulfillment.

Sarika's background includes working in the corporate world and on Wall Street for over fifteen years before deciding to pursue her dream full time of creating a movement around healthy love and empowerment for women over ten years ago. She is a student of energy healing, psychology, feminine leadership and relationships and has studied Life Centered Therapy with licensed clinical psychologist Dr. Andy Hahn. She's been called a "Relationship Sorceress" by her clients.

Sarika has an undergraduate degree in Computer Science & Engineering from University of Pennsylvania, an MBA from The Wharton School, and has worked at Bain & Co., Merrill Lynch and the World Bank.

Sarika lives with her husband, Krishan, and three daughters in New Jersey, and leads a playful, passionate life. More information can be found at www.sarikajain.com.

ACKNOWLEDGMENTS

For Love Goddesses in various forms, including my mother(s), sisters, healers, guides and mentors in my life, I honor you, and hold you in deep gratitude for inspiring my sacred gifts. I also thank the various women who have supported me in my journey, including my goddess sister Jill Hoffman, my sisters Smita and Monica (I even received a brand-new laptop from them as I started writing the book!), my clients and students who have become soulmate friends, Nicola Humber for her continued support and mentorship, and of the sisters in the Unbound Writing Mastermind and my other communities who have made my journey so pleasure-filled and juicy.

I want to acknowledge my husband, Krishan, a man with such deep integrity and a physical embodiment of the divine love I've always sought. Thank you for holding sacred space for me in birthing this book and inspiring me to be my best self. I am also grateful for the sacred masculine presences in my life who continue to guide me, love me, and protect me in my path to love.

My children, Lila, Maya and Tara, have been such a source of childlike joy and wonder and have kept my spirit soaring as I went through ups and downs in writing this book.

I am also incredibly blessed to have parents who always show up to support me in all my endeavors, and who have inspired me to seek a life of family, fulfillment and fitness – thank you so much. I also have deep gratitude to my family in India, who hold the sacred flame of faith and unconditional love in my heart.

I also wouldn't be here without the support of my mentors, like Pat, Beth Raps of Raising Clarity, Arielle Ford, HeatherAsh Amara, Dr. Andy Hahn (founder of Life Centered Therapy), and many others who have taught me so much about spiritual healing and relationships.

My mindfulness communities, teachings of the venerable Zen teacher Thích Nhât Hạnh, priestess mentors, Christian philosophy and my Jain upbringing, which have supported me in my spiritual growth throughout the years, for whom I am incredibly thankful.

Lastly, I am eternally grateful to God, without whom my life and all its glory wouldn't be possible; and to the Mother who weaves her way into my life every day and inspires my work.

RESOURCES

Love is a never-ending, divine quest. I truly hope that this book has inspired you to keep learning and growing. As you're exploring the path ahead, I want to share some books and resources to support your journey.

Mindfulness

The Miracle of Mindfulness (Thích Nhât Hạnh)
Radical Acceptance: Embracing Your Life with the Heart of a Buddha (Tara Brach)
The Issue at Hand: Essays on Buddhist Mindfulness Practice (Gil Frosndal)

Love & Relationships

True Love: A Practice for Awakening the Heart (Thích Nhât Hạnh)
The Soulmate Secret: Manifest the Love of Your Life with the Law of Attraction (Arielle Ford)
Perfect Love, Imperfect Relationships: Healing the Wound of the Heart (John Welwood)
The Mastery of Love: A Practical Guide to the Art of Relationship (Don Miguel Ruiz)
Codependent No More: How to Stop Controlling Others and Start Caring for Yourself (Melodie Beattie)
The Five Secrets to Happy and Healthy Relationships (HeatherAsh Amara and Don Miguel Ruiz Jr.)
The Queen's Code (Alison A. Armostrong)

Healing

It Didn't Start with You: How Inherited Family Trauma Shapes Who We Are and How to End the Cycle (Mark Wolynn)

Discovering the Inner Mother: A Guide to Healing the Mother Wound and Claiming Your Inner Power (Bethany Webster)

Life Centered Therapy with Dr. Andy Hahn (https://www.lifecenteredtherapy.com)

Reconciliation: Healing the Inner Child (Thích Nhât Hạnh)

The Body Keeps the Score: Brain, Mind and Body in the Healing of Trauma (Bessel van der Kolk)

The Warrior Heart Practice (HeatherAsh Amara)

Shadow and Rose: A Soulful Guide for Women Recovering from Rape and Sexual Violence (Sarah Wheeler)

Divine Feminine, Health & Sexuality

Mama Gena's School of Womanly Arts: Using the Power of Pleasure to Have Your Way with the World (Regena Thomasheuer)

The Wild Woman's Way: Unlock Your Full Potential for Pleasure, Power and Fulfillment (Michaela Boehm)

Dear Lover: A Woman's Guide to Men, Sex and Love's Deepest Bliss (David Deida)

Womb Wisdom: Awakening the Creative and Forgotten Powers of the Feminine (Padma Aon Prakasha)

Layla Martin (https://laylamartin.com)

In the FLO: Unlock Your Hormonal Advantage and Revolutionize Your Life (Alissa Viti)

Women's Bodies, Women's Wisdom: Creating Physical and Emotional Health and Healing (Dr. Christiane Northrup)

Sex for One: The Joy of Selfloving (Betty Dodson)

Purpose

The Life You Were Born to Live: A Guide to Finding Your Life Purpose (Dan Millman)

Play Your Cards Right: A Sacred Guide to Living Life on Earth (Alexander Dunlop)

You Are a Badass: How to Stop Doubting Your Greatness and Start Living an Awesome Life (Jen Sincero)

The Wisdom of the Enneagram: The Complete Guide to Psychological and Spiritual Growth for the Nine Personality Types (Don Richard Riso)

Divine Masculine

The Way of the Superior Man (David Deida)

King, Warrior, Magician, Lover: Rediscovering the Archetypes of the Mature Masculine (Robert Moore and Douglas Gilette)

Communication Skills & Emotional Leadership

Nonviolent Communication: A Language of Life (Marshall Rosenberg)

The Art of Communicating (Thích Nhât Hạnh)

Taming the Tiger Within: Meditations on Transforming Difficult Emotions (Thích Nhât Hạnh)

Dating

First Date Stories: https://firstdatestories.com

Finding the One Online with Mark Evan Katz: https://www.evanmarckatz.com

Movies

Under the Tuscan Sun

Eat, Pray, Love

Kamasutra: A Tale of Love

Bruce Almighty

Miss Representation

The Mask You Live In

Made in United States
North Haven, CT
13 July 2023

38926543R00180

Are you craving a soulful, uplifting, lasting and evolutionary connection with your soulmate? Are you eager to experience love and intimacy on a profound and deep level – one that nourishes your mind, body and soul?

Do you want to break your dry, single spell (or relationship hell!), heal your heart, and learn what it really takes to find & keep extraordinary love... and you know that your soul won't settle for any less?

If you're ready to...

- **Say goodbye to painful patterns** with emotionally unavailable men
- **Release limiting beliefs** & unhealthy relationship habits with yourself
- Step into a new level of consciousness around love and **claim your feminine power**
- **Feel radiant, magnetic and confident** while dating and in a relationship
- Attract sexy, commitment-ready men and **find "the one"**

...then you are invited you to join a unique adventure. *The 90-Day Soulmate Plan: Get out of your own way and attract the Higher Love you deserve* is a new, revolutionary way of attracting your soulmate and creating the relationship of your dreams. In these pages, you'll find wisdom, practical tips and techniques to help you become the empowered woman you are meant to be and manifest healthy, lasting love. Full of love, laughs and insight, this debut book by Sarika will teach you how to live an extraordinary life with the partnership your heart has yearned for.

"Sarika is the epitome of a feminine goddess. She lives and breathes all that she teaches. This book is truly a vessel for her to share all her innate (and hard earned!) wisdom. If you are ready for deep intimate connection... read this, it will guide you to your ONE!"
Chrisa Zindros Boyce, Executive Coach

Sarika Jain is a leader in love strategy and transformational coaching. Fondly referred to as a Relationship Sorceress by her clients, Sarika combines her nearly two decades of corporate experience on Wall Street with Eastern spirituality which she learned about while living in India as a child. Sarika facilitates workshops about self-love, mindful dating and relationship skills. To learn more, visit **www.sarikajain.com**

theunboundpress.cor
ISBN 978-1-913590-29
900

THE
UNBOUND
PRESS

cover design: Leah Kent

9 781913 590291